The G

"This book by Shane Kapler is an example of the new evangelization... His words exude faith in and understanding of what is being reported and described. He deals with the most profound and complex issues of our faith, and he does so with simplicity and clarity. Throughout the book he is relating the mysteries of our faith to our everyday, concrete experience of living. For example, his explanations of the gifts of the Spirit are anything by abstract and abstruse...I think that this is an excellent book for any Catholic, young or old, who is looking for something to bring Catholic teaching to life. His use of a wide range of resources, going back to the early Church documents, makes this work so enriching, authentic, and believable."

Bishop Robert Hermann, Archdiocese of St. Louis

"*The God Who is Love* is a masterful interweaving of engaging personal narrative and intelligent catechesis and apologetics; steeped in scriptural, philosophical, and historical insight, proudly Catholic, yet benevolently ecumenical, clearly presented and thoroughly detailed — a heartfelt lesson that appeals to the mind and soul as well. A pleasant and straightforward read, it is supported by a wealth of references, footnotes, user-friendly charts and insightful side-by-side textual comparisons. This book is a theological tour de force, packing a wallop in truth and goodness, inspiring the reader to learn more and to live out the faith. In the introduction, Shane Kapler billed *The God Who is Love* as theological 'one stop shopping.' I'd say he delivered."

Kevin Vost, Psy.D., author of *Memorize the Faith!* and *Fit for Eternal Life*

"Shane Kapler has given us a compendium of truth borne along by a compelling narrative. His book is both a moving charismatic testimony and an engaging Catholic catechesis. That's a rare combination — and a grace for the reader."

Mike Aquilina, author of *The Fathers of the Church* and *The Mass of the Early Christians*. Executive Vice President, St. Paul Center for Biblical Theology

"It is a curious fact that Jesus chose to give us, not a gospel in his own hand, but 'the gospel according to...'. We see Him reflected in the eyes of his people. Shane Kapler follows in this ancient tradition of evangelization by showing us how the light of the gospel dawned on him in the teaching of the Church as he encountered it in the rough and tumble of his collisions with everyday life. He shows us how to meet the Truth who is Christ where he has always been found: not in a specially sterilized room full of theological abstractions, but in the concrete ordinariness of everyday life.

Mark P. Shea, author of *By What Authority? : An Evangelical Discovers Catholic Tradition* and *Making Senses Out of Scripture: Reading the Bible as the First Christians Did*

Mr. Kapler has written a superb synthesis of Christian doctrine as taught by the Catholic Church. He passes frictionlessly between discussions of Old Testament scriptures, New Testament scriptures, the deepest mysteries of God, the life and teachings of Jesus, the role of Judaism, and the experiences of his own spiritual journey, to lead the reader effortlessly into a full and deep catechesis of the Catholic faith, always illumined by and reflecting the overarching theme reflected in the book's title. Immensely enjoyable and readable, informed, and surprisingly deep in its explorations of the mysteries of the faith, it solidly deserves a place among the most outstanding recent works of Catholic apologetics.

Roy Schoeman, convert to Catholicism from Judaism, and author of *Salvation Is From The Jews: The Role of Judaism in Salvation History* and *Honey From the Rock: Sixteen Jews Find The Sweetness of Christ*

The God Who is Love:

Explaining Christianity From Its Center

Shane Kapler

OUT OF THE BOX RECORDS
www.outoftheboxrecords.com
St. Louis, Missouri

Imprimatur: Most Reverend Robert J. Hermann
   Vicar General, Archdiocese of St. Louis
September 25, 2007

The Catholic Edition of the Revised Standard Version of the Bible, copyright © 1965, 1966 National Council of the Churches of Christ in the United States of America. Used by permission. All rights reserved.

Scripture quotations marked (NIV) are taken from the *Holy Bible, New International Version*®. NIV®. Copyright©1973, 1978, 1984 by International Bble Society. Used by permission of Zondervan. All rights reserved.

Quotations from William Jurgens' *The Faith of the Early Fathers, Volumes 1-3*, are used by permission of The Liturgical Press. All rights reserved.

Cover Art: Graphic design, Andrew Kapler.
Photograph, Apse of San Calimero church in Milan (Italy), by Giovanni Dall'Orto, May 5 2007.

Copyright © 2009 Shane Kapler. All rights reserved. Printed in the United States of America. No part of this book may be used or reproduced in any manner whatsoever without written permission except in the case of brief quotations embodied in critical articles and reviews.

ISBN: 9780980090932
Library of Congress Control Number: 2009901938

*To my children,
Brennan at seven, a warrior in every sense.
Happy First Communion buddy!
and
Lily at three, intensely beautiful in every way
("No – call me cute!"), with strong-will to spare!*

*And in grateful appreciation to my grandparents,
L.N. "Sparky" & Virginia Mahlandt   and   Arnold & Ruth Kapler
Protestant   Catholic
Profound Teachers of the Christian Faith
in word, and even more so by example*

The Acknowledgment "Chain"

Between an author's writing and the public's reading, there always exists a chain of people who have helped a book reach its destination. The following deserve my special thanks: Patrick & Amy Monaghan (first encouragers), Terry Shepherd (initial editing), Raymond Burke (gatekeeper), Patti Baratta (secondary editing), Monsignor John Leykam (backbone), Rob & Karen Gilbert (a whisper in my ear), Kathi Strunk (*the* idea lady), Kevin Vost (endorsement and networker), Andrew Kapler (constant technical support), and Adam Bitter & Dominic Lozano (publishers).

Table of Contents

Introduction (p.1)

1 – Are You There? (p.3) The author's initial doubts and God's intervention

2 – Discovering the "New" in the "Old" (p.7) God's Triune nature • Humanity's creation and fall • God's plan of salvation enfolded in Israel's history, rites, poetry and prophecy.

3- Jesus, Through the Eyes of Faith (p.32) Jesus' life as the fulfillment of Israel's hopes and window into the dynamic of the Trinity • Complete God, complete man • Relationship with Law of Moses •Fulfillment of prophecy • Passover and Crucifixion •Resurrection and Ascension • How He brings salvation •Entering into Him through Baptism.

4 – Sharing His Anointing (p.49) "Baptism in the Spirit"? • A *Sacrament* of Confirmation? • Attending a "non-denominational" church • Catholicism's authoritarianism and unbiblical elements

5 – Every Boy Needs His Mother (and Brothers and Sisters too) (p.74) Brief sharing of how God used events, but primarily Scripture, to overcome the author's misgivings regarding Catholic and Orthodox teaching on the Virgin Mary: her immaculate conception • life-long virginity • model discipleship • assumption into heaven • motherhood of all Christians • intercessory prayer • The Christian's relation to the whole "communion of saints."

6 – Confession and the Ongoing Nature of Salvation (p.91) Salvation, a life-long process • Faith or Works? •Salvation can be lost • But regained through confession of sin • This practice in Scripture and the early Church. • Purgatory?

7 – Putting the Word in Context (p.117) Interpreting the Bible: inspiration • inerrancy • historical-critical method • literary genres • senses of Scripture

8 – The End of ~~All~~ Some Things (The *Book of Revelation* and "End Times" Speculation) (p.128) *Book of Revelation* • Millenium • Rapture • suffering and persecution • An infallible book cries out for an infallible interpreter

9 – Sharing Jesus' Passion in Our Dating and Marriage (p.147) Marriage as sacrament and image of the Trinity •John Paul II's *Theology of the Body* •contraception • non-marital sex • homosexual behavior • divorce • annulments.

10 – College: Friendships Inside and "Outside" the Church (p.162) Church as Christ's Mystical Body • Christian ecumenism • the salvation of non-Christians

11 – Loose Ends Finally Tied (p.183) Catholic teachers opened author's eyes to the authority of the Church in matters of not just doctrine, but *discipline*.

12 – The Church and the Word of God (p.187) Scripture and early Church writings illustrate: Apostles as foundations for a renewed Israel • Simon-Peter's function as Rock / Primeminister • Apostles' sharing of authority with those ordained to succeed them • God-given Tradition • Church authority determined contents of the New Testament • Loving the Church amidst scandals

13 – Who Are My Brothers and Sisters? (p.230) Strong Catholic convictions do not negate the bonds shared with other Christians; they increase them!

14 – The Eucharist: Christianity's Source and Summit (p.236) Scriptural and early Church testimony: Our entrance into Jesus' Sacrifice • His Real Presence •. Flow of Mass.

15 – Parting Thoughts (p.253)

Appendix I - The Logic of Belief in God (p.256) Science and faith •Aquinas' five proofs • Cosmology reveals a universe fine-tuned for life • the moral order demands a source.

Appendix II – The Uniqueness of Jesus: Why His Claims Deserve a Hearing (p.266)

Appendix III - A Christian View of the New Age Movement (p.270)

Appendix IV - The Old Testament "Aprocrypha" (p.273).

Appendix V – The Validity of Infant Baptism (p.279)

Appendix VI - Does Everyone Receive the Gift of Tongues? (p.283)

Appendix VII - Scripture is Without Error (p.286)

Bibliography (p.295)

Introduction

"Narrative catechesis," that's what you've picked up. Sounds intimidating? It shouldn't. All it means is that it teaches the Christian Faith in the phases that I came to hold it as a teenager and young adult. Now I hope that a more mature reader won't stop here. For whatever reason – maybe you're the reason – God gave me an incredible hunger to know Him while I was still quite young. Not only did He give the desire, but He sent the people, materials and experiences to satisfy it. I write because I know that God hasn't done anything for me that He doesn't want to do for you too.

My hope is to explain, in detail, the Truth that moved me from a crisis of belief, through a series of intermediate steps, to full-fledge participation in the Catholic Church. Along the way we'll immerse ourselves in Scripture and Christian history. We'll open our minds and hearts to the possibility that God can act in us exactly as He did in times past. We want to get beyond the caricatures of Christianity so prevalent today and come to Jesus' vision on matters like marriage, sex, authority, forgiveness, and freedom. We are going to find out *how* God wants to bring us into unending union with Him, and the tools He's given to make it happen. I want this to be an experience of theological "one stop shopping!"

My dream would be that when you finish this book you'll find yourself breathless at the thought of what God has for you – but not too breathless to say, "Come Lord Jesus, do what You *so want to do in me*. Love Your Father, love Your brothers and sisters, *through me*." And then hold on my friend, the ride will have just begun!

Chapter 1 – Are You There?

"Do Jewish people believe in Jesus?" I couldn't believe he'd asked that; you would think that a seventh grader from a Catholic school would have known the answer. I saw our religion teacher roll her eyes. Our hostess at Shaar Emeth Temple was very gracious though, "We reformed Jews believe Jesus was a prophet. We do not, however, believe that he was the Messiah. When we read our Scriptures, what Christians call the 'Old Testament,' we don't see Jesus in the prophecies. We interpret them differently and believe that Messiah is still to come. Another way our belief differs from Christians is that we don't believe God will become human. Messiah will be a human being just like you and I." Of course Jewish people didn't believe Jesus was the Messiah; didn't *everyone* know that?

So why was I so disturbed when I came home from the synagogue? As I thought about it, I slowly realized that I'd never actually met someone who not only didn't believe in Jesus, but had based their whole life on a system of belief that didn't include him. Growing up in a Christian family and attending a Catholic school day-in and day-out didn't give me much opportunity for contact with other belief systems. My classmate's question really wasn't so stupid after all. Yes, I'd known the answer with my head; but the implications had clearly never made it to my heart: the majority of the world did not recognize the person that I'd always been taught was its center. Why not, and even more, *why exactly did I?* If Jewish people didn't recognize Jesus as the Messiah, then why did this Irish-German kid in the suburbs of St. Louis recognize him?

My parents were hit with a barrage of questions: Why do you believe in Jesus? How do you know he was the Messiah? If he was the Messiah, then why do we believe he's God too? How can you be *sure*? Imagine yourself in their position – not easy questions for your thirteen year old to fire at you! They gave it their best shot, "It's a matter of faith Shane. It's not something you can prove absolutely; it's what you know in your heart." Beautiful, heartfelt…but of absolutely no help to me.

In the weeks that followed my field trip to the synagogue I started doing my own research. I read articles on Judaism and Christianity in our family's *World Book Encyclopedia*, slowly branching out to read about Islam, Hinduism, and Buddhism. At the local library I discovered the philosophy and religion section. I was searching for something "authoritative." There was no shortage of books by authors claiming to have communicated with God or lesser spiritual entities, many written by adherents to the so-called "New Age" movement. It didn't take long to realize that these authors were contradicting each other: reincarnation vs. resurrection; karma vs. grace; Jesus the guru vs. Jesus the Lord; God the creator vs. extraterrestrial experimentation, etc., etc. The more I read, the more bizarre the claims became; and yet, what qualifications did I have to dispute them? The more I searched for answers, the more I realized how important it was to find them.

Religion was something I had taken for granted up until that point. When my friends and I weren't at Mass or saying our prayers before bed, it didn't seem to have much effect on our lives. We had heard stories about the miracles in the Bible and the mystical experiences of the saints, but none of us felt "holy enough" to encounter anything like that. Besides, from what we heard, religious people seemed to have replaced a lot of fun with a lot of suffering - not much there to attract a middle school student. That was changing in my case though.

I was coming to see that religion was a matter of truth - objective truth. It meant seeing reality as it truly is. Either God has given us rules to live by or He hasn't. Either the choices we make have eternal consequences or they don't. Either Christianity was true, or millions of people were wasting their Sunday mornings. If God was the creator, and ultimately judge of all, then I wanted to know what He desired of me. If He had become a human being, or sent a human being to speak to us, then I wanted to hear the message.

Needless to say, the more I read and thought, the more questions I had for mom and dad. I think they finally saw that, "you just have to have faith" wasn't going to cut it. My dad had grown up Catholic and, although he hadn't been to Mass in awhile, had developed a love for studying Scripture. When he first started reading the Bible, I feared he'd become a "religious fanatic," but reading Scripture didn't seem so crazy anymore. In answer to my question of whether or not Jesus actually claimed to be God, dad was able to show me verses in the New Testament, in John's Gospel, where Jesus referred to himself as "I Am" - God's personal name in the Jewish Scriptures (Exodus 3:14). All the conflicting views I'd encountered had made me suspicious though; how did he know the New Testament gave us the words of Jesus and not just the mistaken conclusions of his disciples?

I moved from questioning which religion was true to asking how I could be sure there even was a God. With so much confusion on the issue, wasn't it possible that *everyone* had gotten it wrong? That possibility, much to my surprise, took a tremendous toll on me. It was because I could see what a life apart from even the idea of God meant: in the end, our lives could only be loneliness and emptiness. As good as my parents and my brother and sister were to me, deaths in the families of classmates taught me that it could all be snatched away in the time it took for two cars to collide. In middle school my circle of friends (or, "popularity/ protection pacts") could change from month to month, so there weren't really outside relationships to count on. And if there had been, death still would have loomed in the distance.

The gravity of it all caught up with me one night while sitting and talking with my mom. I blurted out, "I need to know if there is a God out there who loves me. I just want to know if I'm loved, and if I can count on being loved. If I had that, then I would be willing to do anything He asked of me. I wouldn't care if people thought I was a religious fanatic; I just have to know. I need to know." I didn't recognize it at the time, but God can't resist that kind of desire.[1]

A few days later I passed by the kitchen and spied my dad sitting at the table working on a project. I decided to put him on the hot-seat one more time, "Dad, tell me again why you believe in Jesus." He didn't tell me to have faith, and he didn't reach for the Bible; instead he looked into my eyes and said, "Shane, Jesus loves you so much that He weeps for you. He wants *you*, but you won't come to Him." And then...

I saw Him.

In my mind's eye I saw Jesus sitting, His head pressed into His hands and His shoulders convulsing as He wept for me.

It happened in an instant, a "flash" in my mind's eye. It wasn't the kind of evidence I had been searching for – objective, verifiable, free from emo-

---

[1] He is its source.

tion[2] – and yet it was *personally undeniable*. Over twenty years have passed since that day, and I'm still feeling the reverberations. I didn't know quite how to explain it to others until I came across this description years later from Caryll Houselander, a Catholic mystic:

> What do I mean by saying that I "saw"? Frankly, in the ordinary way I did not see anything at all; at least I did not see…with my eyes. I saw…*with my mind*…in a way that is unforgettable, though in fact it was something suddenly *known*, rather than seen. But it was known not as one knows something through learning about it, but simply by seeing it…"alive" and "unforgettable."[3]

And what did I know in that moment? I knew that Jesus of Nazareth was alive, bodily and spiritually alive, and that He loved me with everything in Him. I knew that He was God the Father's outstretched hand to me, the Truth I had been seeking. I burst into tears right there at the kitchen table – tears of remorse for doubting, tears of gratitude for what I'd been shown. I can't tell you how my dad reacted to my tears or anything else he said to me that afternoon. I know that I really talked to Jesus though - for the first time in a long time. In the years since, I've come to feel a kinship with the "doubting" Apostle, Thomas. Appearing to him after the resurrection, Jesus said:

> "[Thomas] put your finger here, and see my hands; and put out your hand, and place it in my side; do not be faithless, but believing."
> Thomas answered him, "My Lord and my God!" (John 20:27-28).

In the end, I've realized that it wasn't so much me seeking Jesus, as it was His seeking me. I will eternally thank Him for allowing me my "crisis of faith" because it brought me to my senses, woke me to the reality of being loved by the Living God. How about you, are you awake yet?

---

[2] In time, I would encounter what I consider good, objective reasons to believe in God's existence. To explore these, I refer the reader to Appendix I. Reasons for giving Jesus' claims a fair hearing are explored in Appendix II.
[3] Found in Patricia Treece's *Apparitions of Modern Saints* (Ann Arbor, MI: Servant Publications, 2001), p.35.

Chapter 2 – Discovering the "New" in the "Old"

[Jesus] said to them, "…Was it not necessary that the Christ should suffer these things and enter into his glory?" And beginning with Moses and all the prophets, he interpreted to them in all the Scriptures the things concerning himself (Luke 24:25-27).

After that experience I was hungry for *authoritative* information about Jesus. At some point I had heard my grandmother speak highly of Billy Graham, so I went to the library and grabbed one of his books. He in turn pointed me toward the New Testament and regular prayer, a combination allowing a seeker to hear from Jesus Himself.

The next two chapters are not light reading, but they are essential for understanding *Who* I found myself dealing with. What does Christianity mean when it says God is a *Trinity* of Persons? And why is it so important for understanding the Christian view of humanity, sin, and redemption? With this foundation in place we will better understand God's action in the life of Israel, and then in the next chapter, how it culminated, to the benefit of the entire world, in Jesus of Nazareth. So in the space of two short chapters we are going to try and glimpse the thread running through the entire Bible: Jesus, loving His Father, in the Holy Spirit.

The Triune God [4]

Throughout elementary, and then high school, everything religion teachers and ministers taught me about the Trinity could be summed up in two points: It is a mystery, impossible to completely understand; and the best image for it is the shamrock. Tragically, a vast number of us never progress further. Why is that a tragedy? Because without the understanding of God as a Trinity of Persons, the heart of Christianity will always be elusive. Everything progresses, everything comes into sharper focus, with the realization that God is *interiorly* a relationship of unfathomable, reciprocal Love. To arrive at this, however, we will have to get a bit "abstract" first.

---

[4] I owe a tremendous debt of gratitude for the thoughts shared here to Frank Sheed, *Theology and Sanity* (San Francisco: Ignatius Press, 1986); Gerald O'Collins, *The Tripersonal God* (New York: Paulist Press, 1984); and Scott Hahn, *The Catholic Gospel* (Audiocassette Series by St. Joseph Communications).

8   THE GOD WHO IS LOVE

Like Judaism and Islam, Christianity begins with the conviction that God is infinite;[5] His intellect and power are inexhaustible. Saying that such a Being "knows everything in the universe" is a given. A person of faith can go further and say that God knows all *possible* worlds – even different realms of creation, such as the angelic. But again, for a Being of infinite intelligence - not that spectacular. To say something truly breath-taking about God's intelligence, you would have to say…"He knows *Himself,* His *infinite Self.*"

Allow that statement to sink in. As persons, you and I have an idea of who we are – a picture in our mind of our appearance, a record of our past, and judgments as to strengths and weaknesses. We can flip on the television and hear what a high priority people place on "finding themselves," discovering what they want out of life. I am sure you have found through experience, however, that our self-images are often in error.

If we acknowledge that God is perfect though, then the same has to be said for His idea of Himself. It would have to be a perfect reflection – and more: there would be nothing in the Thinker that was not also present in His thought of Himself. All of God's attributes must be shared in by His idea: His infinite power, intelligence, will, divine life - even *Personhood.* Now I realize that is a lot to take in; I would recommend rereading the paragraph a few times before continuing.

Alright, lets go one step farther now. Because God stands outside of space and time, He has no beginning. He did not develop, did not grow; He, and He alone, simply IS. There could never have been a time when He was without this knowledge of Himself. So we have God and this *living* Thought always dwelling within Him. I suggest taking another pause.

Now, let me come at this from a different direction, the personalist: from eternity there is one divine Person coming forth from Another. One divine Person, a Son, being generated by Another, His Father. *All that the Father is,* He gives; all that the Son is *He receives.* The Son cannot *be* apart from the Father. The Son is the One Who eternally comes forth from Him.

---

[5] To make such a claim for God is not really a matter of faith, but of reason. *Appendix I* illustrates how a fair-minded, scientific observer can conclude that our universe is the product of design, the work of a Creator. Logically, therefore, the Creator would have to exist both "before" and "outside" of it. His existence, intellect, and power would thus transcend the universe – be infinite.

And this is what we find when we turn to the New Testament. There is a slight change in terminology though. When the Son entered the human race, He was not called the Father's Idea, but His *Word* - exactly what we call an idea that has entered the world![6]

The Father's sharing of Himself with the Son is mirrored in the Son's return of love. As perfect Lovers, Each pours Himself out to the Other, holding nothing of Themselves back. Their love shares in Their very *being*; it is *all that They are* - infinitely powerful, filled with Their intelligence, will, *life*. Their Love, precisely because it is Theirs, is divinely alive, is Person – Their Holy Spirit.[7]

"Three Persons in one God," is the statement traditionally used by Christianity to define "Trinity." We can see something of this three-in-one when we look at ourselves; for as Judaism first taught, humanity is made in the "image and likeness of God" (Genesis 1:27). Our existence could be said to image the Father; our thought within us, the Son; and our capacity

---

[6] Consider the following passages: "In the beginning was the Word, and the Word was with God, and the Word was God" (John 1:1). "In this, the final age, God has *spoken* to us through his Son…This Son is the reflection of the Father's glory, the exact representation of the Father's being" (Hebrews 1:2-3, NIV). In John's Gospel we hear Jesus say, "He who has seen me has seen the Father…I am in the Father and the Father in me" (14:9-10). "The Son can do nothing by himself; he can do only what he sees his Father doing, because whatever the Father does the Son also does" (John 5:19, NIV).

This is also what we find in the Nicene Creed, professed by Christians for the past 1600 years: "We believe in one Lord, Jesus Christ, the only Son of God eternally begotten of the Father, God from God, Light from Light, true God from true God, begotten, not made, one in Being with the Father.

[7] In the New Testament the Spirit is spoken of as a distinct Person, but always proceeding from the Father and the Son: "exalted at the right hand of God, and having received from the Father the promise of the Holy Spirit, [Jesus] has poured out this which you see and hear" (Acts 2:33); The Apostle Paul and his companions were "forbidden by the Holy Spirit to speak the word in Asia…they attempted to go into Bithynia, but the Spirit of Jesus did not allow them" (Acts 16:6-7); according to Paul it was God the Holy Spirit Who spoke in the Old Testament's *Psalm 95* , "Therefore, as the Holy Spirit says, 'Today, when you hear his voice, do not harden your hearts'…" (Epistle to the Hebrews 3:7-8).

This again, is what we see reflected in Christianity's Nicene Creed: "We believe in the Holy Spirit, the Lord, the giver of life, who proceeds from the Father and the Son. With the Father and the Son he is worshiped and glorified. He has spoken through the prophets."

to demonstrate love, proceeding as it does from both our existence and thought, the Spirit. I am an individual being and yet these three aspects co-exist in me, flow out of one another, and complete one another. Take any one of these away and I cease to be me. I am but a pale reflection of the Triune God – infinite Existence, Knowledge, and Love intertwined, flowing to and from One Another.

When the New Testament says, "God is Love," (1 John 4:8) it is not describing one of His traits, but defining His very Being! The One God is an exchange of Love - The Father and Son giving themselves to Each Other in the Person of the Holy Spirit.

God the Creator

This brings us to a very interesting point: if God is so complete, then why did He create other beings? What can an angel or a human give Him that He does not already have, and to an infinite degree? Nothing, absolutely nothing; He could not have created us because of anything we could give Him. The only logical alternative is that He created to *give to us*, to allow us to share in the Love that He is! That kind of generosity is beyond our human power to express. No wonder we call the Trinity mystery!

Hebrew Scripture begins with God's act of creation. Pregnant within those first pages is the later recognition of God's Trinitarian nature: while "the Spirit of God was moving over the face of the waters," God (the Father) spoke His Word,[8] "Let there be…" (Genesis 1:2-3). But perhaps the most pregnant words in the Old Testament are heard when God crowned His creation with man and woman:

> "Let *us* make man in *our* image, after our likeness"…So God created man in his own image, in the image of God He created him; *male and female* he created them. And God blessed them, and God said to them, "Be fruitful and *multiply*" (Genesis 1:26-28).

---

[8]The New Testament will bear witness that Jesus, the Son, was the Word "through Whom [God] made the universe" (Heb.1:2). "In the beginning was the Word…Through him all things were made" (John 1:1,3); "He is the image of the invisible God…For by him all things were created: things in heaven and on earth, visible and invisible" (Colossians 1:15-16).

God, Who *is* a bond of Love, created us to live in His image *as a bond of love!* Man and woman reflect the very Oneness of God when they "become one flesh" (Gen.2:24). Their Oneness is so real, so complete, that oftentimes after nine months you have to give their love *his* or *her* own name![9] Man, woman, and child, living as a family, give us a glimpse of God's inner life.

There is a second aspect of what it means to be created in God's "image and likeness." The phrase carries with it the revelation that we were created as God's sons and daughters.[10] God's act of creation is described as forming man from the clay of the earth and "breath[ing] into his nostrils the breath of life," making man a "*living* being" (Gen.2:7).

That "breath of life" is what we today call the soul, spirit, or heart. To bridge the gap between His transcendence and material creation, God created man and woman with an immaterial component. Like all animal life, we are equipped with strong instincts and drives (self-preservation, fight-or-flight, sex). Unlike the rest of nature, however, we have been given a spiritual soul to integrate these drives and channel them so as to give ourselves in love in imitation of God's Love. Where does the human soul receive that kind of strength? From God dwelling in it, filling it with His Own divine Life!

The first man and woman were created as God's son and daughter, and as such bore a special likeness to God the Son. Like Him, we have received all we are from the Father and are blessed with the capacity to give ourselves back to Him. We can allow God to make a gift of Himself to us in the Person of the Spirit (Love), and then cooperate with the Spirit as He moves us in a return of love to the Father and a sharing of that love with our brothers and sisters. Man and woman shared in the Life, the Love, of the Trinity! It was that state that Scripture called Eden, Paradise – and rightly so.

---

[9] Hahn, Scott. *First Comes Love: Finding Your Family in the Church and the Trinity* (New York: Doubleday, 2000) p.46.

[10] Genesis makes this clear when, just a few chapters later it tells us, "When God created man, he made him in the likeness of God. Male and female he created them…When Adam had lived a hundred and thirty years, he became the father of a son *in his likeness, after his image*" (Gen.5:1,3).

Our Self-Inflicted Wound

When the first man and woman chose to disobey the Father's command, that was what they rejected! Instead of continuing to live as children receiving everything from God's hand, learning right from wrong, learning the way of Love, they chose to make those determinations for themselves. It is mind-boggling how they could make such a foolish choice. Scripture makes their action more intelligible telling us that they were deceived, their convictions about God's Love tampered with, by a member of a higher realm in creation. In Scripture this being (elsewhere described as an angel) is called the Devil (in Hebrew "deceiver") and Satan (or "adversary"). Deceived though they were, it was still our first parents' decision to make, their free choice. The results were catastrophic.

Without God living in them, they could no longer be sons and daughters; they had lost their spiritual likeness to God the Son. As such, their souls were wounded. That is what Christianity means when it says our race "fell from grace;" our first parents rejected their position as children and fell to the level of mere creatures. And like the rest of earth's creatures, they had to contend with the strength of their biological and emotional drives. Because God's Love, His Spirit, had been forced from their souls they did not have the power to direct their passions. We human beings have felt the effects ever since: being overwhelmed by our anger, using other people as a means of gratification, hording material blessings, exerting our private will at the cost of others' liberty. That original sin, or act in opposition to God's Love, became the source of all other sins: lies, insults, theft, sexual misuse and abuse, neglect, and murder. Our experience of being human would have been exceedingly different, had our first parents not sinned. Scripture even reveals that our bodies would not have experienced death and decomposition.

As a result of the first sin we find ourselves incomplete. The most intelligent of Earth's creatures, capable of incredible artistic, technological, and scientific accomplishment; and yet we find ourselves ravished by our desires for acceptance and security. These are good desires, but when sought in any way, at any cost, they become destructive. We find ourselves subject to death, the dissolution of body from soul.[11] We are tortured as we look at ourselves and our world because we have the conviction that things *should* be different. We pass through life with an ongoing feeling of incompleteness and no level of achievement, no relationship, fills the void for long. Where do these feelings come from if not from our spiritual poverty, our lack of the loving Spirit of God at our core? Because at root our problem is spiritual, we have no hope of putting things right without God; only His Life at our core can bring us back into balance.

The Promise of Salvation

We have no right, no legal claim to make upon Him to regain our position as children. Being created in that state was pure gift from the start. He had every right to leave our first parents, to leave all of us who have ratified their decision a trillion times over, to our miserable incompleteness. But He did not, and that is what all of Judaism and Christianity deals with: God's action to heal our self-inflicted wound, to raise disobedient creatures up into a Parent-child relationship! Never forget, God is Love: "[He] is patient and kind...[He] is not irritable or resentful...[He] bears all things...hopes all things, endures all things" (1 Corinthians 13:4-5,7).

In the *Genesis* narrative we see God turn immediately from the fallen man and woman to address their angelic Adversary, "I will put enmity between you and the woman, and between your seed and hers; he will crush your head, and you will strike his heel" (3:15, NIV). I find these words incredibly intriguing. First there is the usage of "seed" for the *woman's* offspring. In Scripture, seed is the male's contribution in procreation. What is there about this promised offspring that he is described *solely* as the *seed of the woman*? Is something unusual implied about his manner of birth? Second, how can the promised offspring crush the *Adversary's head*? The Adversary is of a higher realm, a creature of immense spiritual power. Given man and woman's fallen state, how is that possible? Who is this offspring that he can "crush" angels? To wield that kind of spiritual power it is obvious his soul could not be damaged the way yours and mine are. And third, what

---

[11] And what is the experience of a soul divorced from its body, without God's Life dwelling in it? It has no connection to the material world, no union with the Trinity. It exists in a solitary *agony*, "hell."

wound will the woman's offspring suffer? The Adversary "will strike his heel" but be unable to vanquish him. So many questions for such a small verse! And yet, that small verse is where the hope of salvation begins.

Israel: God Begins Healing the Wound

As the human race spread out over the earth, its memory of its loving Creator became distorted. It projected its own disunity and sinful choices onto the divine, arriving at pantheons of gods. Its sense of right and wrong, of what it meant to act in imitation of the God of Love, likewise became clouded. Humanity's Adversary undoubtedly assisted in deepening the darkness.[12]

Out of His mercy and Love, God called a man, Abraham, to step out of the darkness by leaving his polytheistic homeland to set out for another God would show him (the land of Canaan). Abraham's obedient faith allowed God to bestow many blessings on him. He and his wife had been unable to have children. When he was about *eighty years old* God promised that "your own son shall be your heir. Look toward heaven and number the stars, if you are able to number them…So shall your descendants be" (Gen.15:4-5). God gave Abraham the covenant of circumcision to mark his male descendants, on their eighth day of life, as God's chosen ones (Gen.17:12). When he was a hundred years old his promised son, Isaac, was born.

When Isaac was a bit older, God asked Abraham to do something very strange, barbaric even, with the boy. It is an incident we have to spend some time on. God said to him, "Take your son, your only son Isaac, whom you love and go to the land of Moriah, and offer him there as a burnt offering upon one of the mountains of which I shall tell you" (Gen.22:2). What happened to the God Who Is Love we might ask? Scripture continues, "Abraham took the wood of the burnt offering, and laid it on Isaac his son," who carried it up the mountain (Gen.22:6). Abraham told the servants who had accompanied them, "I and the lad will go yonder and worship, and come again to you" (22:5). Did Abraham lie to them, or did

---

[12] I believe he is still quite active; the "New Age" movement is a modern example. For a brief discussion of Christianity's stance on this movement and other occult practices, I refer you to *Appendix III*.

his absolute trust in God reveal possibilities no one else could dare to entertain? God had told him that *through Isaac* he would have descendants as numerous as the stars. If he handed over the son who *meant more to him than life*, then could not God be trusted to give him back, even if it meant raising him from the dead (Hebrews 11:19)? A second possibility presented itself to Abraham: perhaps the Lord would provide a *substitutionary* sacrifice. When Isaac asked him, "Where is the lamb for the burnt offering?" Abraham responded, "God will provide himself the lamb for a burnt offering" (22:7-8). Abraham then:

> put forth his hand, and took the knife to slay his son. But the angel of the Lord called to him from heaven, and said "Abraham! Abraham!...Do not lay your hand on the lad...now I know that you fear God, seeing you have not withheld your son, your only son, from me. And Abraham lifted up his eyes and looked, and behold, behind him was a ram caught in a thicket by his horns; and Abraham went and took the ram, and offered it up as a burnt offering instead of his son. So Abraham called the name of that place The Lord will provide; as it is said to this day, "On the mountain of the Lord it *shall be* provided" (Gen.22:10-14; italics added).

A ram offered in place of a lamb; a subtle difference. Why did Abraham's mind go specifically to a *lamb*? What will be provided on that mountain? The incident closes with God enlarging his promise to Abraham. Not only would he have numerous descendants through Isaac, but "through [Abraham's] offspring *all nations on earth* will be blessed" (Gen. 22:18, NIV)! If you the reader are not stupefied, are not seeing the parallels to events in the New Testament, don't worry – we'll connect the dots before we are done.

Abraham's descendants multiplied exponentially. Isaac had a son, Jacob, whom God renamed Israel. He in turn had twelve boys. Their descendants became known as the Twelve Tribes of Israel. When famine hit the family moved to Egypt where food was more plentiful, and eventually found itself enslaved by the pharaoh and aristocracy.

Four centuries after their arrival, God raised up Moses to return the Israelites to the homeland shown Abraham. Egypt was given one opportunity after the other to comply with God's requests concerning Israel; nine

16   THE GOD WHO IS LOVE

plagues were unable to turn the pharaoh's heart. In rejecting God's path to bringing the world Life, Egypt chose death. As we have said, death is the "full-flowering" of sin. God allowed their choice to materialize by unleashing of one of the angelic realm, "the destroyer" (Exodus 12:23). This angel would strike down the firstborn sons throughout the nation. To differentiate the Israelites from the Egyptians, God commanded that a special rite be celebrated, the Passover:

> The Lord said to Moses and [his brother] Aaron in Egypt, "Tell the whole community of Israel that on the tenth day of the month each man is to take a lamb for his family, one for each household…The animals you choose must be year-old males without defect…Take care of them until the fourteenth day of the month, when all the people of the community of Israel must slaughter them at twilight. Then they shall take some of the blood and put it on the sides and tops of the doorframes of the houses where they eat the lambs. That same night they are to eat the meat roasted over the fire…head, legs and inner parts…along with bitter herbs, and bread made without yeast…If some is left till morning, you must burn it…The blood will be a sign for you on the houses where you are; and when I see the blood, I will pass over you." (Exodus 12:1-3,5-10,13-14, NIV)

The blood of the Passover lamb saved the sons of Israel; had Abraham intuited some part of this when he spoke to Isaac of a sacrificial lamb?[13]

The shedding of the lamb's blood marked Israel's exit (exodus) from Egypt. God led them to freedom through the waters of the Red Sea (Ex.14:21-31). He fed them in the desert with "bread from heaven" (Ex.16:1-16,35) and quenched their thirst by making water flow from a rock (Ex.17:3-6) – two miracles replicated each time they stopped to camp (Ex.16:35; 1 Corinthians 10:4)!

When they reached Mount Sinai, God revealed His Law. The Law instructed them in how to live as a member of the Chosen People, the people through whom God would bring blessing to the world. The Law, its morality summarized in the Ten Commandments, called the Israelites back to the basic recognition of which actions and attitudes were incompatible with

---

[13] Mind you, however, the sacrifice of the Passover lambs occurred in Egypt, not in the "region of Moriah."

DISCOVERING THE "NEW" IN THE "OLD"

love: the worship of false gods, deception, envy, ingratitude, theft, murder. While incomplete, the Law was that first all-important step toward living in God's Truth. Given the damage done to human beings in "the fall," and the ensuing centuries of sin, it was as big a step as men and women could hope to make. All told, the Law "of Moses" contained 619 commandments. In hindsight we can see a symbolic, or instructive, element to many. The prescriptions about clean and unclean animals, for example, made the Israelites very careful about what foods entered their bodies. The step beyond this would be to pay attention to what the mind and heart were exposed to, to be critical and reject what was at odds with the God of Love.

Pledging themselves to obey the Law, the Israelites entered a covenant with God. Covenants, in the ancient world, were looked at as forming family bonds. God and His People were united in a common life. As in the Passover, this common life was enacted through the shedding of blood and the eating of the sacrificial victim:

> [They] offered burnt offerings and sacrifices as peace offerings of oxen to the Lord. And Moses took half of the blood and put it in basins, and half of the blood he threw against the altar. Then he took the book of the covenant, and read it in the hearing of the people; and they said, "All that the Lord has spoken, we will do, and we will be obedient. And Moses took the blood and threw it upon the people, and said, "Behold the blood of the covenant which the Lord has made with you in accordance with all these words."
>
> Then Moses and Aaron, Nadab, and Abihu, and seventy of the elders of Israel went up, and they saw the God of Israel…And [God] did not lay his hand [in anger] on the chief men of the people of Israel; they beheld God, and ate and drank (Exodus 24:5-11).

Almost instantaneously, however, the Israelites failed to keep the covenant (remember the "golden calf"?). Failure was inevitable given the damaged state of the human soul. Their behavior was of no surprise to God, though. Within the Law, in their prescriptions for worship, He had given instructions for the offering of atonement sacrifices. Allow me to back up a step and describe Israel's worship.

Relationship Through Sacrifice

Moses was shown a pattern and given detailed instructions for a Tabernacle, a place for God to "dwell" among His People. During Israel's wandering in the desert it would be a portable tent. Later, once settled in Canaan, it would be translated into a stone structure within Jerusalem. Outside the Tabernacle was a courtyard containing the altar of sacrifice and the "bronze sea," an immense basin for priestly washing. Upon entering the Tabernacle, you would find it illuminated by ten golden lampstands. A table containing twelve loaves of unleavened bread, one for each tribe of Israel, would stand before you. Just past it was an altar for offering incense and at the far end hung a heavy veil leading to the most sacred chamber, the Holy of Holies. It contained the Ark of the Covenant, God's earthly throne. Within the Ark were the tablets containing the Ten Commandments, the staff of Aaron (the original high priest), and a sample of the "heavenly bread" Israel received in the desert. In the Jerusalem Temple, the interior of the Holy of Holies was a perfect thirty foot cube, overlaid in pure gold. The Ark was flanked by statues, golden cherubim (angels), each having a wingspan of 15 feet.

To illustrate worship under the Mosaic Covenant, I will relate a typical visit to the Temple.[14] A father would come, as the representative of his family and give thanks to God, seek His forgiveness of sin, and ask for continued assistance. He would have the blessings of the yearly harvest with him, unleavened bread and wine. Depending on how much money the family had, he would also bring a couple of birds, a lamb, goat, or a bull. Whichever animal, it had to be perfect, without blemish. He would then slaughter the animal before the priests (who came only from one of the twelve tribes, that of Levi).

Sacrifice for the Israelites did not have the limited meaning it does today in English. No, in Israel sacrifice was the symbolic giving over of *life* to God. The God of Love is not blood-thirsty; that is not what the animal sacrifices of the Old Testament were about. Blood was used because it was the symbol of life (Leviticus 17:11). The life-blood of the animal was poured out at the base of the altar of sacrifice. Part of the animal was then

---

[14] For the insights of this section I am indebted to *The New Jerome Biblical Commentary* (Englewood Cliffs, New Jersey: Prentice Hall, 1990), p.1268-1269.

burned upon the altar in offering to God, part of it held back to be eaten by the priests, and part taken home to the family making the offering. The unleavened bread was also placed on the altar and wine poured out at its base – again, the very elements of *life* for an agricultural people such as the Israelites (Exodus 29:38-42; Leviticus 23:18). In offering sacrifice the Israelites were symbolically offering themselves to God. As in the Passover and the ratification of the covenant, so too in the Tabernacle worship - God and His People were being united in the *life* of the sacrificial victim. Communion, a family bond, was being reestablished after a lapse into sin; or in cases of thanksgiving and petition, the bond was reaffirmed and strengthened.

Thus far, worship has not progressed *into* the Tabernacle but has been reserved to the outer court. Only the priests were allowed to proceed inside the structure to offer fragrant incense. Entrance into the innermost room, the Holy of Holies, however, was reserved to the high priest - and only once a year on Yom Kippur, the Day of Atonement. On that day the sins of the entire nation were atoned for and the Temple purified from being surrounded by the world's sins. The high priest would sacrifice a bull and a goat and take their blood with him as he entered the Tabernacle. Only after sprinkling the blood, the life, on the great veil could he enter the Holy of Holies. Once inside his task was to sprinkle the life-blood on the Ark, to symbolically offer God back the gift of life He had originally bestowed. (An image of the Son? Of man and woman *prior* to the Fall? Of the seed of the woman, the descendant(s) of Abraham yet to come?)

Building a Kingdom

God molded His covenant People by keeping them in the desert wilderness for forty years. We are told of rebellion, discipline, and finally the achievement of an obedience sufficient for following God's instructions to take possession of the land. Just prior to his death, Moses foretold the coming of a great personage:

> The Lord said to me, "I will raise up a prophet like you from among their brothers; I will put my words in his mouth, and he will tell them everything I command him. If anyone does not listen to my words that

the prophet speaks in my name, he will be cut off from the people" (Deuteronomy 18:18-19, NIV).

The Israelites entered the Promised Land under the leadership of Moses' successor Joshua ("Jesus" in Greek). For a time they were governed through judges like Samson and Samuel (who also functioned as a prophet). Eventually, the people asked that a king rule the Twelve Tribes in imitation of the surrounding nations. In response, the Lord sent Samuel to anoint first Saul, and then David, as king.

Under David, Israel entered a golden age. They had peace from their enemies and plans were laid for the construction of the Temple, the "Lord's House." Nathan the prophet was sent to David with an amazing promise:

> The Lord declares to you that the LORD will make you a house. When your days are fulfilled and you lie down with your fathers, I will raise up your offspring after you, who shall come forth from your body, and I will establish his kingdom. He shall build a house for my name, and I will establish the throne of his kingdom forever. I will be his father, and he shall be my son…I will not take my steadfast love from him, as I took it from Saul, whom I put away from before you. And your house and your kingdom shall be made sure for ever before me; *your throne shall be established for ever* (2 Samuel 7:11-16).

The Psalms of David

While successful as a warrior, David was first and foremost a man of prayer, prayer set to music to be specific. Almost half of *The Book of Psalms* is attributed to him. The Psalms were unique prayers in that they were acknowledged to be the product of God's Spirit moving the psalmist. As such, portions of the Psalms were looked upon as having a prophetic character. Listen as David gives voice to a righteous sufferer in *Psalm 22*; Jesus quoted the first verse from the cross:

> *My God, my God, why hast*
> *thou forsaken me?*
> Why art thou so far from helping
>   me, from the words of my groan-

ings?...
All who see me mock at me,
    they make mouths at me, they wag
    their heads,
"He committed his cause to the
    LORD; let him deliver him,
let him rescue him, for he delights
    in him."...
Yea, dogs are round about me,
    a company of evildoers encircle
    me;
    they have pierced my hands and
    feet -
I can count all my bones -
    they stare and gloat over me;
they divide my garments among them,
and for my raimente they cast lots...
I will tell of thy name to my brethren;
    in the midst of the congregation I
    will praise thee:
You who fear the Lord, praise him!...
For he has not despised or abhorred
    the affliction of the afflicted,
and he has not hid his face from him,
    but has heard ,when he cried to
    him
(Psalm 22: 1,7-8,16-18, 22-24).

David was also moved to use resurrection imagery in describing God's faithful care of those walking in His ways:

I set the LORD ever before me;
    with him at my right hand I shall
    not be disturbed.
Therefore my heart is glad and my
    soul rejoices,
My body, too, abides in confi-

> dence;
> Because you will not abandon my
> > soul in the nether world,
> > nor will you suffer your faithful
> > one to undergo corruption.
> You will show me the path to life,
> > fullness of joy in your presence,
> > the delights at your right hand
> > forever (Psalm 16:8-11, NIV).

Stirred by the Spirit, David spoke at greater length of God's promise to one of his descendants:

> The kings of the earth set them-
> > selves,
> > and the rulers take counsel to-
> > gether,
> > against the LORD and against his anointed [Messiah]...
> I will tell of the decree of the LORD:
> He said to me, "You are my son,
> > today I have begotten you.
> Ask of me, and I will make the na-
> > tions your heritage,
> > and the ends of the earth your
> > possession.
> You shall break them with a rod of
> > iron,
> > and dash them in pieces like a
> > potter's vessel"
> (Psalm 2:2,7-10).

> The LORD said to my Lord:
> > "Sit at my right hand
> till I make your enemies
> > your footstool."
> The Lord has sworn
> > and will not change his mind,

"You are a priest for ever,
after the order of Melchizedek"[15]
(Psalm 110:1,4).

The Kingdom Crumbles

Under the leadership of David's son Solomon, Israel saw not only the building of the Temple[16] but the nation expand its borders farther than ever before. Solomon built an extensive network of alliances through marriage. Dignitaries traveled great distances to hear Solomon's renowned wisdom.

That is not to say that David and Solomon were immune from the effects of the Fall; they clearly were not. Scripture tells us specifically that David was tempted by, and succumbed to, the Adversary (1 Chronicles 21:1). He likewise gave in to his own unruly passions, committing adultery and arranging a murder! Solomon faired no better, going so far as to follow his foreign wives in the worship of false gods! The effects of sin continued to be felt, shattering the unity of the kingdom shortly after Solomon's death. The two southern tribes, Judah and Benjamin, remained loyal to the line of David and Solomon and became known as the Kingdom of Judah. Its capital remained Jerusalem. The other ten tribes united under a rival monarchy and retained the name Israel.

The political reality was reflected in the spiritual. Both kingdoms suffered bouts of corruption and even idolatry. God sent prophets to call the people back. The words from Hosea are especially striking:

---

[15] That final verse, concerning Melchizedek, had to cause puzzlement. A priest forever? Israelite priests came from the Tribe of Levi, but David and his descendants were from the Tribe of Judah. And Melchizedek – Scripture tells us only two things about him. First, living some six hundred years before David, he was the king and priest of Salem – later Jerusalem, the very city David had captured and made his capital. And second, that Melchizedek offered a thanksgiving sacrifice, a *sacrifice of bread and wine*, on behalf of Abraham, the father of the Israelites (Genesis 14:18-20). How all of this would apply to David's promised descendant remained a mystery

[16] The Temple was constructed on Mount Moriah, where Jewish tradition held that Abraham had brought Isaac to sacrifice.

> Come, let us return to the LORD;
> > for he has torn, that he may heal us;
> > he has stricken, and he will bind us up.
> > ==After two days he will revive us;==
> > ==*on the third day he will raise us up,*==
> > ==*that we may live before him*== (6:1-2).

Through the prophet Isaiah God spoke of His Servant. The designation is intriguing because it is sometimes applicable to God's People as a whole, while at others it clearly refers to an individual within the People. Observe the following passage where the Servant's suffering is said to atone for the sins of the people:

> Behold, my servant shall prosper,
> > he shall be exalted and lifted up,
> > and shall be very high.
> As many were astonished at him –
> > his appearance was so marred,
> > beyond human semblance,
> > and his form beyond that of the sons of men –
> so shall he startle many nations;
> > kings shall shut their mouths because of him...
> He was despised and rejected by men;
> > a man of sorrows, and acquainted with grief...
> Surely he has borne our griefs
> > and carried our sorrows;
> yet we esteemed him stricken,
> > smitten by God, and afflicted.
> But *he was wounded for our transgressions,*
> > he was bruised for our iniquities;

upon him.was the chastisement that
> made us whole,
> and with his stripes we are healed…

He was oppressed, and he was
> afflicted,
> yet he opened not his mouth;

like a lamb that is led to the slaugh-
> *ter,*
> and like a sheep that before its
> shearers is dumb,
> so he opened not his mouth…

he was cut off out of the land of
> *the living,*
> stricken for the transgression of my
> people.

And they made his grave with the
> wicked
> and with a rich man in his death,

although he had done no violence,
> and there was no deceit in his
> mouth…
> he shall see the fruit of the travail
> of his soul be satisfied;

by his knowledge shall the righteous
> one, my servant,
> make many to be accounted
> righteous;
> and he shall bear their iniquities.

Therefore I will divide him a portion
> with the great,
> and he shall divide the spoil with
> the strong;

because he poured out his soul to
> death,
> and was numbered with the trans-
> gressors;

> yet he bore the sin of many,
>> and made intercession for the
>> transgressors
>
> (Isaiah 52:13; 53:3-5,7-9,11-12).

Speaking in the person of the Servant, Isaiah revealed God's plan for using the Servant to bless not just the Chosen People, but the Gentiles:

> And now the Lord say,
>> who formed me from the womb
>> to be his servant,
> to bring Jacob back to him,
>> and that Israel might be gathered
>> to him...
> "It is too light a thing that you
>> should be my servant
>> to raise up the tribes of Jacob
>> and to restore the preserved of
>> Israel;
> I will give you as a light to the na-
>> tions,
>> that my salvation may reach to the
>> end of the earth"
>
> (Isaiah 49:5-6).

The work of this Servant would take place at some point in the future.

During the period under consideration, God removed His protective hand and allowed both Israel and Judah, like Egypt, to experience the flowering of sin. In 722 B.C., Israel was conquered by Assyria. The ten northern tribes were lost among the Gentile nations, taken into exile never to return. Judah fell to Babylon in 586 B.C. David's reigning descendant, Zedekiah, was taken to Babylon in chains, soon to be followed by successive waves of his countrymen.

Promises of Restoration

Conquered though they were, God remained close to the people of Judah, the Jews, calling the prophets Ezekiel and Jeremiah to minister to them. Ezekiel had been among the first of the exiles to Babylon. The Lord

DISCOVERING THE "NEW" IN THE "OLD" 27

used him to ready the exiles for the news that, since their departure, Jerusalem and the Temple had been destroyed. The Ark of the Covenant would not be seen again. The way God showed Jerusalem's destruction, and marked those to be spared, is quite curious from a Christian perspective:

> I saw six men coming from the direction of the upper gate which faces the north, each with a destroying weapon in his hand. In their midst was a man dressed in linen, with a writer's case at his waist. They entered [the Temple] and stood beside the bronze altar. Then he called to the man dressed in linen with the writer's case at his waist, saying to him, "Pass through the city and mark an X on the foreheads of those who moan and groan over all the abominations that are practiced within it." To the others I heard him say, "Pass through the city after him and strike! Do not look on them with pity nor show any mercy! Old men, youths and maidens, women and children--wipe them out! But do not touch any marked with the X; begin at my sanctuary" (Ezekiel 9:2-6, NIV).

God's People were coming face-to-face with their brokenness, their spiritual inability to keep the Covenant made through Moses. They needed a salvation from *outside of themselves* that could somehow reach *inside* and empower them to live as God desired, to Love as the Trinity did. They were ready to hear God's promise of a New Covenant – and not one for Judah alone, but for Israel lost among the nations too:

> I will take you out from the nations, and gather you from all the countries, and bring you into your own land. I will sprinkle clean water upon you, and you shall be clean from all your uncleanness, and from all your idols I will cleanse you. A new heart I will give you, and a new spirit I will put within you; I will take out of your flesh the heart of stone and give you a heart of flesh. And I will put my spirit within you, and cause you to walk in my statutes and be careful to observe my ordinances (Ezekiel 36:24-27).

Simultaneous with Ezekiel's announcement to the exiles in Babylon was Jeremiah's to the survivors in Judah:

> "Behold, the days are coming says the Lord, when I will make a new covenant with the house of Israel and the house of Judah, not like the

> covenant I made with their fathers…But this is the covenant which I will make with the house of Israel after those days, says the LORD: I will put my law within them, and I will write it upon their hearts; and I will be their God, and they shall be my people. And no longer shall each man teach his neighbor and each his brother, saying, 'Know the LORD,' for they shall all know me, from the least of them to the greatest, says the LORD; for I will forgive their iniquity, and I will remember their sin no more" (Jeremiah 31:31-34).

After approximately seventy years in exile God brought the Jews back to their homeland, just as Isaiah, Ezekiel, and Jeremiah had prophesied. Babylon had been conquered by the Persians and its exiles allowed to return home. Under the leadership of people like Ezra and Nehemiah the people set about rebuilding Jerusalem and the Temple.

During this period the prophets had a great deal to say about the restoration of David's Kingdom. Allow me to back up a step, to an oracle of Ezekiel's and then move forward:

> …one king shall be king over them all; and they shall be no longer two nations, and no longer divided into two kingdoms…I will save them from all their backslidings in which they have sinned, and cleanse them; and they shall be my people, and I will be their God. *My servant David shall be king over them*; and they shall all have one shepherd. They shall follow my ordinances and be careful to observe my statutes… David my servant will be their prince *forever*. I will make a covenant of peace with them; it shall be an everlasting covenant with them; and I will bless them and multiply them, and will set my sanctuary in the midst of them for evermore. My dwelling place shall be with them; and I will be their God, and they shall be my people. Then the nations will know that I the LORD sanctify Israel, when my sanctuary is in the midst of them for evermore (Ezekiel 37:22-27).

This mighty king, coming from the line of David, was designated *the Messiah*, Hebrew for "Anointed One."[17] The prophet Zechariah had more to say about him:

> Hear now, O Joshua high priest, you and your friends who sit before you, for they are men of good omen: behold, I will bring my servant the Branch. . .and I will remove the guilt of this land in a single day (Zechariah 3:8-9).

> Rejoice greatly, O daughter of Zion!
> Shout aloud, O daughter of Jerusalem!
> Lo, your king comes to you;
> triumphant and victorious is he,
> humble and riding on an ass,
> on a colt the foal of an ass…
> he shall command peace to the
> nations;
> his dominion shall be from sea to sea,
> and from the River [Euphrates] to the ends of
> the earth (9:9-10).

Listen to one of Zechariah's later oracles. While it does not specifically mention the Messiah, it clearly refers to the time when God would fulfill His promises:

> And I will pour out on the house of David and the inhabitants of Jerusalem a spirit of compassion and supplication, so that, when they look on him whom they have pierced, they shall mourn for him, as one mourns for an only child, and weep bitterly over him, as one weeps over a first-born …On that day there shall be a fountain opened for the house of David and the inhabitants of Jerusalem to cleanse them from sin and uncleanness (12:10; 13:1).

The intervening centuries between the rebuilding of Jerusalem and the birth of Jesus were tumultuous. Alexander the Great conquered Palestine in 332 B.C. At his death, his empire was divided into four and given to his

---

[17] The term was applicable to all of the kings in David's line, for they were all anointed with oil when taking the throne. In popular usage, however, the term came to refer to the prophesied great king, the one to restore Israel and remain with them *forever*.

generals to rule. By 198 B.C. the rulers over the quadrant that included Jerusalem, the Seleucids, began forcing Greek culture upon their subjects. Bath houses were built in Jerusalem and men encouraged to reverse their circumcision. When Antiochus IV (Epiphanes) came to power in 175 B.C., he defiled the Jerusalem Temple by erecting a statue of Zeus in the Holy of Holies. He also outlawed the Jewish Scripture. It was apparently at this time that the *Book of Daniel* was set in its present form. Daniel, a prophet centuries before, at the time of the Babylonian exile, offered words of great encouragement to the persecuted:

> I saw in the night visions,
> and behold, with the clouds of heaven
> > there came one like a son of man,
> and he came to the Ancient of Days
> > and was presented before him.
> And to him was given dominion
> > and glory and kingdom,
> > > that all peoples, nations, and langauges
> > > should serve him;
> his dominion is an everlasting dominion,
> > which shall not pass away,
> and his kingdom one,
> > that shall not be destroyed (7:13-14).[18]

---

[18] Daniel shortly thereafter stated the interpretation of the vision, "the saints of the Most High will receive the kingdom and will possess it forever" (Dan.7:18). We saw a similar creative tension in Isaiah's descriptions of the Servant. I think we can describe Daniel's Son of Man as an individual figure who represents God's people, reconstitutes them himself. Interestingly, "Son of Man" was Jesus' most frequent self-designation.

Strengthened by God's promises and led by the Hasmoneans, a family of priests, the Jews fought a guerilla warfare. By 164 B.C., they had both secured Jerusalem and rededicated the Temple. The Hasmoneans agreed to govern the Jewish people until God sent a prophet to direct them. In 63 B.C. the Roman general Pompey conquered Palestine and the Romans installed their own king, Herod. And with that the stage was fully set, ready for the Almighty God to enter creation in the most unexpected of ways – as a baby!

Chapter 3 – Jesus, Through the Eyes of Faith

"And you," Jesus said to them, "Who do you say that I am?"
"You are the Messiah," Simon Peter answered, "the Son of the living God!" (Matthew 16:15-16, NIV).

"But when the time had fully come, God sent forth his Son, born of a woman, born under the law" (Galatians 4:4). That woman was of course Mary of Nazareth, engaged to Joseph, a descendant of David. Mary, like Abraham, gave God the "yes," the cooperation He so desired to bless humanity (Gen.22:18). With Mary's consent, "the Word became flesh and dwelt [literally "tabernacled"] among us" (John 1:14). This Tabernacle/Temple imagery reoccurs in Luke's Gospel: "The Holy Spirit will come upon you and the power of the Most High will overshadow you; therefore, the child to be born will be called holy, the Son of God" (Luke 1:35). This was the language used in the Old Testament to describe God's coming to dwell in the Tabernacle and Temple (Exodus 40:34; 1 Kings 8:10). God Himself came to dwell in Mary – became her Son! And He did this without a male's contribution; Jesus is the prophesied "seed of the woman" (Gen.3:15). Notice too in the angel's message, the revelation of the entire Trinity (i.e., Holy Spirit, Most High, Son).

We have already seen how man and woman were created to reflect the Son's receiving of Himself and giving of Himself to the Father (in the Spirit). He became a human being so that humanity, in His Person, could finally do what it was created to do – enter into the exchange of Love within the Trinity!

True God and True Man

What does it mean to say that God the Son *became* a man? First, Christianity is *not* saying that the Son surrendered His divinity. The doctrine of the "incarnation" says that Jesus is true God and true man, simultaneously. The two natures are not mixed together in some type of divine-human jumble. Quite the contrary, they remain unconfused. Jesus' humanity is not swallowed up by His divinity. As a man He is not spared any of the fatigue, exertion, etc. that you or I are. His human mind is finite, has a limit. He has a human will that makes decisions. To meet the man Jesus, however, is to meet God Himself. That human nature, that union of body and soul, is His

– is fused to His Divine Person forever. The words and actions are the *human words and actions of God the Son.*

The *only* difference between Jesus and other men and women is in the soul. You and I are born with that gaping hole, the absence of the Holy Spirit. Jesus' human nature, the human nature of the Word, is filled with the Spirit. He is what we were created to be; not only does He show us God, but He shows us ourselves. His soul was not damaged, His passions not out of balance; yet He freely took upon Himself the effects of the Fall, our subjection to physical suffering and death.

There are a lot of things about Jesus' life, simple things, that we fail to recognize. His relationship with Mary and Joseph is a perfect example. They were His *parents*; He was completely dependent on them. If Mary and Joseph didn't feed Him, He would have starved! They changed His diapers and potty-trained Him. He may have been the Word of the Father in His divine nature, but in His human nature it was Mary and Joseph who took him from babbling to conversation. While it is obvious that Jesus received knowledge supernaturally during His public ministry, we have to recognize that a great deal entered His human mind through Mary and Joseph's words and example, His own reading of Scripture and daily experiences.[19] Even though Joseph was not His biological father, he was still His dad – His protector, provider and guide; and when he died, it would have been Jesus' duty to wash his body and prepare it for burial. I can only begin to understand how difficult that had to be for Him. In a culture where women could not work outside of the home, it would have then fallen to Jesus to provide his mother's daily bread. He knew what it was to work and be depended upon to make a living, and the work he did was manual. It took time and sweat, and if His customers didn't like it, He didn't get paid.

Jesus lived as His neighbors did. He was a country boy from Nazareth. No one expected anything different from Him; the Gospels tell us that His neighbors were shocked when He began preaching. Growing up in Galilee, Jews closer to Jerusalem would have thought He had an accent. When we recall His preaching, we do not hear it with a "twang," but the odds are decent that that was how it was delivered.

---

[19] Remember how when He was 12, His parents found Him in the Temple asking questions of the teachers (Luke 2:46-47)?

It is easy to forget that, within Judaism, Jesus was a layperson. He, being a descendant of David, was of the Tribe of Judah; and priests came only from the Tribe of Levi. God the Son didn't have the religious "credentials" to enter the Holy of Holies!

Jesus shared in the same good, healthy human desires we all do. He cherished His friends. Like all of us He also needed time to be alone, to turn to His Father in prayer, and "recharge His batteries." Jesus was a young man; he was able to look at a young woman and appreciate her beauty (both inner and outer).[20] When all of His friends started courting and getting married He didn't; He had to feel like a "third wheel" at times. Jesus, God the Son, knew what it was to be a "nobody" – to live over 90% of His life in a small town, work hard to put food on the table, and *appear* to have absolutely no effect on the world going on around Him.

The Anointed One, The Christ

When Jesus was around thirty, John the Baptist appeared in the desert, announcing that God's long-awaited Kingdom was about to arrive. John described himself as the forerunner of the one who would "baptize with the Holy Spirit and with fire. His winnowing fork is in his hand and he will…gather his wheat into the granary, but the chaff he will burn with unquenchable fire" (Matt.3:11-12). How could John have meant anyone other than the Messiah?

John had to be a sore spot for the Temple establishment. He, the son of a priest, had turned his back on that ministry. Instead of pointing to the Law as the *end* of God's revelation, John pointed forward to a new order established when the Messiah poured out the gift of the Spirit. He called the Jewish people, not to more fervent participation in the life of the Temple, but to a radical repentance from sin as preparation for the Kingdom's arrival. The sign of their desire to repent was to accept baptism from John. At that point in Jewish history, however, it was a shocking thing to do. Baptism was the way a *Gentile*, a foreigner, entered God's Covenant People. For

---

[20] There shouldn't be anything shocking about that. Jesus was a man, and God created men with an appreciation for women. Because we live in a fallen world, though, we are use to seeing this God-given orientation tainted by lust. When Jesus looked at a woman there was nothing self-seeking in His gaze; He saw her for the priceless, beautiful work of God she was.

someone born a Jew, circumcised, and living under the Law, receiving John's baptism was an incredible act of humility. It was equivalent to saying, "Up until now I have barely understood what it means to be one of the Lord's People. I confess my sin, my unworthiness, and want to begin anew."

The penitential nature of John's baptism is what makes Jesus' reception of it so initially confusing. What sin did God the Son need to repent of? Personally, none; but there was a history in Israel of leaders, representatives of the people, praying for forgiveness in the name of the nation, even when they personally did not bear the guilt.[21] By being baptized Jesus tells us something very important: He has come to act in the name of *humanity*. Our first parents made a decision that wounded and brought death to us all. When God the Son became part of the human family, He joined Himself in some way to each member; and took it upon Himself to act in the name of all. Because the human family needed to repent, as its representative before the Father He did just that.[22] Jesus said He was baptized "to fulfill *all righteousness*" (Matt.3:15).

I'm utterly fascinated by Jesus' baptism and the events it set in motion:

> And when [Jesus] came up out of the water, immediately he saw the heavens opened and the Spirit descending on him like a dove; and a voice came from heaven, "Thou art my beloved Son; with thee I am well pleased." The Spirit immediately *drove* him out into the wilderness. And he was in the wilderness forty days, tempted by Satan" (Mark 1:10-13).

Jesus relived the history of Israel in miniature - forty days in the desert as opposed to years. Unlike Israel though, He didn't give in to temptation. The Adversary was extremely cunning; all of the things he set before Jesus were good in and of themselves: satiating His hunger, showing forth God's Power, governing the kingdoms of the world (Matt.4:1-11; Luke 4:1-13). They were all magnificent things, things Jesus knew to be part of the Father's plan; but not at *that moment*, and not in *that way*. And isn't that where

---

[21] See the prayers of Nehemiah and Ezra for instance (Neh. 9:32-37; Ezra 9:6-7).
[22] "For just as through the disobedience of one man the many were made sinners, so also through the obedience of the one man [Jesus] the many will be made righteous." (Romans 5:19)

most of us fall? Instead of simply succumbing to the path of least resistance though, Jesus allowed the Father's will, as witnessed to in the Jewish Scripture, to dictate His responses (Deuteronomy 8:3; Deut.6:13; Deut.6:16). Jesus won a decisive victory in that desert and won it in the name of all of humanity.

The victory Jesus achieved, as a man, was accomplished in the power of the Holy Spirit. Look back at Mark's account and you will see that it was the Spirit Who "*drove* Jesus" into the wilderness (1:12). At the conclusion of his temptation narrative, Luke tells us that "Jesus returned *in the power of the Spirit* into Galilee, and a report concerning him went out through all the surrounding country" (4:14). Of course it did, listen to how Matthew described that period:

> And he went about all Galilee, *teaching* in their synagogues and *preaching the gospel of the kingdom* and *healing* every disease and every infirmity among the people. . .they brought him all the sick, those afflicted with various diseases and pains, demoniacs, epileptics, and paralytics and he healed them. (4:23-25)

This beautiful, powerful participation of the Spirit in Jesus' life is nothing other than God the Son, Loving His Father and siblings, in the Spirit. Jesus had experienced the Father giving Himself in the Spirit at His baptism; and then in a return of love, the Spirit (Love) poured forth from the Son, flooded His human soul, and gushed forth in teaching, preaching, healing and exorcising – the actions the Father had sent Him to accomplish.[23] The Son's human mind and body experienced the Spirit's move-

---

[23] Even though we see the Spirit manifested at Jesus' baptism and in the deeds of power during the public ministry, we need to recognize that the Spirit had been active in His humanity since conception. At every instant of Jesus' life, at whatever stage of development, Jesus was focused on Loving His Father and brothers and sisters. Over ninety percent of His mission on earth was to bring the "hum-drum" into the Trinitarian Life, to reveal its potentiality for Love. Whether it was studying the Torah, assisting Joseph in the carpenter's shop, playing a game with friends, doing a task for his mother, or celebrating a wedding, Jesus was giving Himself in Love – and that is the activity of the Spirit. Jesus, Mary, and Joseph were living family life to its utmost, redeeming, you could say, all of the family dysfunctions before and since. You and I, whatever our daily tasks are, never have to worry about being "nothings." If we are animated by the Spirit of Jesus then everything we do can be a share in Jesus' life.

ment as a *driving force*. The prophet Isaiah had spoken of this in regards to the Messiah – that He would be anointed not with oil as other kings, but with the *very Spirit of God:*[24]

> There shall come forth a shoot
> > from the stump of Jesse,
> > and a branch shall grow out of his
> > roots,
> And the Spirit of the LORD shall rest
> > upon him,
> > the spirit of wisdom and under-
> > standing,
> > the spirit of counsel and might,
> > the spirit of knowledge and the fear
> > of the LORD
> (Isaiah 11:1-3).

The Law Giver

The presence of the Spirit did not mean Jesus' life was easy though; and we shouldn't expect ours to be any different. In the last chapter I said that the giving of the Law to Moses was a tremendous *first* step in bringing humanity to understand Love, to understand God and His purpose for us. Jesus' task was to bring us the rest of the way. Unlike the rabbis of that period, Jesus did not restrict Himself to commenting on the Law and its interpretation. He claimed to be completing it, giving it its definitive meaning; and so we hear Him telling the crowds:

> Think not that I have come to abolish the law and the prophets; I have come not to abolish them but to fulfill them (Matt.5:17).

You have heard that it was said to the men of old, "You shall not kill; and whoever kills will be subject to judgment." [Exodus 20:13] But I

---

[24] We've said before that "Messiah," or "Christ" in Greek, means Anointed One. What we haven't said is that, for a Christian, the term is a constant reference to the Trinity: the Son who is anointed, the Father Who anoints, and the Holy Spirit Who is the anointing. Cantalamessa, Raniero, *The Holy Spirit in the Life of Jesus* (Collegeville, Minnesota: The Liturgical Press, 1994), p.7.

> say to you that every one who is angry with his brother shall be liable to judgment (Matt.5:21-22).
>
> You have heard that it was said, "You shall not commit adultery" [Ex.20:14]. But I say to you that every one who looks at a woman lustfully has already committed adultery with her in his heart (Matt.5:27-28).
>
> Everyone who hears these words of mine and does them will be like a wise man who built his house upon the rock…And every one who…does not do them will be like a foolish man who built his house upon the sand (Matt.7:24,26).

The Mosaic Law's dietary restrictions had been meant as a living parable on the necessity of properly "nourishing" our souls[25] – keeping watch over the thoughts we allowed to dwell therein:

> "Do you not see that whatever goes into a man from outside cannot defile him since it enters not his heart but his stomach, and so passes on?" (Thus [Jesus] declared all foods clean.) And he said, "What comes out of a man is what defiles a man. For from within, out of the heart of man, come evil thoughts, fornication, theft, murder, …[etc.] (Mark 7:18-21)

He pointed *through* the Mosaic Law to a deeper holiness, a holiness based not on minutiae points of ritual but on internal stances and interpersonal relations.

Making Enemies

Love was at the heart of the Law, love for everyone indiscriminate of their behavior toward us. Imagine how difficult that was for Jews living under Roman oppression to hear. The Zealot movement was convinced that God planned to give His People freedom through a political uprising against Rome; only then would David's Kingdom be restored. Jesus, on the other hand, taught the crowds:

---

[25] I do not mean to exhaust the purposes of the dietary restrictions in the Mosaic law, only to point out what is of greatest significance for the present discussion.

You have heard that it was said, "An eye for eye, and tooth for tooth," [Ex.21:24]. But I say to you, Do not resist one who is evil. But if any one strikes you on the right cheek, turn to him the other also…and if any one forces you to go one mile, go with him two miles…You have heard that it was said, "You shall love your neighbor [Leviticus 19:18] and hate your enemy." But I say to you, Love your enemies and pray for those who persecute you, so that you may be sons of your Father who is in heaven…For if you love those who love you, what reward have you?…And if you salute only your brethren, what more are you doing more than others? Do not even the Gentiles do the same? (Matt.5:38-39,41,43-47).

Another group that had difficulty with Jesus was the Temple establishment. Like the Baptist before Him, Jesus conducted His mission without the sanction of the high priest and Temple bureaucracy. Perhaps His most "outrageous" action was forgiving sins. At one level it could be interpreted as an attack on the sacrifices offered in the Temple. This paled in comparison with the much larger implication though; his critics didn't miss it: "It is blasphemy! Who can forgive sins but God alone?" (Mark 2:7).

This brings us to yet another way Jesus disturbed many of the devout; forgiving sins entailed spending a lot of time with the "wrong kind of people." He took meals with those collaborating with Rome (tax collectors), prostitutes, and others publicly known as "sinners." He loved the lost right where they were, and wanted to bring them back to the Father. Many of the "righteous" however, could not understand a man of God keeping such company.

Jesus showed gentleness where it was needed, but He was just as able to show "tough-love" when the situation called. Listen to Him call a group of Pharisees to repentance:

> Woe to you, scribes and Pharisees, hypocrites! For you [give a tenth of your] mint and dill and cumin, and have neglected the weightier matters of the law, justice, and mercy, and faith; these you ought to have done, without neglecting the others…outwardly [you] appear righteous to men, but within you are full of hypocrisy and iniquity" (Matt.23:23,28).

Jesus' Father called Him to tell Israel's most powerful religious leaders that they were not leading as He intended, that they were closing their eyes to their own sin. Although Jesus won popularity among the rank-and-file, His stances were viewed as a threat by the high priest, Caiaphas. He and his allies were consumed with maintaining the present order, the status quo, so as not to draw down Rome's wrath.

Jesus wanted to open His "opponents" eyes. Jerusalem had already experienced destruction from the Babylonians, and Jesus saw that if its leadership and the zealots continued down their chosen paths it would happen again. What the people needed was not political freedom from Rome, but freedom from sin, the healing of that gaping wound in their souls. They needed the prophesied New Covenant, the Spirit of God at their core.

Jesus had a much different strategy for renewing the Kingdom of David. Out of His followers He selected twelve, recalling the twelve sons of Israel, that He began giving in-depth instruction to. He sent them out to share His Father's message and show forth the Spirit's power, grooming them to take His message to the four corners of the earth. Jesus likewise called forth a group of seventy-two disciples, mirroring the seventy-two elders who assisted Moses, and sent them to prepare towns for His arrival. Accepting Jesus' message and His gift of the Spirit was how Israel would be renewed and the Kingdom of David extended throughout the world - not by uprising and conquest but *through missionaries and conversions.*[26] Through these means the Gentiles would be brought into the kingdom as fellow members with the Jews. By refusing Jesus, the high priesthood and the zealots and all those allied with them, were bringing judgment upon Jerusalem.

> And when He drew near and saw the city [of Jerusalem] he wept over it, saying, "Would that even today you knew what would make for peace! But now they are hid from your eyes. For the days shall come upon you, when your enemies... will not leave one stone upon another in you; because you did not know the time of your visitation" (Luke 19:41).

---

[26] Sri, Edward, *Mystery of the Kingdom* (Steubenville, Ohio: Emmaus Road Publishing, 1999), pp.60-61.

Jesus prophesied that Jerusalem and its Temple would be sacked within that generation [a generation being reckoned as 40 years] (Lk.21:32).[27]

Victory Through "Defeat"

It all came to a head the week before Passover in the year 30 A.D. Jesus rode into Jerusalem, already swelling with pilgrims for the great feast, on the back of a donkey, fulfilling the prophecy of Zechariah (9:9). The high priest and those gathered around him had Jesus arrested and, on trumped-up charges, handed him over to the Romans for crucifixion. It was an injustice – He was the sinless one. He had done nothing wrong, nothing to merit such punishment. He could have protested, could have plead His case; but He didn't. He saw His Father's hand at work; His Father wanted to take that injustice and use it to do something that the high priest, Caesar, Pontius Pilate, no one could conceive – receive it as a sacrifice in atonement for the sins of the world!

We remember that the Mosaic Covenant was ratified by the sacrifice of a bull, part if it being offered to the Lord and part eaten by the people in a covenant meal. We saw the same with the Passover lamb and the various Temple sacrifices. We should not be surprised then to see Jesus doing the same. On the night before He died, in the midst of celebrating the Passover:

> he took bread, and when he had given thanks he broke it and gave it to them, saying, "This is my body which is given for you. Do this in remembrance of me." And likewise the cup after supper, saying, "This cup which is poured out of you is the *new covenant* in my blood" (Luke 22:19-20).

That is the only time Scripture records Him using the words "new covenant." That *meal* was half of the ratification of the New Covenant, half of the reality foreshadowed throughout the Mosaic Covenant; the other half was Jesus' self-offering on the cross! And just as the Passover was the yearly renewal and participation in God's salvation of Israel, so the celebration of the "Lord's Supper," or "Eucharist" was to be the Church's con-

---

[27] Jerusalem and its leaders were given a 40 year period in which to repent and enter into the New Covenant that God had established with Israel.

stant renewal and application of Jesus' death, resurrection, and ascension to the Father. Referring to the Eucharist, Jesus identified Himself as the "true manna" rained down from heaven (John 6:31-59).[28]

Just before He was arrested we find Him at prayer in the Garden of Gethsamene. Jesus was in agony; He knew what lay ahead of Him, and like anyone, wanted to run. Something happened in that garden though; an anguish came over Him like nothing ever experienced before.[29] Other men and women have been executed without experiencing what Jesus did; the difference occurred at the level of soul. He was taking on the weight of the world's sin. Every slight, every harsh word, betrayal, rape, murder, every sin - from the dawn of time to its end - was present to Him. He witnessed it, and as humanity's representative, poured forth the contrition, the horror, that the world should feel *but does not*. I am convinced that He should have died in that garden; His human psyche should have cracked, His heart given out. It was only a supernatural infusion of strength[30] that allowed Him to continue.

His torture by the Romans boggles the mind. They used whips with pieces of metal and bone at the end to rip the flesh from His body, then took thorns two inches long, wove them into a cap and pounded them into His skull. They placed a hundred pound beam on His shoulders and forced Him to carry it uphill (as Isaac did in Gen.22:6). The Romans stripped Him naked and gambled for His clothes (Psalm 22:18). Spikes were used to fasten His hands and feet (Psalm 22:16) to the cross. His blood was spattered horizontally and vertically (just as the Passover lambs' on the doorpost and lintel), and He hung there until He couldn't pull Himself up for another breath, finally suffocating by His own weight. All of this occurred on a

---

[28] As foretold in the Psalms, Jesus' priesthood resembled that of Melchizedek: He was Jerusalem's priest-king offering Himself under the appearances of bread and wine (Psalm 110:4; Genesis 14:18-20). Dr. Brant Pitre offers an insightful observation here; when Jesus commanded his Apostles to "do this," to offer the Eucharist, He was associating them in his priestly ministry.
[29] These thoughts about Jesus' agony in Gethsamene are owed to Sheed, Frank, *To Know Christ Jesus* (San Francisco: Ignatius Press, 1980), p.349.
[30] Its fascinating to me that Jesus received strength in that moment, not from His divine nature, but from a part of creation – an angel. "And there appeared to him an angel from heaven, strengthening him" (Luke 22:43).

height in the region of Mount Moriah, while the Passover lambs were being sacrificed in the Temple!

How does His death save us? Think about what our look at the Jewish Scripture showed us. The first man and woman said "no" to God's Fatherhood, no to mirroring God the Son as He receives and gives Himself back to the Father (in the Spirit). Jesus reversed that for us. As a human being, He was not only obedient but obedient to the point of death. He loved the Father with literally everything in Him – His body, blood, soul, and divinity. And His gift of Himself to the Father, His obedience to the Father as He went through a living hell atones for my disobedience and your disobedience as we live in the *blessings* of our families, schooling, work, and friendships. Jesus was the Suffering Servant foretold by Isaiah. The sin of Israel, of the world, was removed in a single day (Zechariah 3:9). Jesus' loving faithfulness filled in that abyss, that gulf, we had dug between ourselves and the Father. And it did not just fill it in – it overflowed to heaven itself!

He not only loved the Father with this intensity, but you and I. On the night before He died He told His disciples, "As the Father has loved me, so have I loved you!" (John 15:9). Infinite, powerful, tender, complete and total Love is what Jesus has for us. Earlier in the chapter I said that Jesus lived as a single man, a bachelor, but it is equally true to say that He was the most married man in history. Not sure what I mean?

We have already seen that God created man and woman to reflect the Father and Son in their complete gift of Self to Each Other. We have also seen, both in Scripture and experience, how sin has twisted relationships between men and women. In reliving human history in miniature, Jesus gave Himself completely to the one He loved, His Bride, God's People. That is the image of profound intimacy Jesus used, taken over from the Old Testament, to convey His Love. He endured the cross to atone for our sins and poured Himself out body, blood, soul and divinity not to the Father alone, *but to you and me*. That is what the Eucharist is! He has made a complete gift of Himself, fulfilling the Father's dream for humanity.[31] And just

---

[31] As St. Paul taught in *Ephesians 5:25-32*, "Husbands, love your wives, just as Christ loved the church and gave himself up for her to make her holy....'For this reason a man will leave his father and mother and be united to his wife, and the two will become one flesh.' This is a profound mystery – but I am talking about Christ and the church."

as the physical union of husband and wife brings forth new life, Jesus' gift of Himself to the Father and His Bride brings forth supernatural life, resurrection life – first for Himself and then for us:

<u>Philippians 2:8-11</u>
[Jesus] humbled himself and became obedient unto death –even death on a cross! Therefore God highly exalted him to the highest place and bestowed on him the name which is above every name, that at the name of Jesus every knee should bow, in heaven and on earth and under the earth, and every tongue confess that Jesus Christ is Lord, to the glory of God the Father.

<u>Hebrews 5:7-9</u>
During the days of Jesus' life on earth, he offered up prayers and petitions with loud cries and tears to the one who could save him from death, and he was heard because of his reverent submission. Although he was a son, he learned obedience from what he suffered and, once made perfect, he became the source of eternal salvation for all who obey him.

Eye Has Not Seen, Ear Has Not Heard…

Jesus' Love, His persistent obedience, culminating on the cross, called forth a torrent of Love from the Father. The Father could not keep Himself from clutching His Son's body and soul and, through the Spirit, transforming them (Romans 1:4; 8:11). Jesus' body was not resuscitated; no, His humanity was raised to a new level of life. Not only was the resurrection the fulfillment of Isaiah's prophecy of the Suffering Servant (53:11-12), of David's words in the psalms (16:8-11; 22:23-25), and Hosea's promise of revival on the third day (6:1-2);[32] it was the great revelation of what the Father had always planned for His human children.

In Jesus we finally see what would have happened if our first parents had continued living as children of God. The sacrificing, the progressive and complete giving away of themselves, would have "left room" for the Spirit to rush in and raise them to this new height. When Jesus was raised His disciples saw a new synergy between matter and spirit: physical death

---

[32] If your head is spinning from all of the Scripture citations and different threads woven in and out of my discussion of Jesus' death / resurrection then good. That movement from the cross to ultimate Life is what all of history up until that point had been traveling toward, and all of history since is predicated upon.

was no longer a possibility; barriers of any kind no longer had meaning for Him. The doors the disciples had locked themselves behind, for fear of being crucified too, could not hold Jesus back. He passed right through them so that He could bestow the gift of union with Him, union with the Father, union *in* the Spirit, upon His beloved:

> "Peace be with you. As the Father has sent me, even so I send you." And when he had said this, he breathed on them and said to them, "Receive the Holy Spirit" (John 20:21-22).

Jesus brought about the New Covenant, the state prophesied since the Fall. The renewal of Israel began with those first disciples, and as this good news (Gospel) was shared with the Gentile nations it likewise spread to Israel's ten lost tribes (Acts 15:15-18).[33] The Kingdom of David was reconstituted within Jesus' Church. He ascended to the Father's right hand, the victorious Son of Man prophesied by Daniel (7:13-14). One Man is eternally in the Father's presence, Loving with the intensity of the Spirit. One Man poured out all He was – and became more than any of us can fathom.

The Victory Shared, The Kingdom Built

The Son became a man and lived the life He did *for us,* to bring us back to the Father. Jesus relived human history, catching it up in His Love for the Father, redeeming it. His human soul and body has reached the pinnacle of union with the Father. But how does His triumph become ours? How do we enter into the union with God promised by the New Covenant?

First, we need to look back to the prophecies. What did God say through Ezekiel?

> I will sprinkle clean water upon you, and you shall be clean from all your uncleanness, and from all your idols I will cleanse you. A new heart I will give you, and a new spirit I will put within you; I will take out of your flesh the heart of stone and give you a heart of flesh. And I will put my spirit within you, and cause you to walk in my statutes and be careful to observe my ordinances ... (Ezekiel 36:24-27)

---

[33] Pimentel, Stephen, *Witnesses of the Messiah: On Acts of the Apostles 1-15*, (Steubenville, Ohio: Emmaus Road Publishing, 2002), p.7,20.

Wasn't this the same thing said through the prophet Zechariah?

> ...when they look on him whom they have pierced, they shall mourn for him, as one mourns for an only child, and weep bitterly over him, as one weeps over a first-born ...On that day *a fountain shall be opened for the house of David and the inhabitants of Jerusalem to cleanse them from sin and uncleanness* (12:10; 13:1).

John the Baptist's great announcement about the Messiah was that He would "*baptize* with the Holy Spirit and with fire" (Matt.3:11). And when Jesus sent out His Twelve Apostles to build the Kingdom, His command was to "make disciples of all the nations, *baptizing them* in the name of the Father and of the Son and of the Holy Spirit" (Matt.28:19).

He took the sign used by John the Baptist and imbued it with Power, made it the channel through which He communicates the Spirit until the end of time! This is why Jesus said, "Truly, truly, I say to you, unless one is born of *water and Spirit*, he cannot enter the kingdom of God" (John 3:5).[34] A person's soul, formerly hard as stone (Ezekiel 37:26), is transformed – made permeable for God's Life to rush in. The baptized's soul is fused to Christ Jesus. We become children of the Father because we are united to, dwelling within, His only Son. The Holy Spirit has spilled over from Jesus, filling us as well. That choice our first parents made to force God out of our souls – the personal choices we have made to ratify it, all of that is undone through baptism! Just as the Israelites passed from the land of slavery to freedom through the waters of the Red Sea, so we enter into the New

---

[34] Some, wishing to avoid the notion of God using something found in nature as a means of communicating His Life, claim that "born of water and the Spirit" refers to our natural birth ("water" being the amniotic fluid of the womb) and then our spiritual birth via faith and confession of Christ. The difficulty with this interpretation, however, is that it completely ignores the context of the passage. Jesus makes this statement in answer to the question of how a man could be "born when he is old." Our Lord's response was that this *second* birth takes place through *water and the Spirit*.

As Dr. Scott Hahn explains, within the context of the *Gospel of John*, this could be nothing but a reference to the sacrament of baptism: 1) Jesus had just experienced an outpouring of the Spirit in His own baptism with water (John 1:29-34), and 2) Right after finishing this conversation, Jesus initiated a ministry of water baptism via the Twelve Apostles (John 4:1). Jesus' words about "being born of water and Spirit" are given in a "water baptism sandwich." *Born Again: Baptism in the New Testament*, (Audiocassette by St. Joseph Communications).

Covenant through the waters of baptism. Baptism is the *act of faith* in Jesus' identity and action as Son of God.

There is so much that an historian can affirm about Jesus of Nazareth. There are criteria that any unbiased investigator can bring to bear on the historical data: 1) multiple attestation, 2) discontinuity, 3) embarrassment, 4) coherence, and 5) the criterion of Jesus' rejection and execution.[35] The most exhaustive study to date using the above criterion has been John Meier's three volume, *A Marginal Jew: Rethinking the Historical Jesus*. Purely on historical grounds a person should be able to affirm Jesus' existence; His baptism by John;[36] His proclamation of the Kingdom;[37] His teaching of the *Our Father* prayer;[38] that He was popularly regarded as an exorcist,[39] healer,[40] and even one who could raise the dead.[41] We can feel confident in affirming Jesus' founding of the Twelve Apostles,[42] the Twelve's membership,[43] and the prominence of Simon Peter.[44] Rock-solid is the knowledge that Jesus attracted the attention of the crowds, clashed with prominent Jewish leaders and was crucified under the Roman procurator Pontius Pilate. A person can affirm these things on the basis of painstaking, human research alone. An observant reader could even read the Old Testament and recognize all of the parallels between it and the life of Jesus. But to take that all-important next step, the one "off the cliff," we need the help of God Himself:

> [Jesus] said to them, "But who do you say that I am?" Simon Peter replied, "You are the Christ, the Son of the living God!" And Jesus answered him, "Blessed are you, Simon [son of] Jona! For flesh and blood has not revealed this to you, but *my Father who is in heaven.*" (Matthew 16:15-17).

---

[35] Meier, John P., *A Marginal Jew: Rethinking the Historical Jesus*, Volume 2. (New York: Doubleday, 1994), p.5
[36] Ibid, p.100-105
[37] Ibid, p.237-270
[38] Ibid, p.291-309
[39] Ibid, p.646-661
[40] Ibid, p.678-727
[41] Ibid, p.773-837
[42] *A Marginal Jew*, Volume 3. (New York: Doubleday, 2001), p.125-163
[43] Ibid, p198-221
[44] Ibid, p221-245

Faith in Jesus is the Father's unmerited gift, sown in our hearts by the Holy Spirit. It is the *foundation* of our Life in Christ. As John's Gospel tells us: "to all who received [Jesus], who *believed* in his name, he gave power *to become* children of God" (John 1:12). Faith is not just an intellectual exercise, a "head-trip." No, absolutely not. Faith is the Holy Spirit moving men and women's damaged souls to say "yes" to God's unmerited Love; it is supernatural. Baptism is that "yes;" it is *the act of faith*. In the writings of the Apostle Paul it was described as incorporation into Jesus' passage to the Father:

> Do you not know that all of us who have been baptized into Christ Jesus were baptized into his death? We were buried therefore with him by baptism into death, so that as Christ was raised from the dead by the glory of the Father, we too might walk in newness of life" (Romans 6:3-4).

Paul reminded his fellow minister Titus that "he saved us, not because of deeds done by us in righteousness, but in virtue of his own mercy, by the washing of regeneration and renewal in the Holy Spirit" (Titus 3:5). The Apostle Peter wrote "Baptism, which corresponds to [Noah's Ark] now saves you" (1 Peter 3:21).

Through the gift of the Spirit, given in baptism, Jesus dwells in, guides, and empowers His disciples until He returns to catch up all of creation into His resurrected Life. Fused to Jesus, the baptized already participate in His Life. All of Jesus' actions during His time on earth were expressions of Love for His Father, performed in the power of the Spirit. When He acts in us the same is true; He is Loving the Father, in the Holy Spirit, *through us* (Galatians 2:20-21). He is praying through us, acting through us, talking through us. Jesus has brought us full circle, brought us to what we were created for - insertion into the Life of the Trinity. At the moment of baptism the Trinitarian Life begins in our souls, progressing outward as we live and love in the Spirit, until we pass through the trustful sacrifice of death to arrive at full participation in Jesus' resurrection and ascension!

Chapter 4 – Sharing Jesus' Anointing

Even a cursory reading of the New Testament reveals the powerful manifestations of God's presence within the early Church. But where is this power today? God's intervention in our world is regarded as something spectacular. I had absorbed the impression that answered prayers were *miraculous* occurrences. Yet, it did not appear that way to the first Christians. God's interaction with them was no more unexpected or unusual than any human father's involvement in the life of his children (Luke 11:12-13).

For me it began in October of my eighth grade year. I stayed home from school one day - mom was great about letting us kids take a day off here or there. Besides, she had just been in a car accident a few weeks before; and I think she enjoyed someone else being in the house as she rested and healed.

I was in one of the bedrooms as mom watched television in the family room. I was looking at television myself, flipping through the channels when I came upon the *700 Club*. I had never really watched the program before, having shared the general opinion about tele-evangelists. For some reason though, I stopped to look at it for a minute or two.

There was a young woman talking about her life. I cannot recall a name, but I know that she grew up in India and had traveled extensively giving her testimony. She related how as a teenager she had become deathly ill. Jesus came to her at the foot of her hospital bed and reached out and touched her legs. At that moment, she said, it felt like electricity shot through her body. She climbed out of bed healed. Ever since she had been speaking of what Jesus had done for her throughout her homeland of India and abroad, reminding people of God's love and power.

When she finished her testimony, she invited anyone viewing the broadcast to pray with her. I took her up on the offer, and as I prayed something very unexpected happened. This joy, this palpable joy, began welling up inside of me. The largest smile began growing on my face; I couldn't help but laugh. God was so close to me in that moment; I felt ecstatic! The woman on the television had ceased praying, but I just kept going – words of love erupting from my heart and pouring from my lips. I heard the woman mention an 800-number that could be called for additional prayer. With mom still recovering from her car accident, additional prayer sounded fantastic.

A man answered the phone, introduced himself as Mike and asked for my prayer request. I related my special intention to him and the two of us prayed right there on the phone. When we finished Mike asked me if I had been "born again." I understood that phrase well enough and answered in the affirmative. Mike's next question was a bit more difficult though, "Have you been *baptized in the Holy Spirit?*" I thought I knew what he was getting at and hesitantly replied, "I know that the Holy Spirit dwells in me because of my faith in Jesus. Is that what you mean?"

"Not completely," Mike answered. "Have you received the gift of tongues?"

"No Mike, I know I've never done that." I remembered reading of the gift of tongues in the Bible and being told by a family friend that there were Christians in every denomination claiming to have experienced it today. In my own prayer I had told the Lord that I didn't need to see signs and wonders; what I desired most was to know and understand Him better. Anything more was at His discretion.

"Shane, would you like to pray to receive the gift of tongues?" Yes, this question was actually being asked of me. The whole time Mike and I had been talking that joy I mentioned before continued welling up; it was like nothing I had ever experienced. Joy like that could only have one Source. My answer to Mike was one word, "Sure." He went on to explain that the "baptism in the Spirit" was a fuller release of the Spirit's activity in our lives; the Apostles had experienced this "baptism" on the day of Pentecost. And, just as on the day of Pentecost, the gift of tongues was a common occurrence following prayer for this intention. Mike encouraged me that as he prayed I should speak out whatever words came to me, however strange they may sound.

As we resumed our prayer, the joy began growing once again. My heart was bursting with this incredible sense of God's love for me and His presence. Inside of myself I could feel words of love, praise, adoration bubbling up. . .and. . .and. . .I could not speak them out. They were stuck in my throat!

My head and my heart were joined together though in the realization that God Himself *dwelt* within me. We Christians make that profession all of the time, but how often are we dumbfounded by the sheer magnitude of it? God had brought me face to face with it, shattering every boundary of happiness I had known. The One Who created the universe with a word, that brought forth our first parents, parted the waters of the Red Sea, brought down the walls of Jericho, cleansed the lepers, healed the sick, raised the dead - Who raised Himself from the dead; He *lives* within us! The intensity of God's love and presence were still welling up, and it felt like the bedroom was filled with the intensity. My hands were literally trembling! When Mike brought the prayer to a close I told him how words seemed to be stuck in my throat. He seemed excited by this and told me that he believed the Lord wanted to bestow this gift on me. He encouraged me to continue praying about it.

After I left the bedroom it only took mom a glance to know that something had taken place. "What happened to you?" she asked, spying my smile and trembling hands.

"Mom, I've met the Holy Spirit," and out came the rest of my story. Mom didn't seem scared or worried. She had not experienced this before, but she expressed no doubt that what I told her was true. Her belief meant the world to me.

When she was up to driving we hit a Christian bookstore. I found a small section labeled "charismatic" and started looking for an introductory work on "baptism in the Spirit" and the gift of tongues. Perhaps it was my good fortune with Billy Graham's *How to be Born Again*; I decided on *How to Pray for the Release of the Holy Spirit* by Dennis Bennett. Hey, I like the straight-forward approach!

For me one of the book's most appealing qualities was its biblical base, demonstrating from Scripture that this lively experience of God by the common guy in the pew was a normative element in the early Church. (In later years, as I read more history, I came to realize that this was true for regions of the Church for the first 300-some years of her existence.)

I want to take this chance to share some of what I have learned about the Holy Spirit and His bestowal of gifts upon the church. The basics of what I relate were contained in Dennis Bennett's book. I am also going to blend in elements I have gleaned from other teachers, as well as my own experience of the Lord.

Opening to the Spirit in a New Way

What exactly is meant by the phrase "baptized in the Holy Spirit?" The word baptism literally means, "to be immersed in, overwhelmed by." The phrase comes from Scripture. John the Baptist used it (Matthew 3:11), but most notable was Jesus' usage just before His ascension into Heaven, "John baptized with water, but before many days, you shall be baptized with the Holy Spirit" (Acts 1:4). Note that Jesus said this to His Apostles, men to whom He had *already imparted the gift of the Spirit* on the night of His resurrection: "he breathed on them, and said to them, 'Receive the Holy Spirit'" (John 20:23).[45] Thus, when Jesus told the Apostles to await the "baptism in the Holy Spirit," He was speaking about something other than an initial imparting. It would be a *new* outpouring of the Spirit's graces, one opening their eyes to understand the Jewish Scriptures and empowering them to speak and act boldly in the name of Jesus. The day of Pentecost was the fulfillment of Jesus' promise. We need to realize however, that God's desire to work through His Church has not diminished in the least. He is the same "yesterday and today and forever" (Hebrews 13:8).

It can be confusing when we speak of the Holy Spirit coming upon us *again* – as if His coming upon us at baptism was incomplete. We can not get "more" of the Spirit; He is a Person after all. When someone comes to my home I do not welcome in just a part of him. "How much of Jim is in your home?" is a nonsensical question. A person could, however, ask, "How much of your home is Jim in?" In other words, is your guest welcome just inside the front door, or is he free to come into the family room, kitchen, bedroom, basement, etc.? In this same way, we can ask how much of ourselves the Holy Spirit has access to? In baptism with water He took up residence in our souls, but have we given Him permission to move about freely within us - in our minds, consciences, speech, bodies?[46] Instead of the term

---

[45] From the earliest of times the Church has recognized a true imparting of the Spirit by this action (Council of Constantinople, 389 A.D.). *The Book of Genesis* records God creating humanity by breathing the spirit of life into the clay He had molded. Jesus appropriates that action in His recreation of humanity, breathing His Holy Spirit into the men He spent three years molding and shaping.

[46] Bennet, Dennis, *How to Pray for the Release of the Holy Spirit*, (South Plainfield, NJ: Bridge Publishing Inc., 1985), p.10.

"baptism in the Spirit," I find people less confused by phrases like "release of the Spirit," or "a new openness to the Spirit."

I say this because these additional "comings" of the Spirit are moments of grace when our souls yield to his activity in a new way. Thomas Aquinas, one of the greatest Christian theologians of all time, wrote:

> There is an invisible sending (of the Holy Spirit) also with respect to an advance in virtue or an increase of grace...Such an invisible sending is especially to be seen in that kind of increase whereby a person moves forward into some new act or new state of grace: as, for instance, when a person moves forward into the grace of working miracles, or of prophecy, or out of burning love of God offers his life as a martyr or renounces all of his possessions, or undertakes some other such arduous thing.[47]

In life there are going to be intense moments we can point to, where we know this has happened. At other times we will look back to who we were two years ago and realize how the Spirit has changed us. On the day of Pentecost He was unleashed in the lives of the Apostles, and they were given the grace to put themselves completely at His disposal.

Charisms, or Spiritual Gifts

The gifts of the Spirit are innumerable, sometimes building upon our natural talents. At other times the Spirit may infuse an ability completely foreign to us. One list of spiritual gifts found in the Bible comes from the Apostle Paul. I wish to discuss it here because the gifts ("charisms" in Greek) mentioned are probably unfamiliar to many:

> Now there are varieties of gifts, but the same Spirit...to each is given the manifestation of the Spirit for the common good. To one is given through the Spirit the utterance of wisdom, and to another the utterance of knowledge according to the same Spirit. To another faith by the same Spirit, to another gifts of healing by the one Spirit, to another the working of miracles, to another prophecy, to another the ability to distinguish between spirits, to another various kinds of tongues, to an-

---

[47]Quoted in Schreck, Alan, *Catholic and Christian* (Ann Arbor, Michigan: ServantBooks, 1984), p.107-108.

other the interpretation of tongues. All these are inspired by one and the same Spirit, who apportions to each one individually as he wills (1 Corinthians 12: 4, 7-11).

I will explain each of these gifts as best I can:
- *Wisdom* - the Holy Spirit prompts someone to speak a word of direction to the Christian community or an individual
- *Knowledge* - the believer is given information via the working of the Spirit. The Catholic Church has a long tradition of saints who were miraculously aware of the secret sins of others and able to call them to repentance. Something like this was seen in the life of Jesus too (John 4:18-19).
- *Faith* - the Holy Spirit gives one an absolute assurance that God will act in a certain manner. This allows the believer to pray with a faith that "moves mountains" (Matthew 21:21). This type of faith can be seen in connection with healing – as with the Apostle Peter's words to a paralyzed man, begging at the temple:
"I have no silver and gold, but I give you what I have; in the name of Jesus Christ of Nazareth, walk." And he took him by the right hand and raised him up, and immediately his feet and ankles became strong (Acts 3:6-7).
- *Healing* - a person is used as a conduit for God's healing power to overcome physical, mental, or spiritual illness. The believer either prays for someone and sees God answer, or acts as a direct instrument of the Lord, as in the example of Peter cited above.
- *Miraculous Powers* - various interventions of God in the natural order. Jesus' and Peters' walking on water come under this heading.
- *Prophecy* - the Holy Spirit impresses a message for the Christian community upon the mind of an individual. Very rarely does such a message concern a prediction of future events. Most prophecies are examples of God fathering His children - encouraging, correcting, chastising, reminding them how intense His love for them is.
- *Discernment of Spirits* - The Lord's people cannot accept *everything* they hear. Confirmation of a message needs to be sought from the Holy Spirit, discerning the Word of God from the imaginings of human beings or the corruption of the evil one. This gift can often manifest in a

number of people to whom a prophecy or word of wisdom has been addressed, discerning the word as a group. The Holy Spirit often brings our powers of judgment to bear on the matter, comparing what was just spoken to the authoritative record of God's word found in Scripture.

- *Tongues & Interpretation* - Tongues literally means "languages." It is a gift of personal prayer as well as prophecy (when used in combination with the gift of interpretation).
  1. As a gift of prayer, the Christian prays aloud in a language he/she has never learned; the words are given by the Spirit. Because the words come directly from the Spirit, it could be called a "perfect prayer," assuming the believer's heart is truly directed toward the Lord and not just the sounds coming from his/her mouth. This gift is for the edification of the individual, and in this sense is unique as the other gifts are directed toward the edification of the community. I think this is why Paul referred to it as "the least" of the spiritual gifts.
  2. Tongues takes on a different significance when used as a form of prophecy. This would occur in the context of Christian worship when one person is prompted to speak a message aloud in tongues. The Holy Spirit then impresses, either upon the one who gave the message or another believer present, the interpretation in the language of the group assembled. Occurrences have been reported where someone within the group understood the language in which the message was originally delivered, and was able to confirm the accuracy of the interpretation.

All of these gifts were present within the early Church, as is witnessed to throughout *Acts of the Apostles* and Paul's *First Letter to the Corinthians* (chp.12-14). Jesus made mention of gifts of this nature as well:

> And these signs will accompany those who believe…they will speak in new tongues…and if they drink any deadly thing, it will not hurt them; they will lay their hands on the sick, and they will recover (Mark 16:17-18).

Paul encouraged the Corinthians to "Make love your aim, and earnestly desire the spiritual gifts, especially that you may prophesy" (1 Corinthians

14:1). So both Jesus and Paul spoke of these charisms as being active in the life of the common believer, not just the Apostles or "great saints;" and in this century we have seen just that.

A new openness to the Spirit's activity has manifested itself in every Christian denomination, often times referred to as the "charismatic," or "Pentecostal" movement. With it has come an explosion of spiritual gifts. The Catholic Church, for one, recognizes these gifts as still valid today. The 1994 *Catechism of the Catholic Church* reads:

> Whatever their character - sometimes it is extraordinary, such as the gift of miracles or of tongues - charisms are oriented toward sanctifying grace and are intended for the common good of the Church (CCC 2003).
>
> Charisms are to be accepted with gratitude by the person who receives them and by all members of the Church as well. They are a wonderfully rich grace for the apostolic vitality and for the holiness of the entire Body of Christ, provided they really are genuine gifts of the Holy Spirit (CCC 800).
>
> It is in this sense that discernment of charisms is always necessary. No charism is exempt from being referred and submitted to the Church's shepherds. (CCC 801)

My Own Experience

How does one open to the spiritual gifts we have been discussing? First, we ask the Spirit to bestow them (Luke 11:13). Then, we take a step in faith. I think the best image for us is the Apostle Peter walking on the water (Matthew 14:24-33): The Apostles were out in a boat, and Jesus came walking to them on the water. Peter wanted to go out and meet Him, and Jesus gave the go ahead. The thing we rarely think about, though, is that Peter had a decision to make - he had to make himself take that first step out of the boat and onto the sea. Jesus had told him to come, so Peter knew that Jesus' power was available to him. But it was the man Peter who had to put that foot outside of the boat and touch down on water. Without Peter's action there would have been no miracle.

For me that step of faith was taken the day I purchased *How to Pray for the Release of the Holy Spirit*. Sitting in my bedroom, I asked Jesus to immerse me in His Spirit. My prayer, learned from author Dennis Bennett, was "Dear Jesus, I receive You as my Baptizer. Please baptize me in the Holy Spirit. Thank You, Jesus! Jesus, I receive! I accept the new language You have given me. Help me to release it."[48]

My heart started filling with the same joy it had while praying on the phone with Mike. The Spirit's presence was so incredible that I started laughing out loud. I knew that the Lord Jesus was releasing His Spirit, holding out the gift of tongues to me. My part was to cooperate with Him, to begin to speak. I needed to speak out with faith, trusting the Spirit to supply the language. I made a sound, "ah," and then added another, "Ah la." I continued speaking - words, phrases, and then what seemed like sentences. As each sound entered my mind I articulated it, praying in this way for about ten minutes, stopping every so often to talk to God in English as well.

The Purpose of Praying in Tongues

If you have never been exposed to it, you are probably wondering why someone would want to pray in a language they do not understand. It is a fair question, no doubt about it. I cannot claim to give God's final answer, His rationale for tongues. I can speculate though, given the texts of Scripture[49] and the opinions of myself and others.

First, I believe that tongues allows us to open our spirits to God - to express our deepest longings, our most profound inclinations of love to Him. Because we have been fused to Jesus, we are caught up into His Loving of the Father (in the Spirit). Praising God in tongues is an earthly manifestation of the Son's eternal adoration of the Father – manifested through

---

[48] Bennet, Dennis, *How to Pray for the Release of the Holy Spirit*, (South Plainfield, NJ: Bridge Publishing Inc., 1985), p.69.

[49] Paul stated in his *First Epistle to the Corinthians* that "A man who speaks in tongues is talking not to men but to God. No one understands him, because he utters mysteries in the Spirit" (14:2). It's evident that St. Paul saw a value in tongues, "I should like it if all of you spoke in tongues" (14:4) and "Thank God I speak in tongues more than any of you" (14:18).

members of His Body. Through this charism we are given the opportunity to express things our conscious mind could never adequately formulate.

The second benefit builds upon the first. Not only does tongues allow someone to praise God, but also to intercede– the Holy Spirit allowing a person to pray Jesus' intentions for the members of His Mystical Body. It is a visible manifestation of something going on within the soul of every Christian:

> ...the Spirit helps us in our weakness; for we do not know how to pray as we ought, but the Spirit himself intercedes for us with sighs too deep for words. And he who searches the hearts of men knows what is the mind of the Spirit, because the Spirit intercedes for the saints according to the will of God (Romans 8:26-27).

The third value I see is the potential for personal spiritual development. Paul said in *First Corinthians* that "He who speaks in a tongue edifies himself" (14:4). One way this spiritual edification occurs is for a person to yield to tongues in the knowledge that they are worshiping and interceding on behalf of other members of Christ's Body. They are, in a sense, allowing the Head of the Body, Jesus, to more fully conform the intercession rising from earth to Heaven to that of His sacred heart. In cooperating with Him, the Christian's soul progresses in grace, being molded more in Jesus' image and thus more responsive to the stirrings of the Spirit. When Paul said that the person who speaks in tongues builds himself up he was not saying that that was the *only* way a Christian is built up interiorly; that is foolishness. The same happens within souls whenever they cooperate with the Lord's will. For example, when a Christian serves someone in need they have allowed Christ to meet that person's need through them, and the Christian's soul grows in the image of the Master.

Humility before God is the final value I see in tongues. What is more childlike than "babbling" before our Father? With the gift of tongues one yields to God in a simple but concrete way, trusting Him to supply each word in turn. Such an act can build faith - the type of faith necessary to pray with a sick person, or speak out what you believe are *His* words to a prayer group (or your classmates). Tongues is a gift which has benefited me personally.

I do not, however, believe that everyone needs to receive it. The Holy Spirit knows what each of us needs to progress in grace, and He wants to bestow those gifts in abundance. It is our part to be open, not to dismiss any gift He wants to give: "as the heavens are higher than the earth, so are my ways higher than your ways and my thoughts than your thoughts" (Isaiah 55:9). Charisms are no guarantee of personal union with God. When a charism is manifested it only means that at that moment, that individual was open enough for God to work through them. Jesus warned that on the Day of Judgment there will be many who say, "'Lord, Lord, did we not prophesy in your name? …and do many mighty works in your name as well?' to whom He will reply, "I never *knew* you; depart from me" (Matthew 7:22-23). The evidence of a person's union with God is not charisms, but how much they *love* with Jesus' Love (His Spirit).

Finding Others Who Shared this Experience

Initially, I spoke of my experience with few people. One person I confided in was the associate pastor of my parish and school. Once a week he came to our classroom to lead a religion class. He was in his mid-thirties and known among us kids for his great sense of humor. One of my mom's friends had told me he was involved in the charismatic movement within the Catholic Church. When I approached him he was very open to talking about his own experience, even the gift of tongues.

At this same time another person entered my life. My mom's old roommate, Nancy, had just moved back from Florida and had been a member of a Pentecostal church for ten years. When my mom told her about my recent experiences, Nancy invited us to check out a new church with her. It was "non-denominational," and very open to charisms such as prophecy, tongues, and healing.

My first visit to the church, Grace World Outreach, was exhilarating. The sanctuary reminded me of a large theater: in the front was an altar/stage, with a pulpit in the middle and a band (guitars, bass, drums, and keyboard) off to the left side. Song lyrics were projected onto the walls at both sides of the stage. Seven to eight hundred people were in the sanctuary, singing their hearts out. Many of them had their hands raised as they sang, and between songs spontaneously spoke out praise, sometimes speaking or singing in tongues. I hope that the scene I am describing doesn't sound chaotic; it was not. The people were sincere, respectful, and it was obvious to me that we loved the same God. I remember wanting to raise my hands to the Lord as I sang, but feeling inhibited. Ever so slowly my hands started to go up. No one cared, and after a time I began to feel more at ease. Towards the end of the service, one of the ministers, Gloria Copeland, moved to the front of the altar as fifty people came forward to have her lay hands on them and pray for their healings. I had read of the gift of healing in the Bible, but had never seen anyone brave enough to pray for it publicly. The experience made a deep impression upon me and my mom.

The energy present in the sanctuary that day and the lack of inhibition people felt to rejoice before God was so different from my experience of Catholic Mass up to that point. "Nondenominational" churches are the fastest growing in the country right now, and it is easy to understand why. People are looking for an *experience* of Church - to be in the midst of God's Family acting like a family. For some reason I had never registered that taking place at Mass. The demonstrativeness of those at Grace World Outreach struck me as an honest reaction for people who had come into contact with the *living* God. The solemnness, or worse yet the indifference, of my classmates and others I saw at Mass stood in stark contrast to Grace World Outreach's vibrancy. People I saw at Mass, like myself up until that point, just seemed to be "going through the motions." What I am saying isn't as simple as, "Grace was exciting, but Mass wasn't." It is just a fact of human psychology though, that people are going to have emotional reactions concerning the things most dear to them; when those reactions are lacking we often wonder what is wrong. If a child never saw his parents hug, kiss, laugh - no show of emotion whatsoever - don't you think he would question how much they really loved each other? In this respect, the worship at Grace seemed more "authentic." My mom and I began attending their Tuesday night services with Nancy.

"Errors" of Catholic Belief and Practice

One benefit from attending Grace was the encouragement to dig even deeper into the Bible. I adopted a plan to read four chapters a night - one from the historical books or prophets, a psalm, a proverb, and then a chapter from the New Testament. For me, studying Scripture was like a child learning the language of his parents. A child learns by hearing his parents use it in their interactions with him and each other. As the language becomes internalized it gives structure to the child's thoughts (your mind is using that language right now). Studying the Bible, and praying before I do so, has been like that child absorbing his parents' vocabulary. Not only do I experience certain verses leaping off the page as I read, but I occasionally experience the Holy Spirit speaking to me in the midst of the day by activating a portion of this "inspired vocabulary." I remember, for instance, a time when I was absolutely furious with my brother for something he had done. I went to my bedroom and punched the wall, growling "I hate him." Instantaneously the words of *1 John 4:19*, a verse read months before, were in my mind, "If anyone says 'I love God,' and hates his brother, he is a liar." I immediately asked the Lord's forgiveness and, after I had cooled off, worked things out with my brother.

For the believers at Grace, the Bible was a Christian's everything. One verse which seemed to capture this sentiment was, "All Scripture is inspired by God and profitable for teaching, for reproof, for correction, and for training in righteousness, that the man of God may be complete, equipped for every good work" (2 Timothy 3:16-17; NIV). Preaching focused on learning to "stand on" passages – to claim passages of Scripture as God's promises for my personal healing of illnesses, financial prosperity, etc.

In retrospect, however, I see real shortcoming in looking at Scripture this way. First, if we really want to hear what God says in His written Word, then we have to pay attention to the context of given statements. To arrive at a verse's true meaning we cannot separate it from those around it. Tied to this is the realization that pulling out individual verses, without consideration of their literary, historical and cultural contexts, promotes a very fundamentalist reading of Scripture. The overall assumption at Grace was that the words we were reading were completely literal by twentieth century standards; no consideration was given to Scripture containing different literary genres: historical narrative, historical myth, anthropomorphisms (Dt.11:12; Ex.13:3), poetry, hymns, prophecy, instruction, apocalypse, or even fiction[50] (as in the books of *Tobit* and *Judith*[51]). How God brought me to study Scripture contextually is the subject of another chapter though.

---

[50] Should it really come as such a surprise that God would make use of fiction in communicating with us? Consider the booming business of Christian fiction in the past twenty

62 THE GOD WHO IS LOVE

Adopting Grace's way of looking at Scripture, and absorbing their preaching on different subjects, I found myself taking exception to many Catholic beliefs. I did not see the Catholic beliefs about Mary in the Bible – her virginity after the birth of Jesus, her immaculate conception, or heavenly intercession. I did not see the term "purgatory" in the New Testament. Nor did I read of the pope. I knew from school that the pope was supposed to be the successor of the Apostle Peter, the first leader of the Church. It seemed to me though, that St. Paul was a much more important figure in the early Church. After all, the Holy Spirit used him to write two-thirds of the New Testament; Peter, in comparison, had written only two epistles. Besides, the thought of the pope being "infallible" was laughable considering the sinful lives led by a number of pontiffs. No one at Grace felt obligated to confess their sins to the minister; it was a matter between them and God. Nor did they propose rules and obligations like fasting during Lent and attending Mass every Sunday. Attending Sunday worship was definitely encouraged, but missing was not considered a sin.

Instead of living in the freedom and intimacy of the Spirit, I saw my Catholic brothers and sisters caught up in unnecessary, and unbiblical, "externals." Confession, Mary, and the Pope seemed like blockages to the direct relationship a Christian was supposed to have with God. Concerning the obligations of fasting and Sunday worship, I appealed to a verse of Scripture as justification for my new-found position, "…let no one pass judgment on you in questions of food and drink, or with regard to a [religious] festival, or new moon [celebration] or a *sabbath*. These are only a shadow of what is to come; but the *substance* belongs to Christ" (Colossians 2:16-17).[52] People already have a hard enough time believing that God

---

years: *This Present Darkness*, and the *Left Behind* series are two examples. Christians buy these books because they are finding what they believe to be God's truths wrapped in exciting narratives. Is it really that hard to believe that God could have made use of the same device in the Hebrew Scripture?
[51] *Tobit* and *Judith* are usually excluded from Protestant publications of the Bible. For a discussion of why I am convinced they belong there, however, please turn to Appendix IV.
[52] This is a perfect example of how helpful context is to understanding Scripture. With study I came to recognize that the Apostle Paul was talking about a Christian's freedom from the worship stipulations of the Mosaic Law (as we saw in the last chapter). He was *not* addressing the worship obligations of the New Covenant at all. Jesus clearly intended

wants us to live life to the fullest - and there the leaders of the Catholic Church were tacking on arbitrary regulations and calling it sin to disobey.

Amazingly though, given my feelings about Sunday Mass, I never really doubted Jesus' presence in the Eucharist (or Lord's Supper). I was surprised that the believers at Grace, so literal in their interpretation of other passages, became inconsistent here. Jesus had said, "This is My Body...this is My Blood." We also had the Apostle Paul's testimony as to what Jesus meant:

> Whoever, therefore, eats the bread or drinks the cup of the Lord in an unworthy manner will be guilty of profaning the body and blood of the Lord...For any one who eats and drinks *without discerning the body* eats and drinks judgment upon himself. That is why many of you are weak and ill, and some have died (1 Corinthians 11:27, 29-30).

I believed in the reality of the Eucharist as an article of faith, but had not *experienced* it as being "life-giving" in the way my personal prayer and Scripture study had become. I can only say, "Thanks be to God," because He was willing to stoop down and meet me where I was at:

On a Friday morning like any other, my class and I went to Mass. Everything was proceeding as usual...until I received Jesus in Communion. In the moments of prayer that followed He unleashed that same ecstatic joy I experienced when I had asked Him to release the Spirit in a new way. I was shocked. Like I said, I knew intellectually that Jesus came to me in Communion, but I had never *experienced* Him coming. He made use of the highly-structured, "ritualized" Mass to communicate His living presence to me!

This coming of Jesus is part of the reality of Eucharist. Let me share another facet of it. While at Mass a few months later, the priest invited the youth present to come up around the altar for the Eucharistic prayer. As we prayed something became very, very real to me: extending upward from the bowl containing Jesus' Body was the vertical beam of the cross. My physical eyes were registering the altar and the golden bowl, but my mind was overlaying it with the dimensions of this square beam. I was there at Calvary. Standing there at the altar, I was standing at the foot of the cross. That is

---

for fasting and the celebration of the Eucharist to be regular parts of His disciples' lives (Matt.6:16-18; Luke 22:19).

what the Eucharist is – the making present of Jesus' offering to the Father; and not just the cross, but the *full offering* of His cross, resurrection and ascension! Jesus' words, "For my flesh is *real food* and my blood *real drink*. Whoever eats my flesh and drinks my blood remains in me, and I in him" (John 6:55-56; NIV) had never held so much awe for me. Needless to say, these experiences, coupled with additional Scripture study, moved me to acknowledge my obligation to, and need for, Sunday Mass:

> On the first day of the week [Sunday], when we gathered together to break bread,[53] Paul talked with them (Acts 20:7).

> ...let us consider how to stir up one another to love and good works, *not neglecting to meet together, as is the habit of some,* but encouraging one another, and all the more as you see the Day drawing near (Hebrews 10: 25).

Now in all honesty I have to tell you that 99% of the time I receive the Eucharist, I do not get a spiritual "rush." The Lord let me experience that to bring the reality home in perhaps the only way I could understand at the time, but it is no longer required. Whatever my emotional state on a given Sunday, I know that I am entering into Jesus' offering to the Father, in the Spirit. I try to make the prayer of the Mass truly my own – putting all the gratitude I can into the words I say and sing.

Should I Be Confirmed?

The majority of Catholic school students in the Archdiocese of St. Louis receive the Sacrament of Confirmation toward the end of eighth grade. It is viewed as completing our Christian initiation begun in Baptism and Eucharist. (Even though Grace World Outreach did not acknowledge the validity of infant baptism, a parish priest had helped me discover its Scriptural and biblical basis. Please consult Appendix V for a discussion.) Confirmation was presented as my personal "yes" to the Catholic Faith, and the Holy Spirit's bestowal of the gifts to help me live it. Given my disagreement with a number of Catholic beliefs, I did not see how I could receive the sacrament in good conscience.

---

[53] The "breaking of the bread" was one of the Church's earliest terms for the Eucharist (see also Luke 24: 30-31).

After taking a standardized test for the archdiocese, I realized that I needed to talk with my teacher about my predicament; I had found myself writing in, "According to Catholic belief. . ." next to several answers. Mom and dad, for their part, were respectful of my feelings. My eighth grade teacher agreed to meet with me during recess.

I was frank, "I don't think I can receive confirmation; I don't believe I could do so honestly. I've been reading the Bible and doing a lot of thinking too. There are quite a few Catholic beliefs that I don't agree with: the Pope, praying to Mary and the saints, confession, 'Tradition' being placed alongside Scripture." By the time I had finished my teacher had a faint smile.

"Shane, I'm going to be honest with you - I myself don't feel drawn to praying to Mary. I need to know two things - do you believe in Jesus as your Lord and do you believe in the Eucharist?"

"Yes. I believe in both completely."

"Then I don't see any reason why you can't be confirmed. The Catholic Church is a big place Shane, big enough for those with a devotion to Mary and big enough for those without. Jesus, Jesus in the Eucharist, is the center. If you believe this then you can find a home in the Catholic Church." She paused to let her words sink in, "I want you to think about that. I respect your coming to talk to me, and I'll respect your decision. I'll be praying for you."

Afterward, any anxiety that I had felt was gone. I knew the reality of the Eucharist as taught by the Catholic Church. I knew good priests such as my associate pastor. I doubted whether I would find a church where I agreed with *everything* that was taught. Whatever "baggage" the Catholic Church was carrying around, I felt sure that God would not forsake such a large body of believers. Slowly a thought began to form, one that appealed to my inner evangelist: "If everyone who experiences the 'release of the Spirit' leaves the Catholic Church, then how can it ever be renewed?" I cringe now - my arrogance at fourteen! What I could not see at the time was how the Church would be the one doing all the giving – and through the very channels I had rejected: Mary, confession, Tradition, the papacy. The Lord has a tremendous sense of humor – using my evangelistic fervor to foster my own ongoing conversion!

I really had no appreciation for the power of Confirmation. Catholics are taught to equate it with the day of Pentecost. I reasoned that since I had already prayed for the Holy Spirit to be released, and had experienced His activity in my life, the sacrament probably did not hold as much for me as for my classmates. Oh, was I in for surprise!

Confirmation stands out as a wonderful memory. The sacrament began with the bishop extending his hands over all of us gathered in the cathedral, praying for the Spirit to anoint us with the same gifts He had anointed Jesus. When I came forward the bishop laid his hand on me, anointed my forehead with blessed oil (chrism) and said, "Be sealed with the Gift of the Holy Spirit." Then he extended Christ's peace to me by shaking my hand. Most memorable though, because it was so unexpected, was the effect of the sacrament. A new "strength" entered me - there was even a quasi-physical sensation in my chest for a week afterward. A sin I had struggled with for months was finally overcome. God taught me that my earlier prayer for the release of the Spirit was a beginning, not a culmination. In Confirmation the Holy Spirit came upon me in a unique way - to strengthen me even further against sin, to mature me, and cause me to take on more of Jesus' character.

A Theology of Confirmation

In the previous chapter, I shared how the coming of the Spirit at Jesus' baptism fulfilled Isaiah's messianic prophecy, "The Spirit of the Lord will rest on him – the Spirit of wisdom and of understanding, the Spirit of counsel and of power, the Spirit of knowledge and of the fear of the Lord – and he will delight in the fear of the Lord" (Is.11:2). As we went on to say, salvation consists in our being fused to Jesus, fully united to Him. Listen to how the Evangelist Luke began his *Acts of the Apostles*, "In my former book [The Gospel of Luke], I wrote about all that Jesus *began* to do and teach" (Acts 1:1); the rest of *Acts* is the story of what Jesus *continued* to do, *in* and *through* His Church. It is one and the same ministry – and thus the Church shares His anointing.

Jesus	*His Church*
Conceived by the Holy Spirit, free from original sin.	*Baptism* – conceived by the Spirit and freed from original sin (and the guilt of personal sins)
Baptized in the Jordan – Anointed with the Holy Spirit and His gifts to perform His ministry	*Pentecost* – anointed with the Spirit, and His gifts, to participate in Jesus' ministry
Gave Himself to the Father, completely and without reservation from the time of His conception right through His Death, Resurrection, and Ascension	*Eucharist* – incorporation into Jesus as He offers Himself to the Father through His Life, Death, Resurrection, and Ascension

Christians today are baptized. We receive the Eucharist. But where is *our* Pentecost? When will we be empowered the way Peter and the others were?"

Lets look at *Acts of the Apostles* again. We hear how the deacon Philip went to Samaria and evangelized and baptized there:

> …when the apostles at Jerusalem heard that Samaria had received the word of God, they sent to them Peter and John, who came down and prayed for them that they might receive the Holy Spirit; for [the Spirit] had not yet fallen on any of them, but they had only been baptized in the name of the Lord Jesus. Then [Peter and John] laid their hands on them and they received the Holy Spirit." (Acts 8:14-17)

Now the Spirit had dwelt in the Samaritans since their baptisms, just as the He had in the Apostles since Jesus had breathed upon them – but it was through the laying on of the Apostles' hands that He "fell upon them" in the power of Pentecost. We see the same thing with the Apostle Paul in Ephesus. After hearing him, a group of people "were baptized in the name of the Lord Jesus. And when Paul had laid his hands upon them, the Holy Spirit came on them; and they spoke with tongues and prophesied" (Acts 19:5-6).

Later on, when St. Paul[54] wrote his *Epistle to the Hebrews*, he listed what he considered the "elementary teachings about Christ": "repentance from dead works, faith in God, instruction about baptism and the laying on of hands..."(6:1-2, NAB). This "laying on of hands" is every Christians' God-given Pentecost! In time it became known here in the western Church as *Confirmation* and in the eastern Church as *Chrismation*.

Very early in Church history, to make this truth of being anointed with the Spirit visible, an anointing with perfumed oil (chrism) was added to the laying on of hands (CCC[55] 1289). Under the Old Covenant oil was used to anoint priests, prophets, and kings. The Church wanted to bring that to the confirmed's mind, as well as using the oil to evoke other truths (CCC 1293):

1. We are *Chris*t*ians (Acts 11:26), anointed ones dwelling in the Anointed One
2. a sign of abundance and joy (Deut.11:14; Ps.23:5; Ps.104:15)
3. cleansing (in the first century people were anointed before and after baths)
4. it loosens the joints (anointing of athletes and wrestlers)
5. a sign of healing – soothing to bruises and wounds (Isaiah 1:6; Luke 10:34)

In this anointing we receive the "mark," the seal of the Holy Spirit (CCC 1295; 2 Cor.1:21-22; Eph.1:13; Eph.4:30). This seal designates our total belonging to Christ Jesus, our permanent enrollment in His service, and God's promise of protection when the Church on earth faces its final trial or we individuals enter the moment of death (Rev.7:2-3; Rev.9:4; Ezekiel 9:4-6). The ordinary minister of the sacrament is a bishop. Just as the Samaritans and Ephesians received the fullness of the Spirit with the laying on of the Apostle's hands, so we today receive this anointing from the successors to the Apostles.[56]

Jesus' intention in Confirmation is to "mature" our souls so that they can participate in the gifts with which the Spirit endowed His own human-

---

[54] Hebrews was traditionally ascribed to Paul, but modern biblical scholarship calls this into question. The letter is unsigned. Paul is called the author in the present talk for the sake of simplicity.
[55] CCC refers to *The Catechism of the Catholic Church*, 1994.
[56] The justification for seeing bishops as such will be provided in the following chapters.

ity. It is not that Jesus received the Spirit, and then we receive the Spirit and the same set of gifts that He did - as if we were miniature copies of the Lord. Rather, because we are living *in* Jesus we can act with the gifts the Spirit poured out on Him - His wisdom, His understanding, His counsel and strength, knowledge, awe, and fear of the Lord! We are empowered to love with His heart and think with His mind (1 Cor. 2:16)! These gifts, listed in *Isaiah 11:2*, have been called the "traditional" gifts to differentiate them from the charisms. They are traditional in the sense that they are *always* given; if you have had hands laid on you in Confirmation then you have full access to these gifts – guaranteed. We have already seen that that is not so for the charisms. Lets take a moment to examine these gifts in more detail and observe how they build on one another:

1. *Fear of the Lord* – the respect a child has for his/her parents. We do not stand in terror of God, but we do recognize that our Father in Heaven loves us so much that He will discipline us if need be. He loves us just as we are, but He loves us too much to let us remain the way we are!
2. *Piety* – our realization of God's Love for us moves us to respond to Him in prayer, both private and communal. We come to hear God's Word for us, both from other believers and within our own souls.
3. *Knowledge* – this entering into the Father's Presence and listening to His Word empowers us to grow in what we know of the Truth.
4. *Understanding* – as we seek His guidance, the Spirit leads us to penetrate this Truth, perceive its meaning for us and other believers.
5. *Wisdom* – we are the led in applying this understanding.
6. *Counsel* – the Spirit will guide us in making specific decisions, and
7. *Fortitude* – strengthen us to persevere in doing what we now know to be right.

The Spirit also manifests what are known as Fruits in our lives: love, joy, peace, patience, kindness, goodness, faithfulness, gentleness, and self-control (Galatians 5:22-23). The "traditional" gifts and the fruits, not charisms, are what testify to a mature union with Jesus.

When the Spirit Opens the Door – Two Examples

Sharing the Good News has to be the work of the Spirit. Most of the time it is a gradual process: two people opening their inner lives to each other. There are those rare instances though, when the Spirit seems to kick a door open so the Good News can be poured in.

The first example I have comes from a few weeks before my Confirmation. The Lord arranged a meeting between me and a young woman at the mall. My mom and little sister were clothes shopping while I made my way to the bookstore. The section with the Christian works was toward the back, so I had to cruise by the New Age section to get there. I usually took a peak, curious what new and misleading works had appeared on the market. On this particular morning there was only one other person there, a woman in her late twenties.

I knew inside that she shouldn't be looking through those books. God had infinitely more to offer her than she could find in those pages. I realized that I needed to speak to her. . .and that realization terrified me! I began to pray, lingering around and waiting for the courage to strike up a conversation. When I heard my mom and sister's voices from the front of the store, I knew it was go-time. Gesturing to the books on the shelf I said, "Excuse me miss, but do you believe in all of this?"

"Well, some of them. . .I've experienced some strange things, and I'd like to understand them better."

"Oh, what kind of 'strange things'?" I asked - with newly imparted boldness.

"I think that's just a little personal, don't you?" she countered. It was as if a wall was flying up between us. I just continued to say what came to mind.

"In the past few months I've experienced things that I never dreamed possible. It happened after I committed myself to Jesus of Nazareth." The tension on her face began to lessen, and I continued speaking about the Spirit and His gifts. While I was relating all of this my mom and sister finally found where we were. Mom stood silently by, allowing me to share what Jesus had been doing in my life.

The story which the woman related back to me was very unusual. A lifelong friend had just revealed that he practiced witchcraft, headed a coven in fact, and would like her to attend a meeting. The woman was repulsed by the invitation. Just prior to all of this, she had let him babysit her newborn son. The whole matter repulsed her, and she was quite fearful. She went on to explain that a great heaviness (she gave me the impression she thought it demonic in nature) had hung over her since receiving the offer. She had sought advice and help from her priest (revealing that she had grown up Catholic) as well as prayer. The heaviness had broken just shortly before we met. She found herself in the bookstore that morning looking for ways to protect herself and her family from spiritual oppression. I could tell that she considered her childhood friend some type of threat to them.

I explained that she was looking for answers in the wrong place. Our Lord and His Word were the answer, not the New Age movement. I led her to where the Bibles were and showed her verses about the need to avoid looking for answers in the occult - as well as the power the Lord Jesus gives His disciples to overcome anything Satan throws at us. She was completely receptive to everything I shared. She asked me to write down my name and phone number for her. As I did she told my mom how unbelievable it was that we had met. When I handed the paper back to her a shocked look came to her face, "*Shane*, your name is *Shane*?"

"Yes," I replied, giving her a glance of *please let me in on the secret.*

"That's the name I chose for *my son!* I can't believe it." For her it meant something, a confirmation. My family was only home from our shopping trip a few minutes before the woman called to say thank you. She had rushed home and told her husband about our meeting; she even called her priest. We spoke on the phone a few more times but eventually lost track of each other. To my knowledge neither she nor her family experienced any further difficulties related to witchcraft.

The second story I want to share concerns the girl who sat next to me at Confirmation. For some reason she really disliked me. We shared mutual friends though, and I soon found myself at other functions with her. One evening she started to share how she had been out joy-riding with some older kids the night before. The guy driving had almost hit someone head-on. Then turning to look at me she said, "When I was looking into the headlights of that other car I saw Shane's face." She was dead serious. Everyone thought it was a pretty wild story, but no one more so than me, especially given her dislike of me. As soon as the two of us could break away from the group I asked her why she thought that had happened.

"I think God was trying to get my attention, remind me how much I need Him." It was incredibly humbling to think about myself being associated with "a relationship with God." She shared with me some of the struggles in her life and then let me pray with her. We prayed that any blockages in her relationship with the Lord would be removed and that He would let her experience the gifts of His Spirit.

Discipleship Has a Cost

Throughout eighth grade, thanks to the Holy Spirit, I participated in religion class much more. It was not that I made a conscious effort; it was simply that I could not keep quiet when the Lord came up. Classmates I had never really gotten along with used it as one more thing to tease me about, and at first I gave tit-for-tat. Slowly however, Jesus convicted me that that was not the way to conduct myself. For starters, it perpetuated the fighting. But in addition, Jesus had taught the Apostles to see persecution as a blessing. When someone made fun of me because of my faith it was actually an honor; they were recognizing me as His.

Eventually I began to experience tension with my best friend. He had begun listening to music that I found troubling; some lyrics were blatantly satanic. I could not get into a song that began by reciting the name of Satan backwards. I told him how I felt about the music and that his enjoyment of it really worried me. I also mentioned a couple of other things in his behavior that concerned me - drawing pentagrams on his book covers and a preoccupation with death.

The different things occurring at school did get me down at times. I decided that it would all be worth it though, if someone, anyone, were drawn to Jesus by something I said. To all appearance it didn't look like that was going to happen.

I had been growing closer to my classmate Jerry though. At first we just joked around at the lunch table. He was a good-hearted guy. I gave him a call after school one day. Before my friends and I were old enough to drive, the phone lines were the evening gathering place. I'm not sure how Jerry and I got onto the subject, but he eventually said, "Shane, I've heard what you've been saying in religion class. I haven't known how to bring this up, but whatever it is that you have with God - I want it." I truly was stunned; there I was convinced that no one heard what I was sharing about Jesus, and God had been at work in Jerry's heart all along. God is amazing - working all around us, many times within us, without our knowing until much later. When Jerry said those words to me it made any teasing I had taken well worthwhile; the excitement of being used by God to speak His word wiped it all away.

Jerry and I spent a lot of time together the summer after eighth grade. I watched the Lord, in a matter of weeks, bless him with a new awareness of the Spirit and the gift of tongues. Apparently Jerry's mom had been involved in the Catholic Charismatic movement some years before and had even founded a prayer group in the parish where we went to school. The group was a lot smaller than what I had encountered at Grace World Outreach, perhaps twenty-five people, but the intensity of their praise was the same. The Spirit of God was in their midst. I found that the smaller number created a heightened sense of intimacy between those present. The leaders of the group were not ordained ministers, simply Catholic lay people gathered on a Tuesday evening to express their love to God and listen to Him. There was no expensive sound system, just the God-given beauty of human voices and a couple of guitars in a parochial school cafeteria. Something that puzzled me about the parish group was how its members could be so completely charismatic, so immersed in Scripture, and at the same time completely Catholic in their belief.

Chapter 5 – Every Boy Needs His Mother (and Brothers and Sisters Too)

Freshman year at an archdiocesan high school was not easy. My classmates from elementary school did not waste any time spreading the word about my "fanaticism." This was at the same time as the Jim and Tammy Faye Bakker scandal. Comments like "son of God," signs on my locker, and crank phone calls were as bad as it got – not exactly a martyrdom. Having Jerry there with me definitely helped. The Lord opened my eyes to a much more extensive support network though, both on earth and in heaven.

As I said, the prayer group at the parish really intrigued me, fully charismatic and fully Catholic. I remember putting the question to one of the worship leaders, "With Scripture being so clear-cut about not trying to communicate with the dead, why do you pray the 'Hail Mary' at the end of every meeting?"

The thoroughness of his response really caught me off-guard, "The first thing we have to get straight is that Mary isn't dead. Don't you remember what Jesus said, '…whoever lives and believes in me shall never die?'(John 11:25-26) That is true for everyone living in Jesus. And for Mary it's one hundred percent true *right now*, she already shares *completely* in His resurrection from the dead. I believe she was assumed into heaven, body and soul." He went on, "It's also very important to make a distinction here: the Bible prohibits trying to communicate with the dead, trying to receive answers from them; but that's not what I do when I pray the *Hail Mary* or ask a saint to intercede for me. I'm asking them to pray for me, the same as if I asked you to pray for me. I'm not seeking a response or asking them to reveal anything to me; it's strictly one-way."

Everything he said was completely logical. The only thing I felt I could fault him on was the belief that Mary was assumed into heaven; I did not see that in Scripture. And yet, the Bible *did* speak of two other people being assumed, Enoch (Genesis 5:24) and Elijah (2 Kings 2:11-12). If it was true for them, then why not Mary too? And if the assumption occurred at the end of her life, then wouldn't the bulk of the New Testament already have been written? Did the Bible have to explicitly say it for it to have occurred?

I later came to learn that many people see an allusion to her assumption in the *Book of Revelation*, chapter 12.

Through the prayer group's leaders I was put in contact with, get this, a Catholic charismatic youth minister. He in turn invited me to check out a prayer group for teens, God's Gang. It met on Wednesday nights in the home of a couple in their sixties and drew youth from all over St. Louis. I was blown away the first time I attended: fifty kids packed into a room, worshiping the Lord. Youth participated in the music ministry and teaching, even manifesting the charisms of prophecy and discernment of spirits. When I was asked to share my testimony, I recounted how I had received the gift of tongues. My sharing that first night opened the door to another awesome experience: the owner of the meeting place, Bill Patty, asked me to pray with him and a young man desiring the gift of tongues.

We adjourned to an "upper room" (Acts 1:13) that Bill and his wife Ruth had set aside for prayer. We turned to the Lord, and the young man received tongues within a matter of minutes. Before we closed our prayer, it was heavy upon my heart to share my questions about Mary with them. Bill responded with an incredible story of how the Holy Spirit had moved him to seek Mary's intercession in a time of crisis. They then prayed with me to have a heart ready to receive everything the Lord Jesus wanted to give me. A spiritual chain-reaction was set off - within a month I was praying the rosary. Jesus opened my eyes to recognize Mary as my much-more-mature sister in faith, the perfect disciple – and in time, as my mother.

Fast forward almost one year to the day. Through a last minute development I found myself addressing 800 people at the St. Louis Catholic Charismatic Renewal Conference:

> "We are being called to become pregnant with the Lord Jesus Christ...We are being called to give birth to the Word. The Lord is calling us to share in the same honor that Mary did. And that is to have the resurrected Son of God, full of life and love and mercy come through us and speak to His Church and a world that is hurting. Mary did it two thousand years ago, and she's praying for us that we can do it today. So I ask for her intercession and give praise to God tonight."

One of the nuns ministering at the conference confided how a month earlier the Lord had impressed upon her a word He would have shared at the

76   THE GOD WHO IS LOVE

conference – "pregnant;" but that she had not a clue what He meant until my sharing.

In the remainder of the chapter we will explore the Scriptural data concerning Mary and the connection between God's People on earth and those in heaven.

Scriptural Insights

Of the four gospels, Luke and John's tell us the most about Mary. Luke's Gospel relates the moment of encounter between Mary and the Angel Gabriel, "Hail, full of grace, the Lord is with you!...Do not be afraid, Mary, for you have found favor with God. And behold, you shall conceive in your womb and bear a son, and you shall call his name Jesus" (1:28-31). Mary's question at that point is beautiful because it is the question of every disciple upon hearing his/her call, "How can this be?" (1:34). Obviously though, for Mary these words have an even greater import than they do for you and I: she was a virgin, and even though she was engaged to be married, apparently intended, or at least felt a strong "calling," to remain such.[57] Observe Gabriel's words, "The Holy Spirit will come upon you, and the power of the Most High will *overshadow* you; therefore the child to be born will be called holy, the Son of God" (1:35). We have already seen how that

---

[57] "Her concern is not that she is unmarried but that she is a virgin at present and that she intends to remain one in the future...nothing about the angel's announcement should have perplexed Mary – whose betrothal to Joseph [a descendant of David] was already a legally binding marriage – unless she intends to forego ordinary sexual relations even as a married woman," Hahn, Scott and Curtis Mitch, *Ignatius Catholic Study Bible: The Gospel of Luke* (San Francisco, 2001), p.19. See also the excellent exegesis and discussion of this passage in Ignace de La Potterie's *Mary in the Mystery of the Covenant* (New York: Alba House, 1992), pp.22-29.

Then what are we to make of passages such as *Matt.13:55-56*, that speak of Jesus' brothers and sisters? Well, in Jesus' culture, the terms "brother" and "sister" could refer to any relation, or even a close friend. OT examples abound (Gen.14:14-*nephew*, Gen.29:15-*uncle*; 1 Chron.23:21-22-*cousin*; Dt.23:7-*kinsman*; 2 Sam.1:26-*friend*; Amos 1:9-*ally*) In fact, Hebrew and Aramaic, the languages of Jesus, had no word for "cousin." Looking at the writings of the early Church, those closest in time to the facts, no one proposed these brothers and sisters as children of Mary until approximately 300 years later. Instead they were spoken of as step-brothers and sisters (from a previous marriage of Joseph) or as cousins. See <http://www.catholic.com/library/Brethren_of_the_Lord.asp>

term "overshadow" was the same used to describe God's coming to dwell in the Tabernacle (Exodus 40:34).

It is fascinating to see how Luke goes on to develop this insight during Mary's visit to her kinswoman Elizabeth. Allow me to set his account next to an Old Testament text concerning the Ark of the Covenant, God's earthly throne:

Luke 1:39-45, 56	*2 Samuel 6:2-3,6-12,16*
In those days Mary *arose and went* in haste *into the hill country, to a city of Judah, and she entered the house of Zechariah* and greeted Elizabeth. And when Elizabeth heard the greeting of Mary, *the babe leaped in her womb;* and Elizabeth was filled with the Holy Spirit and she exclaimed with a loud cry, "Blessed are you among women, and blest is the fruit of your womb! *And why is this granted to me, that the mother of my Lord should come to me?* For behold, when the voice of your greeting came to my ears, *the babe in my womb leaped for joy.* And blessed is she who believed that there would be a fulfillment of what was spoken to her by the Lord"...*Mary remained with [Elizabeth] three months,* and returned to her home	And David arose and went with all the people who were with him *from Ba'ale-judah* to bring up from there the ark of God...And they carried the ark of God upon a new cart and brought it out of the house of Abin'adab which was *on the hill*...And when they came to the threshing floor of Nacon, Uzzah put out his hand to the ark of God, and took hold of it, for the oxen stumbled. And the anger of the LORD was kindled against Uzzah; and God smote him there...And David was afraid of the Lord that day; and said, *"How can the ark of the LORD come to me?"*...[David] took it aside to *the house* of O'bed-e'dom the Gittite. And the ark of the LORD *remained [there]... three months,* and the LORD blessed O'bed-e'dom and all his household...[When] it was told King David...[he] went and brought up the ark of God from the house of O'bed-e'dom into the city of David with rejoicing...As the ark of the LORD came into the city of David, Michal the daughter of Saul looked out of the window and saw *King David leaping and dancing before the LORD*

There are too many similarities between the two passages for it to be coincidence; the Holy Spirit inspired Luke to make these narrative connections between Mary and the Ark. As God's throne, the Ark was the holiest object under the Old Covenant; its presence designated the Temple as His house. Do you remember, from chapter 2, what the Ark contained? The tablets with the Ten Commandments, the staff of Aaron (the original high priest), and a sample of the "heavenly bread" Israel received in the desert (Hebrew 9:4). Jesus was the fulfillment of all of those: the Word of the Father, the eternal high priest, and the Bread of Life – making Mary, who carried Him in her womb, the Ark of the New Covenant. Her lap was the only throne Jesus knew while on earth!

John the Evangelist, in his *Book of Revelation*, made the identification between Mary and the Ark even more explicit:

> Then God's temple in heaven was opened, and the ark of his covenant was seen within his temple; and there were flashes of lightning, voices, peals of thunder, an earthquake and heavy hail. And a great portent appeared in heaven, a woman clothed with the sun, with the moon under her feet, and on her head a crown of twelve stars; she was with child and she cried out in her pangs of birth, in anguish for delivery. And another portent appeared in heaven; behold a great red dragon...the dragon stood before the woman who was about to bear a child, that he might devour her child when she brought it forth; she brought forth a male child, one who is to rule all the nations with a rod of iron, but her child was caught up to God and to his throne... (Revelation 11:19-12:5)

The vision of the Ark gave way to that of the woman giving birth to the Messiah, Mary.[58] In John's writings Mary is always referred to as "woman;" it is the only way Jesus addresses her in John's Gospel (2:4; 19:26). The vision in *Revelation* takes us back to the first pages of Scripture, where the first woman and man were defeated by the cunning of the Serpent. And what were God's words to the Serpent?

---

[58] Mary is the Ark of the Covenant, and in the final book of the New Testament the author sees the Ark in Heaven. A biblical allusion to her assumption?

> *"I will put enmity between you and*
>   *the woman,*
> and between your offspring and
>   hers;
> He will strike at your head,
>   while you strike at his heel"
> (Genesis 3:15, NIV).

Mary of Nazareth was *the* woman at enmity with the Devil; like her Son, she was (and is) Satan's adversary.

These insights were not lost on the early Church. When we look at the writings they left behind, this contrast between Mary and Eve immediately comes to the fore:

> Eve, a virgin and undefiled, conceived the word of the serpent, and bore disobedience and death. But the Virgin Mary received faith and joy when the angel Gabriel announced to her the glad tidings that the Spirit of the Lord would come upon her (Justin Martyr, *Dialogue with Trypho the Jew*, 155 A.D.)[59]

> The knot of Eve's disobedience was loosed by the obedience of Mary. What the virgin Eve had bound in unbelief, the Virgin Mary loosed through faith. (Irenaeus, Bishop of Lyons, *Against Heresies Book III*, 180-199 A.D.)[60]

> Eve had believed the serpent; Mary believed Gabriel. That which the one destroyed by believing, the other, by believing, set straight. (Tertullian, *The Flesh of Jesus Christ*, 210 A.D.).[61]

The Uniqueness of Mary's Salvation

Deep reflection on the Scripture passages we have looked at, guided by the Holy Spirit over centuries, led believers to recognize the uniqueness of Mary's salvation. To receive Jesus into her, she had to have been healed of the brokenness resulting from our first parents' sin. When did that occur? As

---

[59] Jurgens, William. *The Faith of the Early Fathers*, Volume 1. (Collegeville, MN: The Liturgical Press, 1970) p.141.
[60] Ibid, p.93
[61] Ibid, p.147

the New Eve, paralleling Jesus as the New Adam (Romans 5:12-19), then would not she - like Adam, Eve, and Jesus - have been *created* with the Spirit at her core? If John the Baptist could respond to the Holy Spirit while in his mother's womb (Luke 1:41,44), how can we object to Mary receiving the Spirit but a few months earlier, at conception?

Look again at how the angel Gabriel addressed her, "Hail, full of grace, the Lord is with you!...Do not be afraid, Mary, for you have found favor with God" (Luke 1:28,30). "Full of grace," or "O favored one," in some versions of the Bible, is a translation of the Greek term "Kecharitomene." It refers to an absolute plentitude of grace, Mary "'*has been*' and 'is now' filled with divine life."[62] There was never a moment of separation between she and God. This belief is what Catholics mean when they speak of her "immaculate conception."

Mary herself said, "my spirit rejoices in God my Savior" (Luke 1:47). She, like all of us, was saved from sin – only the manner differs. We are saved from sin by being united to Jesus' offering to the Father at some point in our lives. Cutting through time and space, His sacrifice is the source of salvation for people from the beginning of history until its end (Hebrew 9:28; Revelation 13:8; 1 Peter 3:19-20). By the Father's unmerited gift, the effects of Jesus' victory were applied to Mary at conception. She never experienced the brokeness of original sin. She had no way to earn this gift; it was granted at the instant she came into being. Nor was it a requirement to bear the sinless Jesus. It was certainly fitting, but not a requirement.[63] It was God's sovereign choice.

---

[62] Hahn, Scott and Curtis Mitch, *Ignatius Catholic Study Bible: The Gospel of Luke* (San Francisco, 2001), p.19.

[63] If sinlessness was a requirement for Mary to bear Jesus, then her mother would have had to be sinless to bear her, etc., etc. No, the reason for Mary's immaculate conception lies solely in the graciousness of God. This is precisely what Pope Pius IX said in the Apostolic Constitution, *Ineffabilis Deus* (1854), when he formally voiced the Catholic Church's position on the matter: "the most Blessed Virgin Mary, in the first instant of her Conception, by a singular grace and privilege granted by Almighty God, in view of the merits of Jesus Christ, the Savior of the human race, was preserved free from all stain of original sin"

Mary, the Faithful (and Celebrated) Disciple

Our consideration of Mary's discipleship begins with her reaction to Gabriel's message: "I am the handmaid of the Lord; let it be to me according to your word" (Luke 1:38). This is what people refer to as Mary's *fiat* (Latin for "let it be"). She who received all she was from God put herself completely in His hands; she was living the life of the Spirit, the Life of her Son.

This was what the Holy Spirit moved Elizabeth to recognize during Mary's visit to her: "when Elizabeth heard the greeting of Mary, the babe leaped in her womb; and Elizabeth was filled with the Holy Spirit and she exclaimed with a loud cry, "Blessed are you among women, and blessed is the fruit of your womb!...*blessed is she who believed that there would be fulfillment of what was spoken to her from the Lord*" (Luke 1:41-42,45). Mary's faith, her wholehearted and unequaled cooperation with the promptings of the Spirit, is the reason for her place of honor among the People of God. This is brought out later in Luke's Gospel when a woman cried, "Blessed is the womb that bore you!"

"Rather, " Jesus corrected, "blessed are those who *hear the word of God and keep it* " (Luke 11:27-28). He was not denying Mary's blessedness (the Spirit had already testified to it through Elizabeth); but pointing out that Mary's motherhood was more than a matter of flesh and blood – it was the result of her whole-hearted "yes" when God called.[64]

This brings us to a brief, but important, aside. Why do Catholic and Orthodox Christians refer to Mary as *Theotokos*, Mother of God? It has nothing to do with a belief that Mary preceded God in time– that is absolute nonsense! Look at Elizabeth's words again, "Blessed are you among women, and blessed is the fruit of your womb! And why is this granted me, that *the mother of my Lord* should come to me?" (Luke 1:42-43). The six other occurrences of "Lord" in Luke's first chapter refer to God,[65] so for a Christian reader, "mother of my Lord" and "mother of my God" could easily be viewed as synonymous. "Mother of God" became the favored version in

---

[64] Garrigou-Lagrange, Reginald, *The Mother of the Saviour and Our Interior Life* (Rockford, Illinois: Tan Books and Publishers, 1993), pp.18-19.
[65] Hahn, Scott and Curtis Mitch, *Ignatius Catholic Study Bible: The Gospel of Luke* (San Francisco, 2001), p.20.

the course of history, not because of what it said about Mary, but about Jesus.

When heresies arose in the third and fourth centuries questioning Jesus' divine status, confessing Mary as Mother of God was the way orthodox Christianity reaffirmed its belief in His full humanity and divinity. God the Son truly became a man in Mary's womb. It was God the Son, who as a human being, nursed at her breasts, grew up in her home, and loved and obeyed her as mother. It was God the Son, as a little boy, who was helped by her to take His first steps and say His first words. To deny Mary the title Mother of God would be to deny the shocking reality of the incarnation, that the Word became flesh – it is to deny that God the Son died to save us from sin. If Mary was not the Mother of *God the Son*, then the Christian hope of salvation is null and void!

Getting back to our discussion of Mary's discipleship though, we recognize her as a person of profound prayer. Scripture records a beautiful, prophetic hymn of praise that the Spirit put in her mouth:

> My soul magnifies the Lord,
> and my spirit rejoices in God my
> > Savior,
> for he has regarded the low estate of
> > his handmaiden.
> For behold, henceforth all genera-
> > tions will call me blessed
> (Luke 1:46-49).

Mary was a student of God's actions, a student of her Son. We are told that she "kept all these things, pondering them in her heart" (Luke 2:19, 51).

There were surprises along the way, things she did not understand. Imagine her feelings when the prophet Simeon told her, "[Your] child is set for the fall and rising of many in Israel, and for a sign that is spoken against (and a sword will pierce through your own soul also), that the thoughts of many hearts may be revealed" (Luke 2:34-35). What will happen to my Son? How? When? Where? What awaits me? Mary knew what it meant to walk in the darkness of faith. When Jesus stayed behind in the Temple at the age of twelve, she and Joseph spent three days searching for him. When she found him and said, "I've been searching for you in sorrow," His only response was, "Why did you search for me? Did you not know I had to be in my Father's house?" The pain that had to cause! Scripture is blunt, "[She] did not understand" (Luke 2:48-50).

We see her again in the gospels some eighteen years later, when she, Jesus, and His other disciples attended a wedding in Cana. It is here that we see Mary acting as an intercessor on behalf of others. The feast must have went on for some time when the wine ran out. What would the bride and groom serve their guests? (Hospitality was at the top of the virtue list in the ancient world.) John tells us that Jesus' Mother became aware of the bride and groom's predicament. Observe what she did:

> ...the mother of Jesus said to him, "They have no wine." And Jesus said to her,
> "O woman, what have you to do with me? My hour has not yet come."
> His mother said to the servants, "Do whatever he tells you"
> (John 2:3-5).

I am sure you remember the rest of the story. Jesus told the servants to fill six huge jars with water and take a sample to the master of the banquet. When the head waiter tasted it, it was the finest wine. John concludes the story by writing, "This, the first of His miraculous signs, Jesus performed in Cana of Galilee. He thus revealed his glory, and his disciples put their faith in him" (John 2:11, NIV).

Mary did not take "no" for an answer; and Jesus, in His love for her and in response to her faith, did not turn her down. He performed His first miracle *because* of her intercession! I can't help but think that He had her in mind when he told the parable of the persistent widow, telling us that we should be unceasing in our intercession (Luke 18:1-5). The gospels may be limited in the number of verses devoted to Mary, but what they tell us is astounding. Her words to the servants, "Do whatever he tells you" (John 2:5), compresses the whole of Christian morality and discipleship into one sentence!

The next time we encounter Mary is at the foot of the cross. Simeon's prophecy has been fulfilled; watching her tortured Son hang there, her soul was pierced by a sword, "that the thoughts of many hearts may be revealed" (Luke 2:34-35). She did not rail at the Father, did not lash out at the soldiers overseeing the execution or the mockers passing by. She silently entrusted herself, once again, to the Father, in the Spirit. And then her Son asked something more of her:

> When Jesus saw his mother, and the disciple whom he loved standing near, he said to his mother, "Woman, there behold your son!" Then he said to the disciple, "Behold, your mother!" And from that hour the disciple took her into his home (John 19:26-27).

When we look at the accounts of Jesus' death we see that everything He did at the cross was tied up with the new life He was purchasing for us – everything, *including this*.

We see Mary exercising this maternal care as she prayed with the disciples for the coming of the Spirit at Pentecost (Acts 1:14). Scripture is silent on how she continued to live it out; but we can be sure she did, especially in her relationship with John the Apostle, the beloved disciple.

Upon her entrance into glory,[66] the full sharing of Jesus' resurrection, her maternal care could extend directly to every beloved disciple. She could care, with a mother's heart, for every soul that had been fused to her Son's. Look again at what John told us in the *Book of Revelation*:

> And a great portent *appeared in heaven*: a woman clothed with the sun, with the moon under her feet, and on her head a crown of twelve stars...she brought forth a male child, one who is to rule all the nations with a rod of iron...Now war arose in heaven...the great dragon was thrown down, that ancient serpent, who is called the Devil and Satan, the deceiver of the whole world...he pursued the woman who had borne the male child. But the woman was given the two wings of the great eagle that she might fly from the serpent into the wilderness, to the place where she was to be nourished...the dragon was angry with

---

[66] Pope Pius XII formally defined the bodily assumption of the Blessed Virgin Mary into heaven as a part of Catholic faith in 1950. Pius XII didn't propose the belief as a new piece of revelation; Christians had celebrated it since the early centuries. Before he did so, he wrote to all the bishops of the world, asking them if this was the faith held by their part of Christ's Body. Almost unanimously, the bishops of the *entire world* answered "yes," it should be held by all professing Catholics. That Mary's assumption isn't explicity stated in the Bible doesn't mean it didn't happen. It would have occurred decades after the events recorded in the gospels and possibly after the writing of the epistles.

the woman and went off to make war on *the rest of her offspring*, on those who keep the commandments of God and bear testimony to Jesus (Revelation 12:1,5,7,9,13-14,17).

Mary has been empowered by the Spirit to act as mother, not just to Jesus, but to every person united to Him.[67] The chief way she shows her love is to intercede for us, just as she did for the couple at Cana. And here's the thing - as each Christian reaches the full life of the Trinity in heaven, they too enter into intercession for their brothers and sisters still on earth.

The Intercession of Our Mother, Brothers, and Sisters

At some point, most people have asked someone else to pray for them at some point. Prayers, offered for the ones we love here on earth, are acts of love. Just as Jesus prayed for His disciples while on earth, He continues to do so now *through us*. This does not interfere with Jesus' sole mediation (1 Timothy 2:5) between the Father and humanity in the least; we intercede as members *of Jesus*. If that is true for us still being formed in His image, then how much more so for our brothers and sisters in heaven? This was the belief of God's people even under the Old Covenant. We are told of the vison granted to the Jewish freedom fighter, Judas Maccabeus:

> He cheered [his soldiers] by relating a dream, a sort of vision, which was worthy of belief. What he saw was this: Onias, [the deceased] high priest, a noble and good man, of modest bearing and gentle manner, one who spoke fittingly and had been trained from childhood in all that belongs to excellence, was praying with outstretched hands for the whole body of the Jews. Then likewise a man appeared, distinguished by his grey hair and dignity, and of marvelous majesty and authority. And Onias spoke, saying, "This is a man who loves the brethren and

---

[67] The passage from *Revelation* does not refer to Mary alone – but to the whole People of God, symbolized as both Mother Zion (in the O.T.) and Mother Church (under the New Covenant). As the Mother of the Messiah Mary is the highest embodiment of Mother Zion; and as the spotless Virgin, offering Christ to the world, she is the ultimate image of Mother Church. John's "woman clothed with the sun" simultaneously manifests all of these truths.

> prays much for the people and the holy city, Jeremiah, the prophet of God" (2 Maccabees 15:11-14).[68]

It is my conviction that Scripture gives us many additional reasons to believe that those around God's throne have our prayers "in hand."

> At once I was in the Spirit, and lo, there a throne stood in heaven with one seated on the throne!...Round the throne were twenty-four thrones and seated on the thrones were twenty-four elders (Revelation 4:2,4)... each holding a harp, and with golden bowls full of incense, which are *the prayers of the [earthly] saints* (Revelation 5:8).

So who are the twenty-four elders around the throne? "Elder" is used in the Bible only in reference to human beings. In the passage of Scripture just quoted John related his vision of heaven: members of the Body of Christ surrounding the throne of God, offering up the prayers of the earthly saints.

Since our departed brothers and sisters are even closer to the Lord, they have a perfected capacity to love us. What better way would there be for them to love us then to intercede on our behalf? The saints in heaven do have the earthly Church in mind; in the *Book of Revelation* John also said:

> I saw under the altar the souls of those who had been slain for the word of God and the witness they had borne; they cried out with a loud voice, "O Sovereign Lord, holy and true, how long before thou wilt judge and avenge our blood on those who dwell upon the earth?" Then they were... *told* to rest a little longer, until their brethren should be complete, who were killed as they themselves had been (Revelation 6:9-11).

We find the martyrs crying out to God to bring judgment, to intervene on behalf of the Church and vindicate those who had already given their lives. God revealed to them that more brothers and sisters would be martyred before judgment came. Did you catch that? God allowed the heavenly saints to have information about the earthly saints, that more were to be

---

[68] This book of Scripture, *2 Maccabees*, does not appear in Protestant editions of the Bible. For discussion of the differences between Catholic and Protestant editions of the Old Testament, and why I hold the Catholic position, please consult Appendix IV.

killed. It is a precedent, a biblical example of those in heaven having information about us on earth.

I think it is reasonable to assume the heavenly saints are often interceding before we even ask. But isn't that the case with Christians we know on earth as well? Surely you have asked someone, maybe your mother, to pray for you - knowing full well that you are always in her prayers. So why do you ask? Because it brings you relief, as well as calls her prayers to focus on a particular matter. Catholics and Eastern Orthodox asking their heavenly brothers and sisters to pray has a variety of benefits: it *assures* us of powerful intercession; it gives us the security flowing from agreement in prayer (Matt.18:20), and it fosters our love for siblings we will spend eternity with. Against such things there is no law, no Scriptural mandate to the contrary. Instead we find St. Paul teaching about the interrelation of all Christians:

> I kneel before the Father, from whom his *whole* family, *in heaven and on earth* derives its name (Ephesians 3:14, NIV).

> For just as the body is one and has many members, and all the members of the body, though many, are one body, so it is with Christ. For by one Spirit we were all baptized into one body – Jews or Greeks, slaves or free – and all were made to drink of one Spirit… there [should] be no discord in the body…the members [should] have the same care for one another. If one member suffers, all suffer together; if one member is honored, all rejoice together (1 Corinthians 12:12-13; 25-26).

Think about the image of the Body. When your hand is injured and in need of care, doesn't it send the message to your brain via a series of neurons? When in need I want as many neurons in the Body of Christ firing as possible. Consider these two passages in light of each other:

> You have come to Mount Zion and to the city of the living God, the heavenly Jerusalem…to a judge who is God of all, and to the spirits of just men made perfect (Hebrews 12:22-23).

> The prayer of a righteous man is powerful and effective (James 5:16; NIV).

Living these Beliefs

"Therefore, since we are *surrounded by so great a cloud of witnesses*, let us lay aside every weight, and sin which clings so closely, and let us run with perseverance the race that is set before us" (Hebrews 12:1). No matter where we are or what we are doing, through Christ Jesus, we are in constant union with our brothers and sisters. We can have all of heaven united, interceding for the same need, in an instant. It is as easy as saying, "all my brothers and sisters in heaven, please ask the Lord..." Now that is prayer power!

When some people talk about the intercession of the saints, it sounds like some saints have more pull with God than others. Now, I myself have experienced answered prayers as a result of the intercession of Mary and Therese of Lisieux; they are my special prayer partners. I do not, however, believe that they have a special ability to twist the Lord's arm or change His mind in regard to my needs. Rather, my belief is that God leads us to these heavenly prayer partners, and responds to our combined intercession, because He wants to build bonds in His family, bonds we will live out for the rest of eternity. I believe that one of the reasons praying with Mary is so widespread is because God wants each of us to know our mother!

I'm sure you see pictures of your loved ones as you look around your home. Maybe you have someone's picture in a locket. It is those same family sentiments that lie behind the Catholic Christian's use of icons, paintings, statues, and medals (worn around the neck). There is no idolatry here, simply visual reminders of those we love – those who poured out all they were to the Lord. The *Epistle to the Hebrews* spends a whole chapter (11) celebrating the Old Covenant's heroes. The Christian veneration of the saints simply carries this forward, a constant reminder that Scripture records the things Jesus "began to do" (Acts 1:1); His story is continued in the Church as she moves forward through the centuries.

One of the richest fruits I've received from my relationship with Jesus' mother has been prayer - the rosary to be specific. It is a meditation on twenty events in salvation history.[69] As each event is meditated upon, the

---

[69] Although the rosary is made up of twenty mysteries, it is common to pray only five on a given day. The twenty mysteries have been divided into four sub-groups:
The Joyful Mysteries: The Angel Announces Jesus' Birth (Luke 1:26-33,38); Mary's Visit to Elizabeth (Luke 1:39-45); The Nativity (Luke 2:6-12); The Presentation of Jesus in the Temple (Luke 2:25-35); The Finding of Jesus in the Temple at age 12 (Luke 2:41-50).

believer recites the prayer that Jesus' taught us, the *Our Father* (Matt.6:9-13), then ten *Hail Mary*'s, followed by "Glory be to the Father, and to the Son, and to the Holy Spirit. . ." The ten *Hail Mary*'s serve as scriptural/ petitionary "background music" for the meditations:

> Hail Mary, Full of Grace,
> The Lord is with thee [Luke 1:28].
> Blessed are thou among women
> and blessed is the fruit of thy womb, Jesus [Luke 1:42].
> Holy Mary, Mother of God [Luke 1:42],
> Pray for us sinners now and at the hour of our death. Amen."

You would be hard-pressed to find a more biblical prayer than the rosary!

My "Experience" with a Saint

I received an amazing opportunity at the end of my freshman year - the chance to travel to Rome and attend the canonization of a woman buried just miles from my home, Rose Philippine Duchesne. A Religious of the Sacred Heart, she had been a French missionary to the Native Americans in our area. Canonization is that process whereby the Catholic Church recognizes an individual's strong imitation of Christ and proposes them to the world as a model of faith (Hebrews 6:12). After their official recognition the Church refers to them as Saints (capital "S"). The Church had waited almost 135 years to canonize Rose Philippine Duchesne. First, an exhaustive investigation had to be made of her life. This included examining all of

---

The Luminous Mysteries: The Baptism of Jesus (Mark 1:9-13); The Wedding Feast of Cana (John 2:1-11); Jesus' Proclamation of the Kingdom of God (Matthew 4:17,23-25); The Transfiguration of Jesus (Luke 9:28-36); The Institution of the Eucharist (Luke 22:14-16, 19-20).
The Sorrowful Mysteries: The Agony in the Garden (Luke 23:39-46); The Scourging at the Pillar (Mark 15:6-15); The Crowning with Thorns (John 19:1-8); The Carrying of the Cross (John 19:16-22); The Crucifixion (John 19:25-30).
The Glorious Mysteries: The Resurrection (Mark 16:1-7); The Ascension (Luke 24:46-53); The Descent of the Holy Spirit (Acts 2:1-7); The Assumption of Mary into Heaven (Revelation 11:19-12:2; 12:14); The Coronation of Mary (Judith 13:18-20; 2 Timothy 4:8). I should also note that it is possible to meditate on other events from Scripture while praying the rosary. While meditation does not have to be limited to the above mysteries; the life of Jesus as recorded in the gospels is inexhaustible and obviously maintains the pre-eminent place.

her writings and a medical/scientific investigation made of miracles claimed to have been obtained through the saint's intercession. When a candidate for sainthood is someone closer to our own time, the process also includes interviews of surviving family, friends, and acquaintances.

The canonization of Rose Philippine Duchesne was one of those rare instances where my reputation as a "religious fanatic" actually worked to my benefit; my classmates elected me as one of six representatives to attend on behalf of our school. I remember the canonization Mass as being gorgeous. The Pope delivered the sermon in four different languages. The crowd was immense - Italian, Spanish, French, Vietnamese, African, English, American. As I exited St. Peter's Basilica and looked out upon the sea of people filling the square, I remember gasping, "This really is the universal[70] Church." Yes, Christians belong to an immense "family, in heaven and on earth!" (Ephesians 3:14, NIV).

Moving Among Saints on Earth

Back home in St. Louis I found myself growing through participation in the youth group. Friendships with the adult leaders and other teens made the "communion of saints" an everyday reality. They encouraged me to develop talks on a whole variety of subjects – prayer, Scripture, expectant faith, self-esteem. An evangelization team soon formed, and the Lord connected us with teens throughout the archdiocese preparing for Confirmation. Through skits, personal testimonies, teachings, and small group discussions the Holy Spirit opened the eyes of other youth to the intimacy He wanted with them.

---

[70] "Catholic" is Greek for "universal."

Chapter 6 – Confession and the Ongoing Nature of Salvation

A few weeks before Easter I went on retreat with my youth group. Through a series of talks, games, and group projects a priest challenged us to see the goodness God had placed within us, our beauty as His creation. At the same time we were challenged to recognize the giftedness of others, and the magnificence of the earth God had created. The reflection became an incentive for reconciliation between brothers and sisters, and between all of us and the Lord. Hence, part of the weekend was a group reconciliation service.

It was unlike any service I had attended. Father had a small barbecue pit set up in the meeting room and a fire started. The lights were extinguished except for a few candles. We were each given a piece of paper and asked, after a period of prayer, to write our sins on them. When we were ready we could come forward to the fire, allow Father to silently read the sins we needed Jesus' forgiveness for, place the paper in the fire, and allow Father to speak the words of absolution:

> God, the Father of mercies,
> through the death and the resurrection of His Son
> has reconciled the world to Himself
> and sent the Holy Spirit among us for the forgiveness of sins;
> through the ministry of the Church may God give you
> pardon and peace,
> and I absolve you from your sins
> in the name of the Father, and of the Son, and
> of the Holy Spirit.

When I came forward, even though I had not been to confession in two years, I confessed only recent sins. There were more serious sins that I was too embarrassed to mention. When I heard Father speak the prayer of absolution, I let the words sink into my heart. Once again I found myself encountering God in one of the Catholic Church's seven sacraments - and was surprised. Far from the confessional being an intrusion into my relationship with God, it was an instrument of His mercy.

A passage from John's Gospel suddenly made sense. The setting was the night of the resurrection:

> On the evening of that day, the first day of the week, the doors being shut where the disciples were, for fear of the Jews, Jesus came and stood among them and said to them, "Peace be with you...As the Father has sent me, even so I send you." And when he had said this, he breathed on them and said to them, "Receive the Holy Spirit. If *you* forgive the sins of any, they are forgiven; if *you* retain the sins of any, they are retained" (John 20:19-23).

As I looked at it again I allowed myself to acknowledge what I had been unable, or unwilling, to previously - Jesus established a ministry of reconciliation that operated through His apostles. To absolve or retain someone's sins in a responsible manner required that some form of confession be made.[71] At that retreat, through that priest, I came into contact with this Apostolic Ministry, still alive and operating in the 20th century Church.

There was a gratefulness at this finding, but a drawback as well. As I started looking up more about the Sacrament of Reconciliation, or Confession, in a catechism I had received, I came across a troubling stipulation: "It would be a sacrilege, a grave sin of abusing a sacrament of Christ, to deliberately refuse to confess a serious sin in this sacrament."[72] What? I had two years of unconfessed sins, some quite embarrassing. Could God really expect me to bring all of that forward?

My youth mister was no comfort whatsoever, "Shane, keep on asking the Holy Spirit to guide you. This may be something the Lord is asking of you, and if it is then He will make you able to do it." As undesired as it was, the Spirit impressed upon me that believing in the Sacrament of Reconciliation meant accepting that all serious sins be brought to it. After all, it only made sense that the Church that had preserved this ministry of Christ for almost two thousand years should understand how it was to operate.

---

[71] I've heard only one other interpretation of Jesus' words. It claims that Jesus was simply saying the Apostles would forgive or hold bound the sins of others by preaching, or failing to preach, the Gospel. I think it's twisting the obvious meaning of the passage.
[72] Wuerl, Donald W., Ronald Lawler, & Thomas C. Lawler, *The Gift of Faith: A Question and Answer Catechism Version of the Teaching of Christ*, (Hungtingon, Indiana: Our Sunday Visitor, 1986), p.206.

Two weeks later, after an examination of conscience, I visited a nearby parish. The priest who celebrated the sacrament with me was wise and compassionate, not judgmental in the least. I was given the grace to sit face-to-face with this minister of Christ and tell him everything that bogged me down. He encouraged me to be patient with myself and prescribed some Scripture reading. The culmination of the experience was to hear those sweet words of absolution again.

Do I feel that confession to a priest is a necessary part of receiving God's forgiveness? For serious, or "mortal," sins yes. I believe it is the manner in which the Lord Jesus wishes to touch us with His forgiveness. I realize, however, that a large number of Christians do not believe this way, even considering it a serious error of the Catholic Church. The Lord continues to reconcile these believers to Himself when they fall, not allowing confusion or lack of knowledge about the sacrament to come between He and they. I also, however, believe that God desires them to know about this gift and begin reaping the benefits He has packed into it. In this chapter I want to explain the biblical and historical basis of Reconciliation *within* the Scriptural teaching on the Gift of Salvation.

A Complete Salvation

As we saw previously, the New Testament is adamant that salvation does not come through the Law of Moses. Baptism is our birth as sons and daughters "in the Son." We start out as infants, but our Father has no intention of letting us remain infants for eternity (Ephesians 4:13; Hebrews 6:1). He looks forward, eagerly, to our growth and development. In the end we will be like Jesus – loving and pouring ourselves out to Him in the Holy Spirit (Romans 8:29). Faith propels us forward, moving us to not just listen to God's word but to put it into practice (James 1:22-25). Catholics call this "sanctification" or the "ongoing process of justification" – recognizing birth and the subsequent process of growth as stages in one and the same Life.

Regardless of the terminology, the Apostle Paul has some important things to tell us about this process. First and foremost we have to get it through our heads that the actions we perform (you can call them deeds or works and they can be anything from time spent in prayer, to sharing our goods with less fortunate brothers and sisters, to caring for the sick or dying) are never ours alone – they are *primarily* the actions of Christ Jesus Himself. As Paul tells us in *Philippians*, "work out your own salvation with fear and trembling; for God is at work in you, both to *will* and to *work* for his good pleasure," or as the New American Bible translates it, "who begets in you *any measure of desire* or *achievement*" (2:12-23).

Jesus acting in us and through us is what we call the life of Grace.[73] All of His actions during His time on earth were expressions of Love for His Father, and as such they were performed in the Holy Spirit. When He acts in us the same is true; He is Loving the Father, in the Holy Spirit, *through us* (Galatians 2:20-21). We have already talked about how Jesus deepens our participation in His Life through the Sacraments of Confirmation and Eucharist. Talk about the greatest honor in the universe, we have been inserted into the Life of the God Who is Love!

In Jesus, by His Grace, we live in a way that pleases our Father.[74] And the Father, looking at us with eyes full of mercy and Love, regards these

---

[73] For direction to several verses in the next two footnotes I owe thanks to Robert Sungenis's *How Can I Get to Heaven? The Bible's Teaching on Salvation Made Easy to Understand*, (Santa Barbara, California: Queenship Publishing Company, 1998).

Philippians 4:13, "I can do all things in him who *strengthens* me"
2 Peter 1:3-4, "His divine *power* has granted to us all things that pertain to life and godliness …he has granted to us his precious and very great promises, that through these you may escape from the corruption that is in the world because of passion, and *become partakers of the divine nature*.
1 Corinthians 15:10, "But by the grace of God I am what I am, and his grace toward me was not in vain. On the contrary, *I worked harder than any of them*, though it was not I, but *the grace of God* which is with me."
Romans 12:6, "Having gifts that differ according to the grace given to us, let us use them."
Ephesians 4:7, "But grace was given to each one of us according to the measure of Christ's gift."
See *Ephesians 1:11-12* in next footnote as well.

[74] *Hebrews 13:20-21*, "Now may the God of peace…equip you with everything good that you may do his will, working in you that which is pleasing in his sight, through Jesus Christ, to whom be glory for ever and ever."
Ephesians 1:11-12, "In [Jesus], according to the purpose of him who accomplishes all things according to the counsel of his will, we who first hoped in Christ have been destined and appointed to live for the praise of his glory."
Philippians 1:9-11, "And it is my prayer that your love may abound more and more, with knowledge and all discernment, so that you may approve what is excellent, and

actions (or works, or deeds) as truly *ours*. But how can an action be simultaneously Jesus' and ours? Let me offer an analogy.

Suppose you and your sister were standing at the top of a flight of steps when she lost her balance and began to fall. You reached out and grabbed her, pulling her back upright. In her gratefulness she planted a big kiss on your hand, saying, "I love this hand. Thanks for grabbing me." Now that good deed took place because of the instrumentality of your hand; it extended toward her and grabbed onto her. The only way it could do that good deed though, was because it participated in your life and was under your direction. That action belonged totally to you – and totally to your hand, simultaneously.

And what I remind you of is that, as members of Jesus' Body, we are His hands…and feet, mouth, etc., etc. The action *originates* in Jesus but is *actualized* in us, "For we are [God's] workmanship, created in Christ Jesus for good works, which God prepared beforehand, that we should walk in them" (Ephesians 2:10). The idea to perform the work is Jesus', the Love and Power to carry it out is the Holy Spirit pouring through us, but the action doesn't take place without our "yes," our cooperation. And God the Father is pleased by that cooperation – like any father looking at the work his child "helped" him accomplish (even though it required the father to exert more energy than had he just done it himself).

---

may be pure and blameless for the day of Christ, filled with the fruits of righteousness which come through Jesus Christ to the glory and praise of God"

2 Corinthians 5:9-10, "So whether we are at home [in the body] or away, we make it our aim to please him. For we must all appear before the judgment seat of Christ, so that each one may receive good or evil, according to what he has done in the body."

Romans 12:1, "…present your bodies as a living sacrifice, holy and acceptable to God, which is your spiritual worship."

Philippians 4:18, "I have received…the gifts you sent, a fragrant offering, a sacrifice acceptable and pleasing to God."

1 Timothy 2:1,3, "I urge that supplications, prayers, intercessions, and thanksgivings be made for all men…this is good and it is acceptable to God our Savior"

Colossians 3:20, "Children, obey your parents in everything, for this pleases the Lord."

1 John 3:21-22, "Beloved, if our hearts do not condemn us, we have confidence before God; and we receive from him whatever we ask, because we keep his commandments and do what pleases him."

Not only does God the Father regard these works as ours and smile with pleasure, He goes even further and "rewards" us with progressively more of His Grace – until finally He places the crown of life on our heads.[75]

We "merit" this increase of Grace but not in the legal sense of God owing us a payment for our work. We merit in the same way a child who eats everything on his plate merits a second helping – the merit is founded on the Father's Love for His children.[76] Such a progression can be seen in St. Paul's journey. He could write to the Philippians, "Not that I have already obtained this or am already perfect; but I press on to make it my own, because Christ Jesus has made me his own. . .I press on toward the goal for the prize of the upward call of God in Christ Jesus" (Phil.3:12,14); and then years later write to Timothy, "I am already on the point of being sacrificed…I have fought the good fight, I have finished the race, I have kept the faith. Henceforth there is laid up for me the crown of righteousness, which the Lord, the righteous judge, will award me on that Day" (2 Tim. 4:6-8). Paul had fully entered into Jesus' offering to the Father. The refusal

---

[75] *2 Peter 1:3,5-8,10-11*, "His divine power has granted to us all things that pertain to life and godliness. . .make every effort to supplement your faith with virtue, and virtue with knowledge, and knowledge with self-control, and self-control with steadfastness, and steadfastness with godliness, and godliness with brotherly affection, and brotherly affection with love. For if *these things* are yours *and abound*, they keep you from being ineffective or unfruitful in the knowledge of our Lord Jesus Christ…Therefore, my brethren, be the more zealous to *confirm your call and election*, for *if you do this, you will never fall*, so there will be richly provided for you *an entrance into the eternal kingdom* of our Lord and Savior Jesus Christ."

We see the Mystery of our cooperation with God's Grace in Jesus' "parable of the talents"also: A man went on a journey and entrusted differing sums of money to three of his servants. The first servant, receiving five talents (about five thousand dollars), invests them and makes five more. The second servant did likewise with the two talents he was given. The third servant, however, buried the one talent he had been entrusted with for fear of losing it. When the man returned to settle accounts he was enraged with servant #3,

"You wicked and slothful servant!. . .You ought to have invested my money with the bankers, and at my coming I should have received what was my own with interest. [I'll take the talent from you] and give it to him who has the ten talents. For to every one who has will more be given; but from him who has not, even what he has will be taken away" (Matthew 25:26-29).

[76] Hahn, Scott, *Hail Holy Queen: The Mother of God in the Word of God* (San Francisco: Doubleday, 2001), pp.133-134.

of our first parents to enter into the flow of Life going on within the Trinity, and the effects of that sin, are being undone even as you read this. It happened for Paul and it can for us too. If we enter fully into Jesus' offering to the Father by both our obedience to God's will and our perseverance through suffering, then we will also share in His resurrection (Philippians 2:8-9; 3:10).

We are meant to be branches living by the life of the Vine, parts of the Body of which Jesus is the Head. If our lives are not showing forth His Life, and progressively more so over the years, then there is a problem. "As the branch cannot bear fruit by itself, unless it abides in the vine, neither can you, unless you abide in me. . .I am the true vine, and my Father is the vinedresser. Every branch of mine that bears no fruit, he takes away" (John 15:4,1-2).

This is what the *Epistle of James* means when it says, "You see that a man is justified by *works* and *not by faith alone*...For as the body apart from the spirit is dead, so faith apart from works is dead" (James 2:24,26). James was not teaching that we can earn *initial* justification (the gifts of faith and baptism); no, we have been made God's children purely by His favor. What I am convinced he *was* teaching, and the Catholic Church continues to bear witness to, is the reality that justification is not only our unmerited incorporation into Jesus' Sonship; justification *is also* the process of His lifestyle becoming ours. It is a process that has to be continued. Jesus didn't pour Himself out to the Father just interiorly, or spiritually, one time at the beginning of His Life. He gave Himself in His flesh and blood, His words, thoughts and actions continually; and as parts of His Body, motivated and empowered by His Grace, we are called to do the same![77]

Recognizing ourselves as members of Christ's Body guards us from another danger as well – focusing on salvation as if it happens to souls in isolation. The truth is just the opposite: in being fused to Jesus we are simultaneously fused to one another. We even become channels of Grace to

---

[77] *Galatians 5:4-6* "You are severed from Christ, you who would be justified by the law [of Moses]; you have fallen away from grace. For through the Spirit, by faith, we wait for the *hope* of *righteousness*. For in Christ Jesus neither circumcision nor uncircumcision is of any avail, but *faith working through love*."

one another.[78] We have already seen how Jesus acts through His Church's celebration of the sacraments: Confirmation allows us to access the gifts He Himself operated in, and Eucharist is meant to be our constant nourishment. "He who eats my flesh and drinks my blood abides in me, and I in him...and I will raise him up at the last day" (John 6:56,54).[79]

Speaking of the last day, the Lord was very specific about the criteria we will be judged on. Jesus will welcome the just with a word of thanks for their untold kindnesses to Him - kindnesses He received in lieu of His connection to all of humanity. He went on to describe how He will tell the wicked, those condemned to "the eternal fire prepared for the devil and his angels" to leave His sight - they had neglected and rejected Him (Matt.25:41). They in turn will ask, "Lord, when did we see thee hungry or thirsty or a stranger or naked or sick or in prison and did not minister to thee?"(Matt.25:44). Jesus will answer, "As you did it not to one of the least of these, you did it not to me" (Matthew 25:45). Jesus did not even mention our mental or verbal confessions of faith; by themselves they are inadequate. He wants our confession made in our flesh and bone, living as He lived; to do otherwise is to reject the Life He died to give us.

A passage from the *Epistle to the Hebrews* seems to explain the process of salvation rather succinctly:

---

[78] *Ephesians 4:11-16* "It was [Jesus] who gave some to be apostles, some to be prophets, some to be evangelists, and some to be pastors and teachers, to *prepare* God's people for *works of service*, so that the body of Christ may be *built up* until we all reach unity in the faith and in the knowledge of the Son of God and *become mature, attaining to the whole measure of the fullness of Christ.* Then we will no longer be infants, tossed back and forth by the waves, and blown here and there by every wind of teaching. . .Instead, speaking the truth in love, we will in all things *grow up into him who is the Head*, that is, Christ. From him the whole body, joined and held together *by every supporting ligament*, grows and builds itself up in love, *as each part does its work.*

[79] The centrality and power of the Eucharist in the Christian life will be explored more in depth in Chapter 14.

The New Covenant Process of Salvation	Hebrews 10:19-25
Jesus' Life *Given* to the Father in the Holy Spirit	Therefore, brethren, since we have confidence to enter the sanctuary by the **blood of Jesus**, by the new and living way which he opened for us through the curtain, that is through his flesh
We *enter* by **Faith** and **Baptism**	and since we have a great high priest over the house of God, let us **draw near** with a true heart **in full assurance**, with our **hearts sprinkled clean** from an evil conscience and **our bodies washed with pure water**. Let us **hold fast to the confession of our hope without wavering**, for he who promised is faithful;
We *continue* and *grow* in Him by our **Grace-Filled Works, Membership in Jesus Body** and Participation in her **Prayer /Eucharist**	and let us consider how to stir up one another to **love** and **good works**, **not neglecting to meet together**, as is the habit of some, but **encouraging one another**, and
And, in the end, *inherit* Final Salvation	all the more as you see **the Day drawing near.**

Christians have an even briefer way to proclaim the New Covenant – by making the Sign of the Cross.[80]

Touch your:	Signifying that through the Cross of Jesus we enter into the inner Life of the:	And we have been empowered to do so with:
Forehead	Father	all our mind
Heart	Son	all our heart
and Both Shoulders	and Holy Spirit	and all our strength

Our Need for (the Sacrament of) Reconciliation

When we become Christians we retain our free will. It gives us the ability to cooperate with the grace of salvation or deny it – at any point. We can choose, through our actions, to separate ourselves from the God of Love.

I realize that this possibility seems like heresy to some brothers and sisters. Some passages of Scripture, upon first glance, appear to say that a Christian cannot commit an action so grave as to divorce them from the life of grace, forfeiting their salvation. The more I studied Scripture, however, such a position became untenable for me. We have seen how God comes to us sinners and offers us His Life freely – that action on God's part is *not* something we can *earn*.[81] If we depart this world with that Life within us then we rejoice in God forever. If we force that Life from our souls though, through deadly sin and refuse to repent, then when our body

---

[80] The insight for column two belongs to Scott Hahn and that for column three to youth minister Paul Masek.

[81] As we progress through our lives, however, we can open our lives to a greater in-flux of God's grace by responding to the desires He sows in our minds and hearts: reading His Word, praying, allowing the Lord to serve His People through us, etc. These things can be said to "merit" an increase in grace – *but it has to be understood properly*. It's not like any of our actions can ever demand some one-to-one payment from God. Instead, God, by His Own choice and in His Own great mercy, has established channels of grace and promised us further growth in the image of Christ when we persevere in using them.

stops functioning, our soul will experience the absence of God for eternity (hell).[82]

---

[82] Scripture illustrates the belief I'm sharing. One verse people appeal to justify the belief that we cannot forfeit salvation is *1 John 5:13*, "I write this to you who believe in the name of the Son of God, that you may know that you have eternal life." I agree wholeheartedly; anyone in relationship with the Lord Jesus possesses Life Himself. But notice, John didn't say rejecting the Lord was impossible. In fact, I note a number of places where he clearly states that our relationship to the Father is conditional upon our maintaining a lifestyle consistent with the Gospel:

> ..but *if* we *walk* in the light, as he is in the light, we have fellowship with one another, and the blood of Jesus his Son cleanses us from all sin. (1 John 1:7)
> *If* what you heard from the beginning *abides* in you, *then* you will abide in the Son and in the Father (1 John 2:24).
> By this we may *be sure* we are in him; he who says he abides in [Jesus] ought to *walk* in the same way in which he walked (1 John 2:5-6).

Consider the warnings the Lord Jesus gave in the gospels:

> Because wickedness is multiplied, most men's love will grow cold. But he who *endures to the end* will be *saved* (Matthew 24:12-13).
> That day [of judgement] will come upon you suddenly like a snare...watch at all times, praying that you may have the strength to escape all these things that will take place, and stand before the Son of man (Luke 21:34, 36).

The earliest leaders of the Church must have understood Jesus in this way because the same idea is conveyed in their writings. St. James, our Lord's cousin, wrote:

> Blessed is the man who endures trial, for when he has stood the test he will receive the crown of life which God has promised to those who love him...each person is tempted when he is lured and enticed by his own desire. Then desire when it is conceived gives birth to sin, and sin when it is full-grown brings forth death (James 1:12-15).

Paul seems very blunt to me. He wrote, "I do not run aimlessly, I do not box as one beating the air; but I pommel my body and subdue it, *lest after preaching to others I myself should be disqualified*" (1 Corinthians 9: 26-27). If Paul thought that he could still blow it, then I don't see any reason to consider myself a shoe-in; I just keep on asking the Lord for the strength to be found standing in His grace when my judgment comes. I consider the *Epistle to the Hebrews* frequently, probably written by Paul through a secretary. In it we are cautioned:

> Take care, my brothers, lest there be in any of you an evil, unbelieving heart, leading you to *fall away from the living God*. But exhort one another every day, as long as it is called "today," that none of you may be hardened by the deceitfulness of sin. For we share in Christ, *if only we hold our first confidence firm to the end* (Hebrews 3:12-14).

Or look at what Paul wrote to the Corinthians:

> I want you to know, brethren, that our fathers were all under the cloud, and all passed through the sea, and all were baptized into Moses in the cloud and in the sea, and all ate the same supernatural food...Nevertheless with most of them

Distinctions in the Gravity of Sin

Do I bring every sin I commit to the confessional? No, if I did that I do not know if I would ever make it out of church. Strictly speaking, a Christian is only bound to bring sins which are mortal, or deadly, to the confessional (even though the Church encourages us to bring any matter we need Christ's intensive touch to overcome). I realize that a distinction in the seriousness of sins will seem strange to non-Catholics, so I will try my best to clarify the matter. I will start with Scripture:

> But who can discern his errors?
> Clear thou me from hidden faults.
> Keep back thy servant also from *presumptuous sins*;

> God was not pleased; for 'they were overthrown in the wilderness.' Now these things are a warning *for us*...they were written down for our instruction, upon whom the end of the ages has come. Therefore, *let any one who thinks that he stands take heed lest he fall* (1 Corinthians 10: 1-3, 5-6, 11-12).

The Apostle Peter was just as plain:

> For if, after they have escaped the defilements of the world through the knowledge of our Lord and Savior Jesus Christ, they are *again entangled* in them and overpowered, the last state has become worse for them than the first. For it would have been better for them never to have known *the way of righteousness* than after knowing *it to turn back form the holy commandment delivered to them* (2 Peter 2:20-22).

> Beware lest you be carried away with the error of lawless men and *lose your own stability*. But grow in the grace and knowledge of our Lord and Savior Jesus Christ (2 Peter 3:17-18).

Some believers have tried explaining to me that someone who falls away from Christ must have never really belonged to Him - never made a valid commitment to begin with. That's not what these verses have been saying, though. The Lord Jesus addressed His words to His disciples, and the apostles were writing their epistles to committed members of the Christian community. When I became a Christian I retained my free will; all of us did. And *because we have a free will* we continue to have the ability to forfeit Heaven. The final biblical support I can offer comes from the creation story. Consider our first parents – molded and fashioned by God, filled with sanctifying grace (the grace to which Christ returned us). They were in *intimate union* with God and one another. And yet, they yielded to temptation – cut themselves off from the Life of God and brought spiritual death to our race. If they could be in the state of sanctifying grace – and fall from it – then I have to believe we could do the same.

> let them not have dominion over
> me!
> Then I shall be blameless,
> and innocent of *great transgression*
> (Psalm 19:12-13).[83]

> If anyone sees his brother committing what is not a mortal [deadly] sin, he will ask, and God will give him life for those whose sin is not mortal. There is a sin which is mortal; I do not say that one is to pray for that. All wrongdoing is sin, but there is sin which is not mortal (1 John 5:16-17).

St. Paul gave us examples of serious, or mortal, sins:

> Do not be deceived; neither the immoral, nor idolaters, nor adulterers, nor [practicing] homosexuals, nor thieves, nor the greedy, nor drunkards, nor revilers, nor robbers will inherit the kingdom of God. (1 Corinthians 6:9-10).

For a sin to be truly deadly it must: 1) be a serious matter [such as those listed above]; 2) the person must realize the gravity of the sin; and 3) freely choose to sin nonetheless.

Such an act strangles the supernatural life within us, separating us from God. It is not that God has disowned us; we in effect have disowned Him. To reestablish our union with Him we require the apostolic ministry of "loosing" us from our sins (John 20:23). Again, not all sins are deadly (consult 1 John 5:16-17 above). For example, do you feel completely estranged from God when you make up an excuse not to go out? You have sinned, but you have not done something so grave that you feel completely cut off from God, devoid of life. We should definitely confess such things when we examine our consciences each night, but if we have committed adultery or slander we should be overwhelmed by guilt. We can not just "dust ourselves off" from one of those; spiritually we are dead. We need resurrec-

---

[83] The psalmist is praying first to be cleansed of any failings or faults that he may be unaware of; all of us should be able to identify with his predicament. But note that he then offers a second petition to be free of *presumptuous* sin, which unlike his faults and failings, would be serious transgressions of God's Law.

tion. We need the sacrament - the special touch of Jesus established to revive and heal us in those moments.

Reconciliation in Scripture

I have already discussed *John 20:23* where Jesus told His Apostles, "If you forgive the sins of any, they are forgiven; if you retain the sins of any, they are retained." But what are we to make of scriptures such as, "If we confess our sins, he is faithful and just, and will forgive us from all unrighteousness"(1 John 1:9)? Friends and authors of other denominations have shown me passages to this effect, which did not specifically mention a minister being involved in confession. To come at the matter from another angle though, there is no verse of Scripture that *prohibits* a minister from being involved in confession; silence is a far cry from a denial. It could be just as possible that the Christians to whom John and the other Apostles wrote understood confession to naturally involve a minister - in that case there would have been no need for the Apostles to spell it out. Verses such as *1 John 1:19* (If we confess...) just do not tell us one way or the other. We need to cross-reference them with *John 20:23* (If you forgive...) and others involving the Apostles' ministry.

Take *Matthew 18:15-18* for example. Jesus spoke of the role His Church and its Apostles were to play in correcting erring members:

> If your brother sins against you, go and tell him his fault, between you and him alone. If he listens to you, you have gained your brother. But if he does not listen, take one or two others along with you, that every word may be confirmed by the evidence of two or three witnesses. If he refuses to listen to them, tell it to the church; and if he refuses to listen even to the church, let him be to you as a Gentile and a tax collector [an outsider]. *Truly, I say to you, whatever you bind on earth, shall be bound in heaven, and whatever you loose on earth shall be loosed in heaven.*

Again, Jesus' Apostles are given the ministry of binding and loosing - an ability such that they could exclude people from the Church if they did not live lives consistent with the Gospel, but only after several unheeded calls to repentance. Throughout the whole passage Jesus spoke of using members of His People, His Church, to bring healing to the sinner. Earlier in

The *Gospel of Matthew* Peter had been granted the ministry of binding and loosing in a preeminent way (Matthew 16:18-19).

It seems that this ministry was not only exercised by the Apostles, but also by the ministers they in turn ordained, the presbyters. James instructed the readers of his epistle:

> Is any among you sick? Let him call for the *elders* [presbyter in Greek] of the church, and let them pray over him, anointing him with oil in the name of the Lord; and the prayer of faith will save the sick man, and the Lord will raise him up; and *if he has committed sins, he will be forgiven*. Therefore, *confess your sins to one another*, and pray for one another, that you may be healed (James 5:14-16).

This passage gives us the image of God reconciling sinners to Himself in the midst of, and through, the community of faith. I do not believe this interpretation novel or innovative in any sense, quite the contrary. It was, in fact, the belief of the early Church. Let me justify that statement.

The Sacrament of Reconciliation in History

In recent years I have begun reading the writings of the early Christian Church, the writings of Christians contemporary with and immediately following upon the Apostles. When I was in high school I was ignorant of these great leaders, as are so many Christians today. I think it makes a great deal of sense though to ask ourselves how the first readers of the New Testament would have understood these passages we have been looking at.

The first source I want to look at is the *Didache*, or *Teaching of the Twelve Apostles*. It was composed sometime between 70 and 120 A.D., and appears to be the first written instruction, or catechism, for new converts. It was held in high esteem by the primitive Church, as we can see from its translation into six languages (Greek, Latin, Coptic, Ethiopic, Syriac and Georgian) and its citation in several other works. In the *Didache* new converts were instructed to:

> Confess your sins *in church*, and do not go up to your prayers with an evil conscience. This is the way of life (4:14).[84]

---

[84] Jurgens, William A., *The Faith of the Early Fathers*, Volumes 1 (Collegeville, Minnesota: The Liturgical Press, 1970), p.2.

> On the Lord's Day. . .gather together, break bread and give thanks, after confessing your transgressions so that you sacrifice may be pure. Let no one who has a quarrel with his neighbor join you until he is reconciled, lest your sacrifice be defiled (14:1-2).[85]

Tertullian, a Roman lawyer prior to his conversion, wrote a treatise on repentance between 203 and 204 A.D. As in the *Didache*, he spoke of confession as something done publicly:

> It is not conducted before the conscience alone, but is carried out by some external act...we confess our sin to the Lord, not indeed as if He did not know it, but because satisfaction is arranged by confession, of confession is repentance born, and by repentance is God pleased.

> It commands one. . .to bow before the presbyters, to kneel before God's refuge places, and to beseech all the brethren of the embassy of their own supplication. Confession is all of this, so that it may excite repentance (*Repentance 9:1-5*; compare this passage with James 5:14-16 already cited).

> Most men, however, either flee from this work, as being an exposure of themselves, or they put it off from day to day. I presume they are more mindful of modesty than of salvation. . .The Body [of Christ] is not able to take pleasure in the trouble of one of its members. It must grieve as a whole and join in laboring for a remedy (*Repentance 10:1,5*; compare with 1 Corinthians 12: 25-26).[86]

I find it hard to just speak to a priest about my sins, but what if I had to speak to him in front of the whole Church? Yet, that was how the vast majority of Christians practiced reconciliation for more than three hundred years (Irish monks popularized "private" confession in the fifth century).

Earlier, when quoting from the *Epistle of James*, I stated that the Apostles communicated the ministry of reconciliation to the ministers they ordained, the presbyters and bishops. Hippolytus of Rome recorded the prayer used to consecrate bishops circa 215 A.D. :

---

[85] Ibid, p.4
[86] Ibid, p.130-131

Grant this to your servant, whom You have chosen for the episcopate, to...have the authority to forgive sins, in accord with Your command (*The Apostolic Tradition*).[87]

The final author I wish to make mention of is Origen, a priest as well as one of the greatest scholars of Christian antiquity. Origen taught the Christian faith in Egypt, Palestine, Rome, and Greece as well as found time to write prolifically. The different geographic locales in which he saw the Church function makes his testimony especially important because he is not telling us how an isolated group of Christians practiced reconciliation. He wrote that:

> If we will do this, and reveal our sins not only to God but also to those who are able to remedy our wounds and sins, then our sins will be blotted out by Him Who says, "Behold I have blotted out your iniquities like a cloud, and your sins as the mist" [Isaiah 44:22] (*Homilies on Luke* - Homily 17; 233 A.D.).[88]

In all of Origen's travels he must have come across some bishops or presbyters who had begun administering the sacrament of reconciliation privately, instead of within the church assembly. He counseled his readers to:

> Be careful and circumspect in regard to whom you would confess your sins. Test first the physician to whom you would expose the cause of your illness. Finally, when he has shown himself to be a physician both learned and merciful, do whatever he might tell you...If after much deliberation he has understood the nature of your illness and judges that to be cured, it must be exposed in the assembly of the whole church, follow the advice of that expert physician, and thereby others may perhaps be able to be edified, while you yourself are the more easily healed (*Homilies on the Psalms* -Psalm 37, Hom.2).[89]

Besides coming to see reconciliation, or Confession, as biblical and historical, I also came to see strong benefits to the practice. First, it reminded me that only a small number of sins involved only myself and God; the majority were wrongs committed against brothers and sisters. I think that it is a

---

[87] Ibid, p.167
[88] Ibid, p.201
[89] Ibid, p.204

beautiful gesture, as well as a proper one, for a member of the human race to hear my confession to the Lord, and then for that same person to speak Jesus' words of absolution to me.

Another benefit I see is one being realized by Christians in other denominations as well. Friends of mine have been joining "accountability groups" through their churches. It is an all-male or all-female small group where the members confide their faults, or outright sins, to the other members. The groups meet once a week for members to share their successes as well as failures and to pray for and encourage one another. Anything said in the group remains confidential. One friend described to me how "coming clean" before other people really brought home to him how ugly his sins were, how hurtful they must be to God. He was very candid about how confessing to God during private prayer was a much less humbling experience, and that attending the accountability group had actually been a deterrent when he found himself tempted - he did not want to relive that humbling experience of confession. I smiled, assuring him that I understood everything he was relating. For Catholics the Sacrament of Reconciliation has preserved that sense of accountability for centuries.

I think I need to flesh out the Sacrament of Reconciliation in a bit more detail for you. The most important thing I can say is that, in the final analysis, it is Jesus to Whom we make confession. The priest is Jesus' minister, a man called by the Lord and sent into the world to convey His presence. As St. Paul wrote:

> All this is from God, who through Christ reconciled us to himself and gave us the ministry of reconciliation; that is, God was in Christ reconciling the world to himself, not counting their trespasses against them, and entrusting to us the message of reconciliation. So we are ambassadors for Christ, God making his appeal through us. We beseech you on behalf of Christ, be reconciled to God (2 Corinthians 5:18-20).

You see, each time confession is made, it is the Sacrifice of Christ on Calvary that our sins encounter. That one sacrifice obliterates them!

Well, if this is the case then what is a "penance"? If it is Jesus' atoning sacrifice that our sins come into contact with then why, how, could we do anything else to further atone for them? Isn't His sacrifice sufficient? Yes, it is; we need to come at penance from a different direction.

When people are baptized they are supernaturally born. Anything they did before that time is dealt with as the Holy Spirit recreates them. They are called to repentance and the living of Christ's Life. They are not asked to make a confession of sin to a priest nor is a penance required of them. The Sacrament of Reconciliation is meant to deal with those sins committed *after* baptism, committed by those who are God's sons and daughters. My mind is called to the words of *Hebrews*:

> . . .have you forgotten the exhortation which addresses you as sons? —
> "My sons, do not regard lightly the discipline of the Lord,
> nor lose courage when you are punished by him.
> for the Lord disciplines him whom he loves,
> and chastises every son whom he receives."
> It is for discipline that you have to endure. God is treating you as sons; for what son is there to whom his father does not discipline? If you are left without discipline, in which all have participated, then you are illegitimate children and not sons (12:5-8).

I think of it like this: when we sin we have engaged in a behavior opposed to our Heavenly Father's will. A "penance" is a positive behavior that we perform to correct, or to replace the negative - taking a step in the right direction. I consider Jesus' words:

> When the unclean spirit has gone out of a man, he passes through waterless places seeking rest, but he finds none. Then he says, "I will return to my house from which I came." And when he comes he finds it empty, swept and put in order. Then he goes and brings with him seven other spirits more evil than himself, and they enter and dwell there; and the last state of that man becomes worse than the first… (Matthew 12:43-45).[90]

Without that concrete step of penance being taken, it is easy to fall into the sin again. Look at the way Jesus set Peter back on the road of discipleship after Peter had denied Him three times:

---

[90] I do not mean to equate all sin with demonic infestation or possession. I use the quotation only to illustrate that holiness is not about emptiness, rejecting what is bad. No, holiness is about being *filled*, filled with God's Life and the corresponding behavior.

> When they had finished breakfast, Jesus said to Simon Peter, "Simon, son of John, do you love me more than these?" He said to him, "Yes, Lord; you know that I love you." He said to him, "Feed my lambs." A second time he said to him, "Simon, son of John, do you love me?" He said to him, "Yes, Lord; you know that I love you." He said to him, "Tend my sheep." He said to him the third time, "Simon, son of John, do you love me?" Peter was grieved because he said to him the third time, "Do you love me?" And he said to him, "Lord, you know everything; you know that I love you." Jesus said to him, "Feed my sheep. Truly, truly, I say to you, when you were young, you girded yourself and walked where you would; but when you are old, you will stretch out your hands, and another will gird you and carry you where you do not wish to go." (This he said to show by what death he was to glorify God.) And after this he said to him, "Follow me" (John 21:15-19).

Penances are meant to benefit not just ourselves, but Jesus' Body. With His grace moving us, we seek to repair whatever harm we have done to another. Reconciliation is not a "get out of jail free card." It recognizes that sin is destructive and it enmeshes us in Jesus' work of undoing evil.

Priests have a great responsibility to listen to the Holy Spirit in dispensing penances, to impart practices that will truly help people grow in their love and service of Christ. I will share a particularly good penance I received. I once confessed that I was holding on to anger at a family friend who had spoken badly of my mother. As a penance I was asked to take five minutes in prayer to concentrate on good, fun moments that had been shared with this friend. As I did, the Holy Spirit began to release some of that anger I had been holding inside for close to two years; six months later I felt free of it.

On television priests are always represented as giving so many "Hail Marys" or "Our Fathers" as a penance. Most people probably wonder what the value of that could be. Occasionally I have received a penance like this, and as I meditated on the value, came to see that it was inestimable. If a penance is a virtuous behavior to replace the sinful with, then what could be more effective than praying with the Mother of Jesus for the Spirit to give me more strength, or to petition God the Father in the words Jesus gave us? Penance, at least for me, has become another one of those benefits flowing from confession.

Reaching Full Maturity in Christ

With all this talk about salvation, purity and healing, we need to hear a very important statement from Jesus, "from within, out of the heart of man, come evil thoughts, fornication, theft, murder, adultery, coveting, wickedness, deceit, licentiousness, envy, slander, pride, foolishness. All these evil things come from *within*, and they *defile* a man" (Mark 7:21-23). What we have not considered yet, is what happens when a Christian reaches the moment of death but not totally free of the self-centeredness that characterizes much of our sojourn on earth, and keep us from being the disciples we want to be? What if the damage of sin has not been completely undone?

Even though we are in Christ, there are still impurities within us; we may not commit murder but the unkind thoughts or harsh judgments we harbor toward others (the roots of murder) may still be very much with us. These are not acts so great as to completely severe our union with the Lord, but they do inhibit the flow of His grace, His life within us. When we shed our bodies at death do the impurities, the imperfections in our capacity to love, just disappear? If they are in the heart, and *we take that with us*, then I don't think so. It gets interesting when we recall that "nothing unclean shall enter" the Heavenly Jerusalem (Revelation 21:27). God loves us just as we are, but He loves us too much to let us stay as we are. So how does an impure, yet "born again," soul enter? Through a purification, or *purgatory:*

> Our souls demand Purgatory, don't they? Would it not break [our] heart if God said to us, "It is true, my son, that your breath smells and your rags drip with mud and slime, but we are charitable here and no on will upbraid you with these things, nor draw away from you. Enter into the joy"? Should we not reply, "With submission, sir, and if there is no objection, I'd rather be cleaned first." "It may hurt, you know" - "Even so, sir."[91]

---

[91] Lewis, C.S. *The Joyful Christian* (New York: McMillan Publishing Company, 1984), p.222.

When I looked into purgatory a little further I found that the Catholic Church really had very little to say on the matter officially. When it was all said and done only two doctrinal points emerged, at least that I could see. First, "All who die in God's grace and friendship, but still imperfectly purified, are indeed assured of their eternal salvation; but after death they undergo purification, so as to achieve the holiness necessary to enter the joy of heaven" (CCC 1030).[92] So God loves us right now, unconditionally; but He loves us just too much to let us to remain the way we are. Second, that those passing through this process of purification somehow benefit from our prayers.

The belief has its *roots* not in Christianity but in its predecessor, Judaism. The first written mention that I am aware of is from the *Second Book of Maccabees*. The work as a whole chronicles the Jewish revolt against occupation and persecution under the Seleucid kings. The Jewish reclamation and cleansing of the Temple is still celebrated today in the feast of Hannukah. The hero from whom the book takes its name was Judas Maccabeus; let us examine an event which took place in approximately 163 B.C.:

> Judas and his men went to take up the bodies of the fallen and to bring them back to lie with their kinsmen in the sepulchers of their fathers. Then under the tunic of every one of the dead they found sacred tokens of the idols of Jamnia, which the law forbids the Jews to wear. And it became clear to all that this was why these men had fallen...*they turned to prayer beseeching that the sin which had been committed might be wholly blotted out* ...[Judas] also took up a collection, man by man, to the amount of two thousand drachmas of silver, and sent it to Jerusalem to provide for a sin offering. In doing this he acted very well and honorably, *taking account of the resurrection*...Therefore he *made atonement for the dead, that they might be delivered from their sin* (2 Maccabees 12: 39-40, 42-43, 46).

---

[92] Purgatory isn't a third option for the afterlife. I remember a grade school teacher saying that purgatory was for those "not quite good enough for heaven, but not bad enough for hell." That's not the teaching of Catholicism. If you don't have the grace of Christ adhering in your soul at the moment of death then you experience the consequences; purgatory is not a "second chance." I think the best image for it is the "front porch of Heaven." You're welcome on the property but you need to take off the muddy shoes before you step through the front door.

ONGOING NATURE OF SALVATION   113

At the time of Judas the belief in afterlife among the Jews was still incomplete, awaiting the fuller revelation that was to come in Christ. There was a notion of Sheol, an underworld, mentioned in the Old Testament. What was coming to take hold among the people, due to the revelation given through the prophets, was the belief in the resurrection of the dead. To take part in it one apparently needed to be cleansed of the guilt of their sins. If not cleansed at the time of death then it was considered an act of charity to have sacrifice made on their behalf.

The Jewish belief has continued to develop over time, some branches of Judaism mirroring Christianity in its belief that the "soul" of the departed can draw near to God. When a parent dies it is customary for a son to pray the "mourner's Kaddish" daily for eleven months;

> According to Jewish tradition, the soul must spend some time purifying itself before it can enter heaven…[To pray the Kaddish] insures to the merit of the deceased in the eyes of G-d, because the deceased must have been a very good parent to raise a child who could express such faith in the face of personal loss.[93]

As I investigated the belief in purgatory further I found that though it was not spelled out clearly in the New Testament, it did seem to resonate with some passages. For example, St. Paul told the Corinthians that he had founded their community on Christ and that:

> if any one builds on the foundation with gold, silver, precious stones, wood, hay, stubble – each man's work will become manifest; for the Day [of Judgment] will disclose it, because it will be revealed with fire, and the fire will test what sort of work each one has done. If the work which any man has built on the foundation survives, he will receive a reward. If any man's work is burned up, he will suffer loss, though he *himself will be saved*, but only as *through fire* (1 Corinthians 3:12-15).

Paul spoke on a large scale, talking about the follow-up work of other ministers among the Corinthians and the purification that would sweep through the Church on the great Day of Judgment. The doctrine of purgatory is this same process but scaled down to the individual soul - how it yields to and

---

[93] Accessed at http://www.jewishvirtuallibrary.org/jsource/Judaism/death.html#Kaddish

cooperates with Christ in growing to spiritual maturity. At the moment of death the grace-filled soul experiences the "Particular Judgment," the fire of God's love burning away all that is not of Him. As the impurities within our souls are burned away we will likely experience discomfort - seeing ourselves as we truly are before God's righteous eyes always entails discomfort. What remains after the purification is a heart finally ready to give itself to the Lord *completely*; it is then that we can truly *enjoy Heaven*.

Sometimes I hear people talking about purgatory as a process of "making satisfaction for our sins." Taken one way that statement can be very confusing – as if God were looking to take it out of our hides. I offer this: Every action we perform, good or bad, either conforms us more closely to the image of Christ Jesus or disfigures that image in our souls. When we confess sins God truly forgive us; and yet we still have to undergo a process, prompted and lead by God's grace, of correcting the damage these acts have done in our own souls and psyches *as well as in the world around us*. We try to make "satisfaction;" we cooperate with God's grace to undo the damage of sin. Many times this is a difficult process, rather humbling – again, a true purgation. If the damage caused by sin is not fully repaired, if we have not fully cooperated with God's redeeming grace to this end prior to death, then we encounter His purifying love after. We can not possibly open our sin-weakened "arms" wide enough to embrace the Trinity without this purification.

Looking at the above one can see how I have come to equate the fire of purgatory with God's love, God Himself (1 John 4:16). I feel justified in doing so because in Scripture, not only is the Day of Judgment a day of fire[94], but it is the Day of God's Visitation – God Himself coming to set all things right. In the Epistle to the Hebrews we find these two images fused, "*our God is a consuming fire*" (Hebrews 12:29). When we speak of the purifying fires of purgatory I think we remain on safe ground describing purgatory as that final purifying and healing *personal* encounter we will have with God before entering into the full Life and joy destined for us in the em-

---

[94] Besides the above quotation from 1 Corinthians we also have the Apostle Peter's words, "The day of the Lord will come like a thief, and on that day the heavens will vanish with a roar; the elements will be destroyed by fire, and the earth and all its deeds will be made manifest" (2 Peter 3:10; see verse 12 also).

brace of the Trinity. As we already know, sometimes God's healing touch, which gradually transforms us into the image of His Son, causes us momentary pain and suffering - but that is looking at it from the side of earth. When we look back at it from the side of Heaven we will recognize the pains as "joys" because of Who they brought us to. I believe that this type of thinking was what lead one of the saints to say that the pains of purgatory are better than any pleasure we could experience on earth.

In recent years I have been able to confirm that Christians in the early centuries believed in such a purification following death. The practice of making intercession for the departed by having the Eucharist celebrated seems an ingrained practice by the third century. In 211 A.D. Tertullian, already quoted from, wrote in his work *The Crown*, "We offer sacrifices for the dead on their birthday anniversaries."[95] Two years later in his work *Monogamy* he stated, "A woman, after the death of her husband. . .prays for his soul and asks that he may, while waiting, find rest; and that he may share in the first resurrection."[96] Cyril, the Bishop of Jerusalem, stated in his *Catechetical Discourses* delivered circa 350 A.D. that during the Eucharist, "we make mention. . .of all among us who have already fallen asleep; for we believe that it will be of very great benefit to the souls of those for whom the petition is carried up, while this holy and most solemn Sacrifice is laid out."[97] St. Augustine, writing in the year 421 A.D. said that:

> We read in the books of the Maccabees that sacrifice was offered for the dead. But even if it were found nowhere in the Old Testament writings, the authority of the universal Church which is clear on this point is of no small weight, where in the prayers of the priest poured forth to the Lord God at His altar the commendation of the dead has its place.[98]

---

[95] Jurgens, William A., *The Faith of the Early Fathers*, Volume 1(Collegeville, Minnesota: The Liturgical Press, 1970), p.151
[96] Ibid, p.158
[97] Ibid, p.363
[98] Jurgens, William A., *The Faith of the Early Fathers*, Volume 3(Collegeville, Minnesota: The Liturgical Press, 1970), p154

116 THE GOD WHO IS LOVE

The Lateran Museum in Rome houses two fragments of a burial monument belonging to Abercius, the Bishop of Hierapolis in Phrygia (West-Central Asia Minor), written 180-200 A.D., which reads:

> [I am] a disciple of the chaste shepherd who feeds his sheep on the mountains and in the fields, who has great eyes everywhere, who taught me the faithful writings of life...Standing by, I, Abercius, ordered this to be inscribed; truly, I was in my seventy-second year. May everyone who is in accord with this and who understands it *pray for Abercius*.[99]

Prayer has always been considered beneficial for souls going through this purification, from the beginnings of the belief among our Jewish brothers and sisters, through the early Church, and up to our day. How prayer eases the purification process I'm not sure; how our prayers can assist in bringing about conversion here on earth I'm not sure about either – but I believe they do. As Thomas Aquinas postulated in his *Summa Theologica*, perhaps it has always been in our Lord's plan that some graces are dispensed only through the intercession of Christ's Body.[100]

---

[99] Jurgens, William A., *The Faith of the Early Fathers*, Volume 1 (Collegeville, Minnesota: The Liturgical Press, 1970), p.78
[100] Kreeft, Peter, *Summa of the Summa*, (San Francisco: Ignatius Press, 1990) p.179.

Chapter 7 – Putting the Word in Context

Joseph Burns was my religion teacher during my freshman and sophomore years. For the majority of that time I was probably a thorn in his side. Mr. Burns styled himself a "contextualist," meaning that he read the Bible as a collection of documents which, even though they were inspired, needed to be read in their proper historical and cultural contexts. To be read correctly, one needed to ascertain what literary form the author of a particular book was making use of - history, poetry, parable, etc. I, on the other hand, was very much a fundamentalist: the biblical text meant exactly what it said on the surface, just as it was written, with no room for discussion.

At first I considered his outlook as a watering down of Scripture. The contextualist viewpoint seemed an attempt to make the face-value meaning of Scripture more palatable to modern believers who could not stomach talk about the creation of man, plagues of Egypt, or parting of the Red Sea. My concern was that it would reduce the experience of the Jewish people and early Christians to a purely human level, relegating salvation history to merely an inspiring fable.

I came to see, however, that Mr. Burns did not fall into the pitfalls I had feared. He very much believed that God was involved in the unfolding of human history. Viewing Scripture through a contextualist lens did not rob him of his faith. Quite the contrary, it produced insights I valued.

As a teacher in an archdiocesan high school, it should not come as a surprise that his outlook simply reflected that of the Catholic Church. The insights I came to value were arrived at through Catholic principles of interpretation. In passing them along to you I am going to eliminate the middle man and let you hear it straight from the horse's mouth. What I am about to share comes predominantly from Vatican Council II's 1963 *Dogmatic Constitution on Divine Revelation, Dei Verbum* in Latin.

Inspiration

In English the word inspiration is used to translate the Greek *theopneustos*, which literally means "God breathed."[101] Our minds probably go to the story of creation, when God breathed into the clay He had shaped, making it a living, an "in-spirited" being. Perhaps we recall the night of Jesus resurrection, when He breathed upon the Apostles and said, "Receive the Holy Spirit" (John 20:22). In *Dei Verbum* the Church explained inspiration in this way: "To compose the sacred books, God chose certain men who, all the while He employed them in this task, made full use of *their powers and faculties* so that though He acted in them and by them, it was as *true authors* that they consigned to writing whatever He wanted written, and no more."[102] You will undoubtedly notice the words I chose to emphasize, "true authors" …their powers and faculties."

Similar to our understanding of salvation, the action of composing Scripture was completely divine *and completely human*.[103] The free, authentically human task of composing and writing became God's instrument. The human author's "entire personality and experience, with his own peculiar gifts of mind and heart, is applied by God to express that which God wishes to say."[104] This is an action only imaginable of the God Who called the universe into being from nothing – not a mechanical dictation of words but

---

[101] Collins, Raymond F, "Inspiration," in *The New Jerome Biblical Commentary*, Ed. R.E. Brown, J.A. Fitzmeyer, and R. E. Murphy, p.1028 (Englewood Cliffs, NJ: Prentice Hall, 1990).

[102] Flannery, Austin, *Vatican Council II: The Conciliar and Post Conciliar Documents*, (Northport, New York: Costello Publishing Company, 1992), p 756-757. Italics added

[103] It appears that the Church is here drawing upon the thought of St. Thomas Aquinas in regards to efficient causality: "one may distinguish between a principal efficient cause (God or the Spirit) and an instrumental efficient cause (human author). In scriptural composition a distinct but conjoined role is attributable to God and to the human writers, just as in sawing lumber a distinct but conjoined role is assigned to the carpenter (principal efficient cause) and the saw (instrumental efficient cause)" Collins, Raymond F, "Inspiration," in *The New Jerome Biblical Commentary*, Ed. R.E. Brown, J.A. Fitzmeyer, and R. E. Murphy, p.1028 (Englewood Cliffs, NJ: Prentice Hall, 1990).

[104] McKenzie, John L. *The Two-Edged Sword: An Interpretation of the Old Testament* (Garden City, New York: Image Books, 1956), p.30.

but the seemingly paradoxical feat of employing the free actions of human authors to write "what He wanted written and no more" (*DV*, 11).[105]

In Their Entirety

This leads directly into the next point, that all of Scripture, and not just individual portions or ideas, is the product of God's inspiration. As *Dei Verbum* tells us:

> Holy Mother Church, relying on the belief of the Apostles (see John 20:31; 2 Tim.3:16; 2 Peter 1:19-20; 3:15-16), holds that the books of both the Old and New Testaments in their entirety, with all their parts, are sacred and canonical because, written under the inspiration of the Holy Spirit, they have God as their author and have been handed on as such to the Church herself (*DV*,11).[106]

This means that the books of Scripture, as we now have them, in their final form, are recognized by the Church as inspired. The *Gospel of John*, with its evidence of editorial activity; *Mark 16:9-20*, probably not originally part of the Gospel; the deuterocanonicals, etc., form part of the Church's inspired Scripture.[107]

Without Error

If not just human beings, but God Himself, is the author of Scripture, in its entirety, then how could it contain error? If God is truth, how could His written word be at odds with reality, deceive? In *Dei Verbum* the teaching Church reiterated its ancient conviction[108] that it cannot:

---

[105]Flannery, Austin, *Vatican Council II: The Conciliar and Post Conciliar Documents*, (Northport, New York: Costello Publishing Company, 1992), p.757.

[106] Ibid

[107] Montague, George T., *Understanding the Bible: A Basic Introduction to Biblical Interpretation* (New York: Paulist, 1997) p.194.

[108]The following quotations are taken from Jurgens, William A. *The Faith of the Early Fathers*, Volumes 1-3.(Collegeville, MN: Liturgical Press, 1970):

Clement of Rome, *Letter to the Corinthians* (c.80-101 A.D.), "You have studied the Holy Scriptures, which are true and are of the Holy Spirit. You well know that nothing unjust or fraudulent is written in them." Vol.1, p.11.

Justin the Martyr, *Dialogue with Trypho the Jew* (c.155 A.D.), "I am totally convinced that no Scripture is contradictory to another, I shall admit instead that I do not understand what is spoken of, and shall strive to persuade those who assume that the Scriptures are contradictory to be rather of the same opinion as myself." Vol.1, p.61.

Since, therefore, all that the inspired authors, or sacred writers, affirm should be affirmed by the Holy Spirit, we must acknowledge that the books of Sacred Scripture, firmly, faithfully and without error, teach that truth which God, for the sake of our salvation, wished to see confided to the sacred Scriptures. Thus, "all Scripture is inspired by God, and profitable for teaching, for reproof, for correction and for training

---

Irenaeus, *Against Heresies Book II* (180-199 A.D.), "The Scriptures are certainly perfect, since they were spoken by the Word of God and by His Spirit." Vol.1, p.88.

Hippolytus of Rome, *Commentary on Daniel* (200 A.D.), "Neither does Scripture falsify anything, nor does the Holy Spirit deceive His servants, the prophets, through whom He is pleased to announce to men the will of God." Vol.1, p.164.

Epiphanius of Salamis, *Against All Heresies* (c.374), "...nothing of discrepancy will be found in Sacred Scripture, nor will there be found any statement in opposition to any other statement." Vol.2., p.74.

Augustine of Hippo, *Letter of Augustine to Jerome* (394-395 A.D.), "I think it is dangerous to believe that anything in the Sacred Books is a lie...For if we once admit in that supreme monument of authority even one polite lie, no shred of those books will remain. Whenever anyone finds anything therein that is difficult to practice or hard to believe, he will refer to this most pernicious precedent and explain it as the idea or practice of a lying author." Vol.3, p.2.

Augustine of Hippo, *Letter of Augustine to Jerome* (405 A.D.), "I have learned to hold those books alone of the Scriptures that are called canonical in such reverence and honor that I do most firmly believe that none of their authors has erred in anything that he has written therein. If I find anything in those writings which seems to be contrary to the truth, I presume that either the codex is inaccurate, or the translator has not followed was said, or I have not properly understood it...I think that you, dear brother, must feel the same way. And I say, moreover, that I do not think you would want your books to be read as if they were the books of Prophets or Apostles, about whose writings, free of all error, it is not lawful to doubt." Vol.3, p.4.

Augustine of Hippo, *Harmony of the Evangelists* (c.400 A.D.), "For since it is in no one's power, however well and faithfully he knows his facts, to determine the order in which he will remember them, - for whether one thing comes into a man's mind before or after another depends not upon our will, but is simply as it occurs, - it is probable enough that each of the Evangelists believed he ought to proceed with his narrative in the same order in which God had willed to suggest to his memory the events he was narrating, at least in those matters the order of which, whether it were this or whether it were that, in no way diminished the authority and truth of the gospel." Vol.3, p.62.

in righteousness, so that the man of God may be complete, equipped for every good work. (2 Tim.3:16)" (DV,11) [109]

Because all of Scripture was produced under the action of the Holy Spirit, for the sake of our salvation, it must be acknowledged as teaching the truth "firmly, faithfully and without error." The Church is not subscribing to fundamentalism, taking every word at face-value; but it is saying that once we take account of literary genres and figurative language, whatever Scripture does in fact affirm is without error.[110]

Interpreting Scripture

With great wisdom, *Dei Verbum*, turns immediately from these truths to matters of interpretation. Knowing by faith that Scripture is free from error doesn't erase difficulties in the text, apparent contradictions, etc. Faith does not magically bridge the miles and centuries between us and the biblical writers. These texts, "inspired by God and committed to writing once and for all time,"[111] forever tie us to our ancestors in the ancient Middle East. We need to:

> …carefully search out the meaning which the sacred author really had in mind, that meaning which God had thought well to manifest through the medium of their words…attention must be paid to literary forms for the fact is that truth is differently presented and expressed in the various types of historical writing, in prophetical and poetical texts," and in other forms of literary expression. Hence the exegete must look for that meaning which the sacred writer, in a determined situation and given the circumstances of his time and culture, intended to express and did in fact express, through the medium of a contemporary literary form…due attention must be paid both to the customary and characteristic patterns of perception, speech and narrative which prevailed at the age of the sacred writer, and to conventions which the

---

[109] Flannery, Austin, *Vatican Council II: The Conciliar and Post Conciliar Documents*, (Northport, New York: Costello Publishing Company, 1992), p.757. Italics added

[110] Their Church's position is a point that is misunderstood by a number of Catholics today. For a more in-depth examination please consult Appendix VII.

[111] Flannery, Austin, *Vatican Council II: The Conciliar and Post Conciliar Documents*, (Northport, New York: Costello Publishing Company, 1992), p.762.

people of his time followed in their dealings with one another (*DV*, 12).[112]

We need to make an important distinction: we do not want to be literalist, but we do want to arrive at what has traditionally been called Scripture's *literal* sense. ***Dei Verbum*** **speaks to us of the literal sense; it is "the meaning which the sacred authors really had in mind, that meaning which God thought well to manifest"** through the literary forms and devices (and yes, even figurative language) we find in Scripture. To arrive at this meaning the Church, while recognizing its limits, endorses the use of the historical-critical method.[113] The historical-critical method uses scientific criteria to establish the original form of the text, sources used in its composition, its literary genre, and modifications the text likely underwent before reaching its final, fixed form.

Scripture contains a variety of literary forms (genres) and devices; and these have to be taken into account if we are to understand what the sacred writers, what God, wanted to express and teach us. Examples of these forms are: historical narrative (Ex.14:21- 22,29); historical myth (Genesis 1-11); poetry and hymns (Psalm 137:7-9); prophecy (Malachi, Amos); apocalyptic (Isaiah 13:10; Matt.24:29; Book of Revelation); pastoral instruction (Titus, 1&2 Timothy); and edifying fiction (Tobit, Judith). An example of a literary device would be anthropomorphisms, ascribing human characteristics to the Lord (Dt.11:12; Ex.13:3).

Recognizing this great variety of expression rules out fundamentalism, taking each word literally, at face-value. That is not the way we moderns express ourselves either; our daily speech is peppered with idioms and our television filled with everything from news reports and documentaries to soap operas. Knowing the form of expression is absolutely essential to knowing what its producers want us to take from it. I will watch a sitcom like CBS's *Everybody Loves Raymond* for a humorous morality tale, not for current events or political analysis. Recognizing the genre of a piece is essential to correctly interpreting its message.

---

[112] Ibid, pp.757-758.
[113] It does this implicitly in *Dei Verbum* and Pope Pius XII's *Divino Afflante Spiritu*, and then explicitly in the Pontifical Biblical Commission's 1994, *The Interpretation of the Bible in the Church*.

The first chapter of *Genesis* serves as a classic example. The author was not writing a scientific paper; he did not intend to make any scientific assertions about the age of the earth or to make a preemptive denial of an evolutionary process at work in the formation of the human body.[114] No, instead he made use of a genre often labeled mythic narrative.[115] Mythic symbols, already available in the surrounding culture,[116] were used to teach that Yahweh, the God of Israel, was the God of all of creation. He granted man and woman the unheard of dignity of being made in His image and likeness. Historical-critical study of *Genesis* has been able to show that there are actually two independent creation accounts, the first extending from 1:1 to 2:4a and the second from 2:4b-3:24. This is yet another proof for us that the inspired editor, who set the accounts next to each other, did not mean for them to be understood as blow-by-blow accounts of *how* the earth and humanity were formed; no, these stories were meant to communicate the "why" in language that even the simplest could understand. Among the truths we are meant to take from the accounts are: 1) the original goodness of humanity; 2) that a single couple stand at its beginning; 3) that our race enjoyed intimacy with God at its beginning; 4) Our first parents were tempted and chose their own will over God's will; 5) thus our parents and the race descended from them entered spiritual death, and 6) God gives a first hint of redemption (Genesis 3:15).

We would think we could let our interpretive guard down a bit when we turn to the genre of historical narrative, but we would be mistaken. Re-

---

[114] If a Christian thinks that God called forth the human body through evolution that's fine, so long as he/she holds that once the body was fully evolved the Lord united a rational soul with it - bringing the first man and woman into existence. It wasn't until the Lord "blew into his nostrils the *breath of life*, [that] *man* became a *living being*" (Genesis 2:7).
[115] Pope John Paul II, in his general audience of Nov.7, 1979, referred to the first three chapters of Genesis as "myth," going on to explain that "the term myth does not designate a fabulous content, but merely an archaic way of expressing a deeper content." Most, William G. *Free From All Error.* (Libertyville, Illinois: Prow Books/Franciscan Marytown Press, 1985), p.66.
[116] The order of creation largely follows the same sequence as that in the *Enuma Elish*, an ancient Babylonian creation myth. Images such as a "plant of life" and a serpent can be found in the Babylonian *Epic of Gilgamesh*. "Genesis, Reading Guide," in *The Catholic Study Bible*, Ed. D. Senior, M.A. Getty, C. Stuhlmueller, and J.J. Collins. (New York: Oxford University Press, 1990), pp.61-62.

cently I came across a book by Dr. Barbara Organ, *Is the Bible Fact or Fiction?: An Introduction to Biblical Historiography*. In true "contextualist" fashion she asks us to realize that ancient historians had access to, "a far narrower range of materials...and they also had a clear intent to teach a moral lesson and to entertain, to make their histories interesting...The aesthetics of history writing was an important component. The ancient historian had more freedom in rearranging material – even chronology – in order to make a point."[117]

Of particular interest to me was Dr. Organ's treatment of the chronology running through *Joshua, Judges, 1 & 2 Samuel*, and *1 & 2 Kings*. 1 King 6:1 states that the temple was established 480 years after Israel came out of Egypt. When one looks closely at the individual time periods recounted from the *Book of Judges* to that point in *1 Kings* however, a grand total of 534 years emerges.[118] Organ suggests that we recognize that patterns were often inherent in ancient chronologies. The 480 years may be symbolic, forty multiplied by the twelve tribes.

> The number forty appears frequently in biblical texts as a round number signifying fullness or completion...a completed cycle...The people of Israel spent forty years in the wilderness (Num.32:13)...David reigned for forty years as did Solomon (1 Kings 2:11; 11:42). Prior to the monarchy, Eli the priest is said to have "judged" Israel for forty years, and the hero Samson for twenty years. The pattern is especially noticeable in the Book of Judges, where the period of rest from the enemies are measured in forty or eighty years for a total of 200 years...David and Solomon, as Israel's greatest kings, could not have reigned for less than a full cycle of years. Clearly these numbers are "round figures," probably symbolic numbers to account for what must have been gaps in the historian's narrative.[119]

This type of historical-critical insight resolves what on the surface appears to be an historical error, but in reality is only a narrative device; the ancient author was not asserting a rigid chronology but organizing and structuring

---

[117] Organ, Barbara E., *Is the Bible Fact or Fiction?: An Introduction to Biblical Historiography*. (New York: Paulist Press, 2004), p.7.
[118] Ibid, p.120
[119] Ibid, p.120

his narrative. Historical texts operated by a different set of rules in antiquity than they do today. How well *Dei Verbum* captures this harmony between Scripture's complete inerrancy and its use of ancient forms:

> In sacred Scripture, *without prejudice to God's truth and holiness*, the marvelous "condescension" of eternal wisdom is plain to seen "that we may come to know the ineffable loving-kindness of God and see for ourselves how far he has gone in adapting his language with thoughtful concern for our nature." Indeed the words of God, expressed in the words of men, *are in every way like human language*, just as the Word of the eternal Father, when he took on himself the flesh of human weakness, became like men (*DV*, 13).[120]

The Catholic Church also recognizes that God can impregnate the text with additional meanings not discernable by historical-critical methodology. This additional sense, the spiritual sense, is often spoken of as taking three forms: the analogical (or typological), the moral, and the anagogical.[121]

---

[120] Flannery, Austin, *Vatican Council II: The Conciliar and Post Conciliar Documents*, (Northport, New York: Costello Publishing Company, 1992), p.758.

[121] I'll try to provide a brief explanation for each:

The analogical, or typological, sense becomes manifest when persons or events in the pages of the Old Testament take on an added significance in light of Christ Jesus. The writer of John's Gospel (19:33-36) sees Jesus' legs not being broken during the crucifixion as a fulfillment of a prescription concerning the Passover lamb, "Do not break any of the bones" (Exodus 12:46, NIV). In the New Testament's *1 Peter* we read, "God waited patiently in the days of Noah while the ark was being built. In it only a few people, eight in all, were saved through water, and this water symbolizes baptism that now saves you also" (3:20-21). The examples could be multiplied. As Catholics we recognize this type of exegesis as going back to Jesus Himself, who on the night of His resurrection "opened [his disciples] minds so they could understand the Scriptures...beginning with Moses and all the Prophets, he explained to them what was said in all the Scriptures concerning himself" (Luke 24:45,27; NIV).

The moral sense indicates how "the events reported in Scripture ought to lead us to act justly." The Apostle Paul, after reflecting on how even though all of the Israelites who departed Egypt were "baptized into Moses in the cloud and the sea...[and] all ate the same spiritual food and drank the same spiritual drink," still ended with their bodies scattered over the desert (1 Cor.10:2-5; NIV). "These things happened to them as examples and were written down as warnings for us...So, if you think you are standing firm, be careful that you don't fall! No temptation has seized you except what is common to man" (1 Cor.10:11-13). C.S. Lewis, the British author, made an application of the moral sense that I cannot resist sharing with you:

According to *Dei Verbum*, once we have labored to understand the words according to their literary genre, time, and culture, we have only gone half the way: "since Sacred Scripture must be read and interpreted with its divine authorship in mind, no less attention must be devoted to the content and unity of the whole of Scripture, taking into account the Tradition of the entire Church and the analogy of faith, if we are to derive their true meaning from the sacred texts" (*DV*, 12).[122] Personally, I could agree with interpreting individual passages in light of the whole – but to say that Tradition and Church teaching were a *necessity*? I could agree with everything up until that point; the Catholic teaching on inspiration, inerrancy, and interpretation was well-thought-out, wise. That last element, however, gave the

---

> I can use even the horrible passage in Psalm [137] about dashing the Babylonian babies against the stones. I know things in the inner world which are like babies; the infantile beginnings of small indulgences, small resentments, which may one day become dipsomania or settled hatred, but which woo us...with special pleadings that seem so tiny, so helpless, that in resisting them we feel like we're being cruel to animals. They begin whimpering to us, "I don't ask much, but" or "I had at least hoped", or "You owe yourself *some* consideration." Against all such pretty infants (the dears have such winning ways) the advice of the psalm is best. Knock the little bastards brains out. And "blessed" is he who can, for it's easier said than done. (Shea, Mark P., *Making Senses Out of Scripture: Reading the Bible as the First Christians Did* [San Diego: Basilica, 1999] p.116-117.)

The anagogical sense emerges when we begin to view the earthly realities spoken of in Scripture in terms of eternity. The Tabernacle and Temple of the OT become images of heaven (Heb.9:1,23), as does the city of Jerusalem, "You have come to the Mount Zion, to the heavenly Jerusalem, the city of the living God. You have come to thousands upon thousands of angels in joyful assembly, to the church of the firstborn whose names are written in heaven. You have come to God, the judge of all men, to the spirits of righteous men made perfect" (Hebrews 12:22-23). Using the anagogical sense, the Songs of Assent (Psalms 120-134), the psalms sung by the ancient Jewish pilgrims as they approached Jerusalem, become our psalms of pilgrimage as well.

These spiritual senses of Scripture were obviously perceived by the inspired writers of the New Testament. For we interpreters living two millennia after the writing of the NT, and almost three after the OT, caution should be observed. The chief rule to follow is that the spiritual sense can never contradict the literal; it can build on it but never contradict it. The spiritual sense also, because of the greater subjectivity of the interpretation, should not be used to prove doctrine. Theology should restrict itself to the use of the literal sense.

[122] Flannery, Austin, *Vatican Council II: The Conciliar and Post Conciliar Documents*, (Northport, New York: Costello Publishing Company, 1992), p.758.

Church a little too much authority for my taste – at least at that point in my journey.

In Conclusion

   Mr. Burn's view, the Catholic view, did justice to the Bible as a work of both God *and* man. I saw that a rigid fundamentalism was not necessary to protect Scripture's authority; in fact, it could stand in the way of a proper interpretation. I began reading Scripture more and more as a contextualist, paying greater attention to study notes in the margin and consulting commentaries as to genre and cultural information. I never told Mr. Burns how deeply he affected me. I feel confident that he knows though; he went to be with the Lord almost five years ago. If you could, would you say a prayer that his soul's growth will be completed soon, if it hasn't been already? Thank you.

Chapter 8 – The End of ~~All~~ Some Things (*The Book of Revelation* and "End Times" Speculation)

By senior year I finally felt like a part of my high school "community." The change at school was due to several factors. First, there was a change in the way I was looking at those around me. Instead of viewing my classmates as being in need of encountering Jesus for the first time, I had had a few years to live with my beliefs on infant baptism, as well as listen to what classmates said when it was just myself and them. Many of them came from faith-filled families and had a deep, deep desire to know God. The difficulty was that they had not been told how simple it was to begin, that God desired it even more than they. I had begun to sense a change in the way peers perceived me back in junior year. I was being included in more of the conversations before class and in the hallways, and that allowed me to let my guard down and show my sense of humor. I was still just as open about my faith, but it was not a source of ridicule anymore; my class went so far as to vote me "most well-rounded."

Senior year also saw spiritual developments taking place that I had barely dreamt possible. A new young priest, who I will call Fr. Mike, came on board as a religion teacher, and that summer between junior and senior year had taken a group of students on pilgrimage to Medjugorje. When they returned a school prayer group was formed!

Medjugorje and Private Revelations

If you are unfamiliar with Medjugorje, it is a small township in present-day Bosnia-Herzegovina where the Virgin Mary reportedly began appearing to six young people in 1981, and has continued to do so. The apparitions have yet to receive the Church's official approval, a statement that there is nothing in them contrary to the Faith. Such approval cannot be granted until the events have reached their culmination and investigators given a chance to reach a conclusion.

Before I go any farther I want to make something clear. I am not trying to take pot shots at anyone who believes that Jesus is sending His Mother to call people and nations to repentance. The Lord sending saints from heaven to earth isn't without biblical precedence. When Peter, James, and John witnessed our Lord's transfiguration they saw Him speaking with

THE END OF ~~ALL~~ SOME THINGS   129

Moses and Elijah (Luke 9:31). When John the Apostle was later granted a vision of Heaven, he was spoken to not only by the Lord and His angels, but by one of the human elders before God's throne (Revelation 5:5). If you read accounts of Church-approved "Marian" apparitions you will undoubtedly notice the fruits of holiness that flow from them: sincere conversion, evangelistic zeal, fasting and prayer for the conversion of the world. Physical, emotional, and spiritual healing also seems to abound. While Medjugorje has yet to be granted Church-approval, I have met several people for whom it has had a positive effect.

Apparitions belong to what the Church terms "private revelation." Public revelation consists of all that Jesus revealed to us, during His own ministry and then that of the Twelve Apostles. Nothing can be added to or subtracted from it. The purpose of private revelation is not to bring new truths *but to spur us on in living the public revelation.* When the Catholic Church approves one of these private revelations it is affirming that there is nothing in it that contradicts public revelation. While the bishops of the Church may find a private revelation credible, they can never impose it upon the faithful. Private revelations are just that, private – left to the prayerful consideration of the faithful as to how, or if, they will incorporate them into their faith lives.

A Prayer Group at My School

Fr. Mike and the trip he led to Medjugorje were instrumental in establishing a prayer group at my high school. I didn't make the trip but instead got to know Fr. Mike by having him as a religion instructor senior year.

Jerry was one of the students who had accompanied Fr. Mike, so when he invited me to the prayer group I was happy to go. The thought of praying with classmates was pretty exciting. We met at the rectory where Fr. Mike resided, not too far from school. There were ten to twelve students; all the different grades were represented. Father barbecued for us and after the meal we retired to the second floor of the rectory for the meeting proper. We sat in a circle and engaged in silent prayer for the majority of the time, ending with the *Our Father, Hail Mary,* and *Glory Be.* Most of the group then went to the window as the sun became low in the sky. Many pilgrims to Medjugorje report seeing figures in the sun or the sun seeming to "dance" in the sky. Fr. Mike and some of the youth claimed to continue experiencing this after their return to St. Charles.

Father invited me to look with them, to let my eyes rest on the sun. I noticed a red and then a green cast at its outer edge. My eyes didn't hurt though, I could look at it for as long as I wanted. The strangest thing was that when I took my eyes off of the sun, and looked around the room, I could see a distinct image. You know how when you look at a light and then turn away you still have that bright spot in your field of vision? Well, my bright spot was a red heart with a gold cross in the center. It lingered for a minute, maybe two, and was gone. It was an experience. I didn't really have an emotional reaction or receive any illumination from it. It did, however, encourage me to pay attention to this little group.

Strange Teachings

As I said, Fr. Mike was my religion teacher for senior year. We were slotted for three areas of study: church history, death and dying, marriage and family. No matter the subject though, Father had a way of interjecting interests of his own. He frequently spoke of "the Chastisement" and the dawning of a new interval in history. He gleaned these ideas from a number of alleged apparitions of the Lord Jesus and the Blessed Mother occurring around the world – apparitions not fully investigated nor approved by the Catholic Church.

One of the "revelations" he passed along to us, with the disclaimer that it was a matter of private revelation, was that AIDS was a plague sent by God. I took opposition to this on the simple grounds that I could never imagine my Father conceiving such a ravaging disease. God had told us throughout salvation history that fornication and adultery were not in His plan for our lives. Why not? He knew what would happen if we abused the gift - syphilis, gonorrhea, herpes, AIDS. These diseases are not just contracted by people who commit sexual sin; as with all sin, the innocent suffer the effects as well - like the child who contracts HIV through blood transfusion. Even though Father Mike had given a disclaimer, this did not seem appropriate for classroom discussion.

While that was troublesome, I had the most difficulty accepting Father's remarks on "the Chastisement." Because of its sins the world would be plunged into three days of darkness. The only light during that time

THE END OF ~~ALL~~ SOME THINGS   131

would be that given off by blessed candles. Demons would be let loose upon the earth to torment unbelievers. A few of the school prayer group members later told me that the only safe-haven during that period would be church buildings. The teens closest to Father seemed to focus on these catastrophes more than a personal relationship with Jesus or the desire to evangelize.

This differed from other people I knew of who had visited Medjugorje. While believing that the world could very well be on the brink of a chastisement, they did not bring in strange side revelations like seeing only by the light of blessed candles or demons being let loose on the earth. Instead, the chastisement was spoken of more in terms of war and environmental upheaval - God's disciplining of a wayward world, reminding it that there are consequences to selfishness, pride, and the devaluing of human life. They also believed that such a chastisement was to a large degree *conditional*; if the world repented then it could be mitigated. A biblical correlation may be the repentance of the city of Nineveh at the preaching of Jonah; when the Lord said that there would be a reckoning for their sinfulness:

> They proclaimed a fast, and put on sackcloth, from the greatest of them to the least of them,. . .[The king ordered the people to] 'Cry mightily to God; yea, let every one turn from his evil way and from the violence which is in his hands.'. . . When God saw what they did, how they turned from their evil way, God repented of the evil which he had said he would do to them; and he did not do it" (Jonah 3:5,8,10; information within brackets added).

Father Mike peppered his version of the chastisement with references to the *Book of Revelation*. After the three days of darkness the earth would be cleansed and history continue, with Jesus ruling from Jerusalem for a thousand years. Only after the thousand years had elapsed would history come to a close and the world be transformed.

For me, the most authoritative information about the end times came not from private revelations, but the Bible. If something didn't jive with it then I was on my guard. This talk of three days of darkness and demons let loose to torment people was way out there. I knew there were a number of Christians who believed Jesus would establish a thousand year reign, ruling politically from Jerusalem, before a final rebellion and the Day of Judg-

132   THE GOD WHO IS LOVE

ment. They based their belief on the twentieth chapter of the *Book of Revelation*. But that was the only piece of what Fr. Mike said with which I was familiar.

Besides the strange teaching, Fr. Mike claimed a variety of spiritual phenomena. I was shocked to walk into class one afternoon and find Father and a group of students at the back of the room with an 8x10" image of the Virgin Mary. One by one the students were invited to run their hands over the photo as Father asked, "Can you feel the heat coming off of that?" He would also speak of seeing auras around people.

The final straw came with the outbreak of the Gulf War, when he identified Saddam Hussein as the antichrist. That was when I knew I had to begin studying the *Book of Revelation* and offer my classmates a more balanced, more authoritative vision, of Christianity's belief about the end times.

My dad supplied me with a couple of books he had used to study *Revelation*. The first thing I noticed was that most modern scholars interpreted it within the context of first-century Christianity, the original recipients of John's revelation, and the world in which they lived. That was what Mr. Burns had taught me to do; the method was endorsed by the Catholic Church. Besides, in its very first verse *Revelation* says it concerns "what soon must take place." It was addressed to "the seven churches in the province of Asia" (1:4). So whatever additional meanings we glean from this book, we first have to identify the literal sense – the meaning its author intended for his original readers!

I found the research fascinating. I got the chance to sort through not just the scenarios offered by Fr. Mike, but to look at other popular beliefs such as the "rapture." As you will shortly see, my experience with Fr. Mike brought me not just to a deep appreciation and fondness for the most misunderstood book of the Bible, but a growing appreciation of both tradition and the papacy! Before I get to that though, I should tell you how things worked out with Fr. Mike.

Once I felt prepared, I spoke up in class. Father Mike and I carried on a discussion/debate that left most classmates looking on in silence. Father told me that I was too black and white, especially in my outlook on the Bible; and I told him that he had departed from the Catholic Church in his teaching about the end times. Things quieted down for a bit after that, but Father gradually began slipping in more "private revelations." In despera-

THE END OF ~~ALL~~ SOME THINGS   133

tion I went to my school's administrator, who listened patiently. He promised that the matter would be addressed, but quietly and in his own way. I, for my part, was to continue going to class and to try to avoid confrontation as best I could. Three weeks later Fr. Mike announced that he would not be returning to our school, that he was being transferred to a parish in a neighboring town.

The Book of Revelation

When we look at Revelation from the perspective of the early Church, instead of reading it with a newspaper in the other hand, I think that the message becomes very plain: in the midst of the horrible persecutions suffered by the Church, Jesus *is* Lord; and in the end His Kingdom will be manifest to all of creation. In the fourth chapter of the book, the author John heard a trumpet-like voice calling him to, "Come up [here]," (4:1) and begin viewing the scene through God's eyes.

The book belongs to a whole genre of literature that flourished among the Jews, and then the Christians, from roughly 200 B.C. to 200 A.D., known as *apocalyptic*. Much of its imagery is taken from the Old Testament. In *Revelation*'s 404 verses, scholars can identify at least 278 allusions to the O.T. It borrows imagery already familiar to the people of God - the pictures painted in *Exodus, Daniel, Ezekiel, Isaiah*, and the *Psalms*. Jesus made use of this same imagery, using the language of cosmic and environmental upheaval to prophesy of the destruction of Jerusalem (see Matthew 24:1-35, with parallels in Mark and Luke).

Revelation was written in code, written to give strength to a persecuted Church - being ostracized by the Jewish community on one side and put to death by the Romans on the other. When you are a group hunted by the authorities you can not say things straight out, you have to veil it in symbols, much like the resistance in World War II did in their radio messages. Thus we find Roman Empire referred to as a Beast "with ten horns and seven heads...the seven heads are seven hills" upon which the city of Rome was built (Revelation 17:3, 9).

So much speculation about the end times is wrapped up in the idea of "antichrist" - who is he and when he will make his appearance. In World War II people naturally pointed to Hitler. Others in the 1930's, opposed to the New Deal, held up Franklin Delano Roosevelt. As I said, Fr. Mike pointed to Saddam Hussein. While Saddam and Hitler may be called antichrists, in the sense that they oppose our Lord's will, neither of them was that diabolical personage, or "man of lawlessness" (2 Thessalonians 2:3), prophesied to immediately precede our Lord's return.

Many commentators on the *Book of Revelation* identify the "First Beast" of chapter thirteen with this "man of lawlessness" spoken of by St. Paul. We are told that this first beast will have received a mortal wound to one of its seven heads. The healing of this wound would entice the whole world to follow after it out of wonderment (13:3). The beast waged war against God's people and conquered them. "Authority was given it over every tribe and people and tongue and nation" (13:7). The "Second Beast" is said to have "had two horns like a lamb and it spoke like a dragon" (13:11). It led the whole world in worshipping the first beast, making an idol in its honor. Further, the second beast did not allow anyone to "buy or sell unless he has the mark, that is, the name of the beast or the number of its name" (13:17).

When we interpret these images in the context of first-century Christianity we arrive at a pretty likely candidate for John's "First Beast," or Antichrist. Consider the following: The Emperor Nero was the first Roman Emperor to persecute Christians; Peter and Paul were martyred under his reign. Nero died by a self-inflicted wound to the throat (the Beast with a mortal head wound?)[123] Nero, as well as the emperors who followed, insisted on being worshipped as gods. The "Second Beast" may correspond to the pagan priests of Rome, leading people throughout the Empire in sacrifice to the false god. It may also refer to "asiarchs," the Roman officials who enforced emporer worship. When we are told of people who did not accept the mark of the beast on their forehead or in their hand (13:17) it may refer to a dilemma faced by the early Church - they would have been unable to swear oaths invoking the emperor's divinity during business transactions. They may also have refused to use coinage stamped with the inscription "Caesar is Lord."[124]

---

[123] Tickle, John, *The Book of Revelation: A Catholic Interpretation of the Apocalypse*. (Ligouri, Missouri: Ligouri Publications, 1983), p.94.
[124] Perkins, Pheme, *Collegeville Bible Commentary: The Book of Revelation* (Collegeville, Minnesota: The Liturgical Press, 1983), p.63.

THE END OF ~~ALL~~ SOME THINGS   135

Allow me to flesh out this identification of the First Beast with the Roman Emperor a bit more. The most telling detail concerns the most picked-over verse in *Revelation*:

> This calls for wisdom: let him who has understanding reckon the number of the beast, for it is a human number, its number is six hundred and sixty-six (Revelation 13:18).

One has to wonder how many heavy-metal tunes have pondered this verse. What does John mean by "the man's number"? As said earlier, the Hebrew alphabet - as well as Greek and Latin - have a number associated with each letter. The Jews had a "science" called gematria - discovering the hidden meanings of words by studying and comparing their numerical values. And whose name, when written in Hebrew, has the numerical value 666? You guessed it - Nero Caesar. What I found to be convincing about this identification was that early Latin manuscripts of *The Book of Revelation* exist in which this verse reads 616 instead of 666. When the name Nero Caesar is written in Latin, 616 is its value. From what I read, scholars postulate that the early Church, believing it understood John's code, made the adjustment when the book was translated into Latin.

Chapter 17 of *Revelation* further narrows the identity of the Beast to the Roman Emporers, personified by Nero at the time of the work's composition.[125] We are told that the beast's "seven heads are seven hills...they are also seven kings, five of whom have fallen, *one is*, the other has not yet come, and when he comes he must remain only a little while" (17:9-10). Five emperors had preceded Nero; he was the last of the royal blood-line. With his suicide the empire was plunged into civil war as competitors vied for the throne. Galba succeeded Nero but was assassinated six months later, making him the seventh king, who "must remain only a little while" (17:10). Only Vespasian's ascendancy to the throne returned stability to the empire; the "mortal wound" inflicted by Nero's suicide "was healed, and the whole earth followed the beast with wonder" (13:3).

---

[125] For this information I am indebted to Kenneth L. Gentry and his works *Before Jerusalem Fell: Dating the Book of Revelation* (American Vision, 1998) and *The Beast of Revelation* (American Vision, 2002). These can also be accessed online at http://freebooks.entrewave.com/freebooks/docs/_bksauth.htm.

Reading *Revelation* in the historical context of the early Church made sense to me. It didn't rob the book of its prophetic character either. As I have said before, prophecy is predominantly God giving His people a reality check. In this case He reminds us that even when the Church on earth looks like it is being crushed Jesus is still Lord of the situation; He will bring deliverance to His holy ones and rule the Earth as her King. Whenever the Church finds herself persecuted, under the gun, martyred - *Revelation* is God's word addressed to the situation. The Roman Empire did fall; its former capitol is now the center of Christ's Universal (Catholic) Church! Will the Church undergo another great persecution immediately before Christ's Second Coming? Will there be a definitive antichrist? Taking the New Testament as a whole, as well as two thousand years of constant Christian interpretation, I believe we have to say "yes." When that time, often called "the great tribulation," comes the symbols in *The Book of Revelation* may speak very clearly and precisely to the Church once again. That is the beauty of God's Word – because its author is beyond time, its applicability is also timeless. Right now though, I think it is a mistake to interpret *Revelation* in terms of the evening news; it presupposes that we are living in not only the Final Age but in the final days. I do not see the warrant for that.

Above I mentioned Christian interpretation having spanned two thousand years. The Church had meditated on the Scripture for close to two millennia - asking what particular verses meant while struggling to keep one ear open to the previous generation and the other to the Spirit for greater insight. The thought occurred to me that blindly setting all of this "tradition" aside would be very arrogant; after all, who did I think I was?

One area in which I found the Church's interpretive tradition helpful was in looking at the Millennium, or thousand year reign of Christ, before the Last Judgment. As I stated earlier, Fr. Mike believed its commencement was just around the corner. The *Book of Revelation* did speak of Jesus, and those who had given their lives in testimony to Him, ruling for a thousand years. During that time Satan would be chained; at the end of the millennium he would be released for a short time to incite the nations against God's people. This final insurrection would then be crushed and the world judged. There are groups of Christians today who accept these verses as a literal forecast.

THE END OF ~~ALL~~ SOME THINGS   137

What I discovered, however, was that theirs was a minority opinion. Historically it was not how the vast majority of Christians had interpreted the millenium. One of the early Christian apologists, Justin Martyr (writing in 155 A.D.) *did* expect a literal thousand year reign of Christ, but was candid in saying that there were "many Christians of a pure and pious faith who do not share this belief" (*Dialogue with Trypho the Jew*).[126] In the second century it was a point open to honest debate, but by the fourth century the Christian Church had made up its mind. Eusebius Pamphilus, the first Christian historian, vehemently condemned the literal interpretation in his *History of the Church, Book III* (325 A.D.). St. Augustine of Hippo held the literal interpretation in the early years of his conversion but later abandoned it. He saw an alternative that fit the data better. It was accepted throughout the Christian Church from the fourth century up until the resurgence of millennial belief in the late nineteenth century. Allow me to go into more depth.

I stated my belief that *Revelation* is not to be read as a blow-by-blow account of the Last Days. Some of the visions describe particular incidents; others seem to zoom out and describe a whole epoch of history in a few lines. I believe the section of *Revelation* dealing with the millennium is a good example of a "zoom-out." Chapters four through nineteen deal with the persecution of the Church and Christ's victory. I say this because chapter nineteen ends with Christ returning to earth - defeating the two beasts and having them thrown into the pool of burning sulfur. Chapter Twenty pans out and gives us a look at the whole period between Christ's first and second comings. First, we are told that an angel came down from heaven and:

> . . .seized the dragon, that ancient serpent, who is the Devil and Satan, and bound him up for a thousand years, and threw him into the pit, and shut it and sealed it over him, that he should deceive the nations no more, till the thousand years were ended. After that he must be loosed for a little while (20:1-3).

---

[126] Jurgens, William A., *The Faith of the Early Fathers*, Volume 1(Collegeville, Minnesota: The Liturgical Press, 1970), p.57.

Augustine and others felt that this chaining of Satan refers to the "driving out" of Satan accomplished by Jesus' death, resurrection, and ascension (John 12:31). *Revelation 20* continues:

> Also I saw the souls of those who had been beheaded for their testimony to Jesus and for the word of God, and who had not worshiped the beast or its image and had not received its mark on their foreheads or their hands. They came to life, and reigned with Christ a thousand years. The rest of the dead did not come to life until the thousand years were ended. This is the first resurrection (20:4-5).

This first resurrection was understood by Augustine as a *spiritual* resurrection; everyone who has fully surrendered their lives to Christ behold Him face-to-face *in Heaven* and share in His victory over Satan, sin, and death. They are even said to share in Christ's heavenly priesthood. The *Epistle to the Hebrews* tells us that, as High Priest, Jesus "always lives to make intercession for [His people]" (7:25); earlier we saw how the saints in heaven offer intercession through Him for the Church on earth. For members of the Church still in need of purification (purgatory) the full experience of Heaven is postponed briefly. But when Jesus returns to earth, *every person* will be *physically* raised from the grave - the second resurrection.

Before this "second" resurrection, though, we are told about the final assault launched against the Church:

> And when the thousand years are ended, Satan will be loosed from prison and will come out to deceive the nations which are at the four corners of the earth, that is, Gog and Magog, to gather them for battle; their number is like the sand of the sea. And they marched up over the broad earth and surrounded the camp of the saints and the beloved city; but fire came down from heaven and consumed them, and the devil who had deceived them was thrown into the lake of fire and brimstone (20:7 10).

Now if Christ had been physically reigning on earth for a thousand years, then how could anyone, even the most feeble-minded, think that a revolt could be successful?" And yet, Satan is said to raise an army whose "number is like the sand of the sea." That doesn't make sense; granted, we human beings can do some outrageously stupid things, but that's just suicide!

THE END OF ~~ALL~~ SOME THINGS   139

I would have to say that Augustine's interpretation, that accepted by the Christian Church for almost 1600 years, makes more sense of the data than a literal thousand years: the Millennium is Christ's reign from heaven, occurring right now; Satan's release from his chains will be the final persecution, "the Great Tribulation" to come upon the people of God. Thus, Jesus' Second Coming and deliverance of the Church will be immediately followed by the Judgment (20:11-14).

No Place for the "Rapture"
One of the first books I read, after becoming serious about my faith, was Hal Lindsey's *The Rapture*. It was my introduction to a very popular belief in American Christianity – even more so after Tim LaHaye and Jerry Jenkin's *Left Behind* books. In a nutshell, proponents of the rapture expect Jesus to instantaneously transport believers from earth to Heaven, just prior to the final antichrist's rise to power. True believers, living at that time, will not have to suffer the Great Tribulation; it is reserved for those left on earth, who finally recognize the signs of the times and come to a belief in Jesus.

Although proponents of the rapture appeal to Scripture, no one – and I mean *no one* - in the first eighteen hundred years of Christianity saw it there. The two key verses I have heard appealed to by its proponents are *1 Thessalonians 4:16-18* and *Matthew 24:37-41*. Allow me to address them each in turn.

I will start my quotation from *1 Thessalonians* before, and end it after, the verses alleged to concern a rapture prior to the time of tribulation:

> For this we declare to you by the word of the Lord, that we who are alive, who are left until the coming of the Lord, shall not precede those who have fallen asleep. For the Lord himself will descend from heaven with a cry of command, with the archangel's call, and with the sound of the trumpet of God. And the dead in Christ will rise first; then we who are alive, who are left, shall be caught up together with them in the clouds to meet the Lord in the air; and so we shall be with the Lord. Therefore, comfort one another with these words. But as to the times and the seasons, brethren, you have no need to have anything

> written to you. For you yourselves know well that *the day of the Lord will come like a thief in the night* (1 Thess.4:15-5:2).

Note the words I have italicized. Paul is talking about the great Day of the Lord, the Day of Judgment. He is talking about the glorious, triumphant manifestation of Jesus and His Body when He returns in glory. Paul says nothing about the Church being raptured away so as to escape persecution. Instead, those translated directly from earthly existence to glory are those who are "alive," who are "left."

Read within its historical context, Paul is probably likening the Lord's return to that of a victorious general. As the conqueror returned to Rome, he would stop outside the city, and wait for his family to be brought to him. Once his entourage was fully assembled they would enter the city together, amidst fanfare and celebration.[127]

Lets turn now to Matthew's Gospel. After just employing apocalyptic imagery to describe the fall of Jerusalem, Jesus tells the Apostles:

> But of the day and hour no one knows, not even the angels of heaven, nor the Son, but the Father only. As were the days of Noah, so will be the coming of the Son of man. For as in those days before the flood they were eating and drinking, marrying and giving in marriage, until the day when Noah entered the ark, and they did not know until the flood came and swept them all away, so will be the coming of the Son of man. Then two men will be in the field; one is taken and one is left. Two women will be grinding at the mill; one is taken, and one is left. Watch therefore, for you do not know on what day your Lord is coming. But know this, that if the householder had known in what part of the night the thief was coming, he would have watched and would not have let his house be broken into. Therefore you also must be ready; for the Son of man is coming at an hour you do not expect (Matt.24:36-44).

Like *Thessalonians*, we have that image of the Lord coming like a thief in the night. It was a common motif for talking about the Second Coming; that is what both of these passages are dealing with. In *Thessalonians* we saw the Lord sweeping up His beloved. Not so in this passage. Who is taken? In

---

[127] Thigpen, Paul, *The Rapture Trap* (West Chester, Pennsylvania: Ascension Press, 2001).

THE END OF ~~ALL~~ SOME THINGS   141

this passage it is the *un*righteous! "As [in] the days of Noah,...the flood came and swept them all away." Much to the chagrin of Tim Lahaye and Jerry Jenkins, in Jesus' example it is the righteous who are "left behind." Jesus gave a similar description earlier in Matthew:

> The Son of Man will send his angels, and they will gather out of his kingdom all causes of sin and all evildoers, and throw them into the furnace of fire, there men will weep and gnash their teeth. Then the righteous will shine like the sun in the kingdom of their Father. He who has ears, let him hear...
>
> So it will be at the close of the age. The angels will come out and separate the evil from the righteous and throw them into the furnace of fire; there men will weep and gnash their teeth (Matt.13:41-43,49-50).

This idea that the Church will not suffer the great tribulation is completely unbiblical, and at odds with historic Christianity. Jesus, the Master, suffered. Eleven of the twelve Apostles died as martyrs; there have been martyrs throughout Jewish and Christian history. To believe in a rapture of the Church, so as to save it from suffering, flies in the face of this.

So how did belief in the rapture begin? With a man named John Nelson Darby (1800-1882), a former Anglican priest and founder of the Plymouth Brethren.[128] The teaching made its way to the United States and was disseminated through the study notes of the incredibly popular *Scofield Refernce Bible*. Dallas Theological Seminary, Moody Bible Institute, and Talbot Seminary then incorporated it into the training of future pastors. Hal Lindsey, whom I have read for example, was a graduate of Dallas Theological Seminary. His first blockbuster, the 1970 *The Late Great Planet Earth* brought the idea to the masses.[129] As we have seen, however; this belief has no ground in Scripture and runs counter to almost two thousand years of Christian belief.

---

[128] There is conjecture that the rapture was seen in a vision by a fifteen year-old Scottish girl, Margaret McDonald, and that this private revelation then found its way into the teaching of Darby.
[129] See Currie, David,. *The Rapture* (Manchester New Hampshire: Sophia Institute Press, 2003), p.14-17.

So What Should Christians Expect Before "the End"?

There are three things I feel safe in affirming.[130] First, that although "many antichrists have come" (1 John 2:18), there will be one final personage. Paul speaks of him quite plainly in *2 Thessalonians 2:3-4*. Second, that the Church will pass through his great persecution. And third, that the Jewish people will recognize Jesus as their Messiah (Romans 11:13-32). Notice that none of these are affirmations arrived at from *The Book of Revelation*. As I said before, when the final persecution arrives *Revelation* will speak the message it always has, "Jesus is Lord. Stand firm throughout this persecution and await the establishment of His Kingdom in power." The book's symbols may very well take on new significance at that time – but it is not a blow-by-blow, prophetic account of the last days. That was not its purpose, not its author's intent.

I think it best to end our examination of the end times with the words of Jesus, "that day or that hour no one knows, not even the angels in heaven, nor the Son, but only the Father" (Mk 13:32); "The Son of Man is coming at an hour you do not expect...Happy the servant whom his Master discovers at work on His return!" (Matt 24:44,46, NIV).

A New Take on Tradition

My research into end-time beliefs helped show me that Church tradition did not have to be some horrible monster distorting God's word. I had absorbed that impression early on from believers I respected, and it was hard to shake. Instead, tradition was a wise voice – the Christian Church speaking about the Word it had pondered for close to two thousand years. In considering the millennium and rapture, and answering the "end-time fever" of my religion instructor, it had proved invaluable.

But that was not the only green light I had received in its favor. Around this same time I came across three New Testament passages that forced me to rethink my position. The first was *2 Timothy 3:8* in my copy of *The Student Bible (New International Version)*. Paul warned Timothy about the type of person who would be plentiful in the last days, "Just as Jannes and

---

[130] See *The Catechism of the Catholic Church*, 670-682.

THE END OF ~~ALL~~ SOME THINGS 143

Jambres opposed Moses, so also these men oppose the truth." The study note for this passage read, "These names, *not mentioned in the Old Testament*, were handed down in Jewish *tradition* as the names of the Egyptian magicians who opposed Moses during the ten plagues against Egypt" (Exodus 7:11; 9:11). For a strict fundamentalist this should create a problem because Paul's *inspired* inclusion of these names would put a stamp of approval on the tradition! We might be able to sweep this under the rug; after all, it's just two names. The other two examples I found in *The Epistle of Jude* were much more blatant though.

Jude, only a chapter in length, demonstrates a real fusion between appeal to Scripture *and* tradition. Jude saw it as a valid Christian stance, using both to encourage readers to "fight hard for the faith delivered once for all to the saints" (v3). He asked his readers to remember "...the archangel Michael, [when] contending with the devil, disputed about the body of Moses, he did not presume to pronounce a reviling judgment upon him, but said, 'The Lord rebuke you'" (v9). What was Jude referring to? The Old Testament recorded no such confrontation - and yet Jude expected his readers to know it. And they did - from tradition; it is recorded in the Jewish apocryphal work, *The Assumption of Moses*.[131]

The second example Jude gives us may be the strongest argument in favor of tradition yet. Jude wrote:

> Enoch in the seventh generation from Adam, prophesied, saying, "Behold, the Lord came with his holy myriads, to execute judgment on all, and to convict all the ungodly of all their deeds of ungodliness which they have committed in such an ungodly way, and of all the harsh things which ungodly sinners have spoken against him" (14-15).[132]

Again, this prophecy is not found in the Old Testament, and yet an inspired New Testament author witnesses to its authenticity. This word of prophecy came down to Jude through Jewish tradition recorded in the apocryphal

---

[131] *The Catholic Study Bible* (New York, Oxford University Press, 1990) Note on page 397 of New Testament.
[132] Notice too how this image of the Second Coming complements Paul's vision (in *1 Thessalonians 4:15-5:2*) of the Church being caught up in the air to share in her returning Lord's triumph.

Book of Enoch, chapter one, verse nine.[133] Now Jude's use of these works does not mean that they were inspired Scripture in the way the books of the Old Testament were, just that the incident and prophecy conveyed are legitimate.

I didn't feel wrong looking to the Church's traditional understanding of the End Times to debate Fr. Mike. Seeing that Paul and Jude looked to tradition in making points to their audiences put me in good company. I found myself admitting the wisdom of *Dei Verbum* once again, "since Sacred Scripture must be read and interpreted with its divine authorship in mind, no less attention must be devoted to the content and unity of the whole of Scripture, *taking into account the Tradition of the entire Church* and the analogy of faith, if we are to derive their true meaning from the sacred texts" (*DV*, 12).[134] The logical question then became, "How do I know which traditions come from God and which do not? If the Apostles Paul and Jude saw some traditions containing the word of God, but Jesus rejected others as being purely human, and even misleading,[135] then how is the Church today able to differentiate? Who in Christianity could make that kind of distinction?"

Oh yeah, that is exactly what my Catholic Church claimed of the Pope! I could finally see the *need* for such an authority. Was the Pope's teaching really any more authoritative than another Christian minister's though? I found myself leaning toward "yes." The Holy Spirit had opened my eyes to the truth of so many other Catholic doctrines (Mary, the Sacraments of Confirmation and Reconciliation, purgatory, infant baptism); the acceptance of each new piece making this one seem all the more likely.[136]

Catholics look to the pope as the successor of Simon-Peter, and to Simon-Peter as the head of the Apostles. That he had held such a position

---

[133] Halley, Henry H., *Halley's Bible Handbook* (Grand Rapids, Michigan: Zondervan Publishing House, 1965), p.682.

[134] Flannery, Austin, *Vatican Council II: The Conciliar and Post Conciliar Documents*, (Northport, New York: Costello Publishing Company, 1992), p.758.

[135] Jesus said to the Pharisees, "You hypocrites! Well did Isaiah prophesy of you, when he said, 'This people honors me withtheir lips, but their heart is far from me; in vain do they worship me, teaching as doctrines the precepts of men'" Matthew 15:7-9.

[136] There was also the realization that, in reality, all of us have a "pope;" it is simply a question of who. It may be a learned writer or scripture scholar, a favorite pastor, or just *ourselves*; but there is someone we look to to interpret the data of faith.

among Jesus' inner circle didn't give me difficulty anymore. (Yes, the Apostle Paul may have written significantly more of the New Testament, but that same New Testament clearly witnessed to Peter's prominence.) Throughout the gospels Simon-Peter always heads the list of the Twelve; throughout the gospels and *Acts of the Apostles* he is their spokesman. Jesus had established him in a unique role, "Blessed are you, Simon…And I tell you, you are Peter [meaning Rock], and on this rock I will build my church, and the powers of death shall not prevail against it. I will give you the keys of the kingdom of heaven, and whatever you bind on earth shall be bound in heaven, and whatever you loose on earth shall be loosed in heaven" (Matt.16:17-19).

Did the pope continue that role? Was he, as Bishop of Rome, the successor to Peter? It struck me as intriguing that great Christian mystics - people who had encounters with God of a magnitude I can only imagine – answered yes. I am talking about people such as Francis of Assisi, Teresa of Avila, and John of the Cross - people admired by Christians of all denominations. Did the Holy Spirit, Who had opened so many other mysteries to them and empowered them to live lives of holiness even amidst corruption in the Church, mislead them on such an important matter?

Learning what the Church meant when it called the pope "infallible" certainly helped me feel more at ease too. It did not mean that the pope could not sin; that really had no bearing on the matter. Not every word that comes out of his mouth is "free of error" either. Rather, infallibility means that when the pope speaks a) in his official role as successor of the Apostle Peter, b) on a matter of *faith or morals,* and c) explicitly defines that what he is saying is an article of faith to be held by the entire Church, the Holy Spirit protects him from error. Such a papal statement is called *ex cathedra,* meaning "from the chair [of Peter]." The Catholic Church did not claim that the pope was infallible when delivering a Sunday sermon, expressing a personal opinion, nor when speaking on matters such as science or politics. His statements are regarded as infallible *only when* they meet the criteria outlined above.

Further, the Church does not teach that the Holy Spirit *inspires* the pope as He did the authors of Scripture, in the exact words he uses. The pope proclaims what the Spirit has brought him to through the usual channels of study. The Spirit does not force him to speak either; the pope could keep from saying what the Church needs to hear out of cowardice, for example. The doctrine of infallibility states that *when* the pope makes an *ex cathedra* pronouncement, the Holy Spirit protects him from teaching anything *false*. Another way to think of it is that the charism of infallibility is completely negative; it is about what the Spirit *prevents the pope from saying*. I cannot stress that enough.

So infallibility had to do with faith and morals, and I could understand Christianity's need. I still didn't feel bound to live by all of the Church and the pope's disciplinary measures. He had a necessary ministry, preserving the integrity of doctrine; but I didn't think that gave him the right to tell me how to pray or when to fast. What was the point in that – what did taking on all these observances have to do with living as a Christian? Being concerned with matters like that struck me as legalism, and wasn't that opposed to the freedom we are supposed to have in Christ?

The End of High School

Graduation finally arrived, and it stands out as an especially fond memory. My parents threw a party, letting me bring together my relatives, long-time friends of the family, and the adults and teens from God's Gang. Dad gave me a letter I still enjoy glancing at: "like another Father I can say that you are 'my beloved son in whom I'm well pleased.'"

Chapter 9 – Sharing Jesus' Passion in Our Dating and Marriage

High school dating had been a mixed bag. The early stages of relationships were always exhilarating: the flirtation, the thrill of a young lady being interested in me, planning the first date. Who doesn't enjoy that? It was the rest of the relationship that gave me trouble. I found things within myself that I never imagined were there.

When I developed feelings for someone they were deep. And usually dating young ladies from my prayer group, God was part of our relationship from the start. Besides all of the usual activities that bond couples, we prayed and even evangelized together. I knew how unique that was, how few young people there were who *could* share that, and I allowed that last point to skew my perspective.

I dated one young lady for a year and a half during high school. She truly cared for me, but was uneasy about labeling our relationship or making too deep of a commitment. Instead of just respecting where she was at and enjoying the time we spent together, I succumbed to this emotional "reflex" to latch on, to press to know exactly where I stood. With it came the question, "How could I share my heart with someone else the way I do with her?" I noticed that theme recurring in later dating relationships too.

On my part it was a lack of faith, and a lack of true love. Instead of trusting God to bring me together with the partner He had chosen, I let myself become consumed with questions like, "What if we're meant for each other, and she's missing it? What if we go our separate ways and never come back together?" Instead of fully loving those young ladies for themselves, I was also loving them for who they could be for me. And that is no way to love; I felt frustrated and so did they. I knew that as a Christian I was called to chastity; at the time I thought that just meant refraining from sex until I was married. But chastity isn't about what we hold back; it is how we give ourselves away.

The Virtue of Chastity

Chastity means, "having the strength to use your sexuality according to God's plan, whether you are single or married…Chastity is a virtue that defends love from selfishness and frees us from using others as objects. It makes us capable of authentic love."[137] Defined as such, chastity is at the very heart of the Gospel. Through the Spirit, Jesus empowers us, at any point in life, in any situation, to love others – to show forth His passion for them. In dating we give our attention, time, and kindness to the person we are involved with – in the knowledge that God is molding us for the future, bringing out the image of His Son that much clearer.

There is nothing to fear in dating. We may experience heartache as we, or our partner, feel called down different paths; but we have a God committed to our well-being. We will never be unloved. Despite our emotional state on a given day, the truth is that we exist within Love Himself. And in the end, we will see that all roads converge before our Father's throne. No relationship is lost, simply postponed for a brief time to be picked up again and deepened throughout eternity.

The Theology of the Body

The *Book of Revelation* ends with the "wedding feast of the Lamb," the consummation of Jesus' courtship of the Church. Like Jesus, many of us experience God's call to share our lives with a spouse. The Catholic Church recognizes the love of a Christian husband and wife as a unique participation in Jesus' spousal love for the Church:

> Husbands, love your wives, as Christ loved the church and gave himself up for her, that he might sanctify her...no man ever hates his own flesh, but nourishes and cherishes it, as Christ does the church, because we are members of his body.
>
> "For this reason a man shall leave his father and mother and be joined to his wife,
> and the two shall become one" [Gen.2:24].
>
> This is a *great mystery*, and I mean in reference to Christ and the church (Ephesians 5:25-26, 29-32).

A great *mystery* – a great *sacrament* in Latin. Because of Jesus' redemptive power, the marriage of Christians is *super*natural. Through their vows to love one another till death do them part, they become sacrament – a material conduit of Jesus' union with the Father and the Church. Let me say it

---

[137] Evert, Jason, *If You Really Love Me: 100 Questions on Dating, Relationships, and Sexual Purity.* (Ann Arbor, Michigan: Servant Publications, 2003), p.17

again, because of a Christian husband's fusion to Jesus, he becomes the Lord's unique, chosen instrument for expressing the Lord's sacrificial love to his wife. The wife, in turn, becomes a conduit of Jesus' love for her husband. They share in His "passion" in the truest sense of the word: through one, Jesus pours Himself out to the other and for the other, unconditionally. The struggles they inevitably face become their participation in the "passion" of Jesus' suffering and death.

The transformation of marriage into sacrament is at the center of Jesus' work of redemption. Remember what we saw in our discussion of humanity's creation in the image of the Trinity? The love between a husband and wife is meant to be a sharing of all they are. It is so real, so completely imbued with life, that it becomes its own person – a son or daughter. The human family is a reflection of the God Who is Love, the Three in One! It is written into our very bodies; man and woman were made for union.

This view, expounded in great depth by Pope John Paul II, has come to be known as the *Theology of the Body*. It calls us to recognize the implications of Jesus' Cross and Resurrection for married life, placing sexual expression within the context of living as images of God. Sex is meant to be an icon of both the Love between the Father and the Son, and a participation in Jesus' Love for the Church. In the sexual act a man and woman *say to each other*, through their bodies, "I am making a complete gift of myself – my body, fertility, mind, and heart – to you, until death parts us." This type of married love is only possible if it is animated by the Spirit, the very Love of God.

As we look at the world around us, perhaps even within us, we see how God's plan for married love has been hi-jacked. Our culture has become obsessed with sex but terrified of commitment. We have allowed Satan to twist our vision of sexuality. Sex without the marriage bond, sex in which our God-given, God-imaging fertility is eliminated, is a bodily lie.

Historically Christianity has focused so much on the lie, the perversion, that it neglected to teach the infinitely more powerful, beautiful Truth that sex is the husband and wife's way of imaging the Trinity. It is only when we have comprehended the magnificence of the original that we can recognize the counterfeits. The Truth is where the Church needs to begin her proclamation, in chastity and the *Theology of the Body*. With that in place, the flaws in the counterfeits of non-marital sex, contraceptive sex, cohabitation, di-

150 THE GOD WHO IS LOVE

vorce, and homosexuality become glaring. Christians cannot be motivated by the desire to condemn, but to bring others to the full experience of God's Life-giving Love. Consider the following:

Counterfeit #1, Contraception

Many Christians today never question the compatibility of such a choice with the Gospel. Historically speaking, however, believers have always seen it as incompatible with God's design, a conscious choice to eliminate human and Divine love's life-giving nature. We think of contraception as being a modern development, but it has existed for thousands of years. Medical papyri have been unearthed which describe contraceptive methods used in China in 2700 B.C. and in Egypt in 1850 B.C. A Greek physician, Soranos, writing circa 120 A.D., listed seventeen medically approved means.[138]

Right alongside this long history has been the protest of God's people. This opposition was ingrained throughout the thought of the Hebrew people. We see it in God's first directive to man and woman, "Be fruitful and multiply" (Gen.1:28). Children are always spoken of as a blessing from the Lord (Gen.4:1; 17:3; Ps.127:3-5; Ps.128:3-4).[139] Throughout Scripture, infertility is a condition to be overcome with the Lord's help. And finally, in *Genesis* we have the case of Onan, a practitioner of *coitus interuptus,* the pull-out method of contraception. The Lord manifested the gravity of his sin by requiring his life (Gen.38:6-10).[140]

In the New Testament we find the terms *pharmakos* and *pharmakeia,* translated into English as "sorcerer" and "sorcery," in lists of mortal sins (Gal.5:19-26; Rev.9:21; Rev.21:8). Listed with sexual sins, some scripture scholars conjecture that they are references to potions used as contracep-

---

[138] Saunders, William. "Contraceptive References in the Bible," *The Arlington Catholic Herald*, May 7, 2003. <http://www.catholicherald.com/saunders/03ws/ws030807.htm>
[139] Kresta, Al. *Why Do Catholics Genuflect?* (Ann Arbor, Michigan: Servant Publications, 2001) p.157.
[140] Modern interpreters try to negate the force of this passage by saying that Onan's sin was in refusing to raise up offspring in memory of his brother, a violation of the levirate law. The levirate law, a common practice in the Middle East, insuring "social stability for the widow and…descendants to continue the family line;"(Ibid, p.158). Onan's sin was two-fold, but death was not the punishment for violating the levirate law, *public humiliation was* (Deut.25:5-10). Onan's mortal sin was clearly contraception.

tives and abortificants. Does the *Didache* (written circa 70-120 A.D.) give an example of this?[141]: "You shall not murder. You shall not commit adultery. You shall not seduce boys. You shall not commit fornication. You shall not steal. You shall not practice magic. You shall not use potions. You shall not procure abortion, nor destroy a newborn child."[142]

Abhorrence to contraception is ingrained throughout the *whole* Christian tradition, as can be seen from the Protestant Reformers. John Calvin wrote:

> Deliberately avoiding the intercourse, so that the seed drops on the ground, is doubly horrible. For this means that one quenches the hope of his family, and kills the son, which could be expected, before he is born…When a woman in some way drives away the seed out of the womb, through aids, then this is rightly seen as an unforgivable crime. Onan was guilty of a similar crime, by defiling the earth with his seed, so that Tamar would not receive a future inheritor.[143]

Martin Luther's denunciation was just as strong:

> [T]he exceedingly foul deed of Onan, the basest of wretches . . . is a most disgraceful sin. It is far more atrocious than incest and adultery. We call it unchastity, yes, a sodomitic sin. For Onan goes in to her; that is, he lies with her and copulates, and when it comes to the point of insemination, spills the semen, lest the woman conceive. Surely at such a time the order of nature established by God in procreation should be followed. Accordingly, it was a most disgraceful crime . . . Consequently, he deserved to be killed by God. He committed an evil deed. Therefore, God punished him.[144]

The first Christian body to allow contraception was the Anglican Church. As late as its Lambeth Conference of 1920, it repeated the traditional Christian opposition, "We utter an emphatic warning against the use

---

[141] Saunders, William. "Contraceptive References in the Bible," *The Arlington Catholic Herald*, May 7, 2003. <http://www.catholicherald.com/saunders/03ws/ws030807.htm>
[142] Jurgens, William A. *The Faith of the Early Fathers*, Volume 1. (Collegeville, Minnesota: The Liturgical Press, 1970), p.2.
[143] Calvin, *Commentary on Genesis*
[144] Wolf, Aaron D. "Hating Babies, Hating God," *Chronicles*, June 2003. <http://www.chroniclesmagazine.org/Chronicles/June2003/0603Wolf.html>

of unnatural means for the avoidance of conception."[145] One decade later however, it reversed itself:

> ...in those cases where there is such a clearly felt moral obligation to limit or avoid parenthood, and where there is a morally sound reason for avoiding complete abstinence, the Conference agrees that other methods may be used...the Conference records its strong condemnation of the use of any methods of conception-control from motives of selfishness, luxury, or mere convenience.[146]

The outcry throughout the Christian world[147] was deafening: And yet, within a few decades contraception became the norm, and questions of conscience as to motives of "selfishness" and "convenience" went the way of the dinosaur.

By the time Pope Paul VI penned his encyclical *Of Human Life*, or *Humanae Vitae*, the Catholic Church was the last denomination publicly teaching this truth; and there were many bishops who wanted to see it fall by the wayside. In the face of this Paul VI, the Successor of Peter, stood up:

> We are obliged once more to declare that the direct interruption of the generative process already begun and, above all, all direct abortion, even for therapeutic reasons, are to be absolutely excluded as lawful

---

[145] Kippley, John F., *Sex and the Marriage Covenant: A Basis for Morality* (Cincinnati, OH: The Couple to Couple League International, Inc, 1991), p.324.
[146] Ibid.
[147] Not to mention the world at large:
> Sigmund Freud, the founder of modern psychoanalysis and an atheist, observed, "The abandonment of the reproductive function is the common feature of all perversions. We actually describe a sexual activity as perverse if it has given up the aim of reproduction and pursues the attainment of pleasure as an aim independent of it."
> ...Mohandas Gandi, the famous Indian nationalist leader and a Hindu insisted that contraceptive methods are "like putting a premium on vice. They make men and women reckless." He predicted that "nature is relentless and will have full revenge for any such violation of her laws. Moral results can only be produced by moral restraint...nothing but degradation can result...[contraception], no matter how well meaning the advocates may be, will still further degrade [women]."

Quotation taken from West, Christopher, *Good News About Sex and Marriage: Answers to Your Honest Questions about Catholic Teaching.* (Ann Arbor, Michigan: Servant Publications, 2000), p.119.

> means of regulating the number of children. Equally to be condemned…is direct sterilization, whether of the man or of the woman, whether permanent or temporary…Similarly excluded is any action which either before, at the moment of, or after sexual intercourse, is specifically intended to prevent procreation—whether as an end or as a means.
>
> …consider how easily this course of action could open wide the way for marital infidelity and a general lowering of moral standards. Not much experience is needed to be fully aware of human weakness and to understand that human beings—and especially the young, who are so exposed to temptation—need incentives to keep the moral law, and it is an evil thing to make it easy for them to break that law. Another effect that gives cause for alarm is that a man who grows accustomed to the use of contraceptive methods may forget the reverence due to a woman, and, disregarding her physical and emotional equilibrium, reduce her to being a mere instrument for the satisfaction of his own desires, no longer considering her as his partner whom he should surround with care and affection.[148]

Talk about prophetic! Since the proliferation of contraceptives the number of teenage mothers has skyrocketed, as have sexually transmitted diseases, abortion, and divorce. Why? Because contraceptives have divorced fertility from love; for the Western world they no longer go hand in hand. And once pregnancy was removed as the natural end of the act, responsibility went into a tail-spin.

This is not to say that married couples may not have valid reasons for wishing to avoid conception at certain times. God designed the female body with periods of fertility and infertility. For a husband and wife to exercise self-control during periods of fertility, refraining from intercourse, is not "contraceptive." It is not trying to frustrate the life-giving nature of love. On the contrary, exercising self-control in such a case is an expression of love. In *Humanae Vitae* Pope Paul VI wrote, "It is particularly desirable

---

[148] Pope Paul VI, *Humanae Vitae (On the Regulation of Birth)*,, (July 25, 1968), n.17. <http://www.vatican.va/holy_father/paul_vi/encyclicals/documents/hf_p-vi_enc_25071968_humanae-vitae_en.html>

that…medical science succeed in providing a sufficiently secure basis for a regulation of birth, founded on the observance of natural rhythms."[149]

Such methods go under the name of Natural Family Planning. By paying attention to the consistency of cervical mucous, basal body temperature, etc., a couple learn to identify the wife's periods of fertility and infertility. There are different methods: Sympto-Thermal, Creighton, Billings; but all have been found to be highly effective at postponing pregnancy – 97% accuracy, the same "success rate" as the birth control pill. Natural family planning, however, doesn't try to eliminate God's right to "intervene" in the couple's love-making and bestow the gift of a child.

Counterfeit #2, Non-Marital Sex and Cohabitation

Sex is being engaged in by men and women with no true guarantee they will be there tomorrow. Human beings are not wired that way. We have said time and again that sex is the body's expression of life-long, loving commitment. It creates a bond between people. This is true from the biological standpoint. The female brain releases oxytocin, a hormone creating a strong emotional attachment.[150] A number of psychologists even speak of "imprinting;" the phenomena of a woman's first sexual partner becoming imprinted on her mind in a permanent way – resulting in feelings of attachment even years after a break.[151]

Sex with multiple partners tends to cripple this bonding process. Each time a relationship ends the two partners become a little more scarred, a little more calloused; sex loses some of its bonding power.[152]

Cohabitation, living together, trying out your compatibility prior to marriage, seems like a step in the right direction – but that is the ingenious part of the deception. In fact, "couples who cohabit before marriage have a divorce rate of about eighty percent."[153] Surveys show that when compared

---

[149] Ibid, n.24.
[150] Bonaci, Mary Beth, *Real Love*. (San Francisco: Ignatius Press, 1996), p.32-33.
[151] Ibid, p.86.
[152] Ibid, p.84. Bonacci goes on to give the analogy of a piece of duct tape: the first time you stick it to your arm and rip it off there's pain; but repeated time and again the pain gradually lessens to non-existence as the tape loses its stickiness.
[153] Evert, Jason, *If You Really Loved Me*, (Ann Arbor, Michigan: Servant Publications, 2003), p.87.

to peers who did not cohabitate prior to marriage, cohabitating couples report "greater marital conflict and poorer communication, and they made more frequent visits to marriage counselors."[154] Cohabitation sets people up for failure:

> The desire to "test drive" a marriage demonstrates a lack of understanding regarding what makes a marriage work. It also shows a real lack of faith in one's love for the other. In one sense, the couple is saying that they desire intimacy, but on the other hand they want to leave a way out if the partner does not measure up. This sows seeds of doubt and distrust from the start…successful marriages are not the result of a lack of annoying qualities in the other; they are the result of choosing to love and forgive the other daily, with all of his or her imperfections. It is the ability to sacrifice that holds marriages together…[155]

"The love required for the sacrament of marriage demands a profound purity, humility, selflessness, honesty, trust, and willingness to sacrifice that can be established *only* by embracing the virtue of chastity – that is, lived respect for the truth and meaning of sexuality outside *and within* marriage."[156]

Counterfeit #3, Homosexual Behavior

Before I say anything else I want to make a sharp distinction between experiencing same-sex attraction and engaging in homosexual acts. Attraction is not under a person's conscious control, *but behavior is*. As we said in our discussion of creation, man and woman differ from other animals precisely in their soul's ability to integrate and channel instincts and drives so as to love in imitation of God. To do this with any kind of consistency, however, our souls need the strength of the Spirit.

Homosexual attraction does not have to be acted upon. However the attraction originated, its expression is in direct conflict with God's design. Obviously our culture is re-thinking its view of homosexual behavior, but

---

[154] Ibid, p.88.
[155] Ibid, pp.88-89.
[156] West, Christopher, *Good News About Sex and Marriage*, (Ann Arbor, Michigan: Servant Publications, 2000), p.72.

even as late as 1973, it was recognized as a disorder by the American Psychiatric Association. God doesn't reverse Himself though. His will regarding sexual union is written into our very bodies; it is male and female. A homosexual couple may come together "freely," may choose to be monogamous, but fruitfulness is an impossibility. Sexual expression closed to life is a contradiction. Everything about human design argues against homosexual expression. For those for whom this isn't enough, God communicated His intention to the shepherds of His people.[157]

Opposition to homosexual behavior, however, must never give way to personal condemnations or mistreatment. "The number of men and women who have homosexual tendencies is not negligible. They do not choose their homosexual condition; for most it is a trial. They must be accepted with respect, compassion, and sensitivity. Every sign of unjust discrimination in their regard should be avoided" (CCC 2358). Just as other persons who struggle with challenging psychological and/or genetic conditions, homosexual persons "are called to fulfill God's will in their lives and, if they are Christians, to unite to the sacrifice of the Lord's Cross the difficulty they may encounter from their condition" (CCC 2358).

Counterfeit #4 – Divorce and Remarriage among Christians

This counterfeit is particularly difficult to talk about because of the pain and circumstances that often lead to divorce: extramarital affairs and abuse (both mental and physical). I would not dare to say, nor would the popes and bishops, that there are not cases where, for the well-being of one or both spouses, a separation needs to occur - maybe a permanent separation; but this a long way from saying that the spouses are no longer married.

---

[157] The Apostle Paul wrote, "Do not be deceived; neither the immoral...nor adulterers nor homosexuals...will inherit the kingdom of God" (1 Cor.6:9-10). This thought was repeated by Paul in 1 Tim.1:10. He explained the reason behind such dire consequences: it is a rejection of God and His design of love: "God gave them up to dishonorable passions. Their women exchanged natural relations for unnatural, and the men likewise gave up natural relations with women and were consumed with passion for one another, men committing shameful acts with men and receiving in their own persons the due penalty for their error" (Rom.1:25-27).

Whenever two Christians have pledged themselves to one another, become sacramental conduits of Jesus' love for the Church, that bond exists for life; only the death of one of them can end its exclusivity. A state court may issue a decree of divorce, but it cannot dissolve the sacramental bond; in God's eyes the two are still united. "Remarriage," in such a situation, is not possible:

> Pharisees came up and in order to test him asked, "Is it lawful for a man to divorce his wife?" [Jesus] answered them, "What did Moses command you?" They said, "Moses allowed a man to write a certificate of divorce, and to put her away." But Jesus said to them, "For your hardness of heart he wrote you this commandment. But from the beginning of creation, 'God made them male and female.' 'For this reason a man will leave his father and mother and be joined to his wife, and the two will become one.' So they are no longer two, but one. What therefore God has joined together, let no man put assunder." And in the house the disciples asked him again about this matter. And he said to them, "Whoever divorces his wife and marries another, commits adultery against her; and if she divorces her husband and marries another, she commits adultery" (Mark 10:2-12).

Divorce and remarriage were tolerated by God up until the time of Jesus, the time of restoration – even though He had already begun to express his displeasure with it through the prophets (Malachi 2:13-16).[158] After Jesus' ascension, with the coming of the Holy Spirit, God's people were supernaturally empowered to live in His image – constant, faithful, life-giving love.

Granted, there are Christian churches that allow divorce and remarriage, citing the parallel passage in *Matthew* :

> And Pharisees came up to him and tested him by asking, "Is it lawful to divorce one's wife for any cause?...Why then did Moses command one to give a certificate of divorce, and to put her away?"
> [Jesus] said to them "For your hardness of heart Moses allowed you to divorce your wives, but from the beginning it was not so. And I say to

---

[158] "So take heed to yourselves, and let none be faithless to the wife of his youth. 'For I hate divorce, says the LORD the God of Israel'" (Malachi 2:15-16).

you: whoever divorces his wife, *except for unchastity*, and marries another, commits adultery; and he who marries a divorced woman, commits adultery"

The disciples said to him, "If such is the case of a man with his wife, it is not expedient to marry." But he said to them, "Not all men can receive this precept, but only those to whom it has been given...for there are eunuchs who have made themselves eunuchs for the sake of the kingdom of heaven. He who is able to receive this, let him receive it" (Matt.19:3,7-12).

Doesn't this passage offer an exception to what seemed like the absolute prohibition on divorce in Mark's Gospel? Wouldn't an act of adultery, unchastity in this passage, break the marriage bond? I maintain that it does not – not when analyzed linguistically and contextually.

The term translated here as "unchastity" is *porneia* in Greek. At the time of Jesus one usage of the term was in reference to incestuous marriages. While such unions did not occur in Judaism (Leviticus 18:18-29), they did in the surrounding Gentile cultures – the very cultures that the Christian Church was expanding into when Mark and Matthew wrote. With these people's acceptance of the Gospel would have come the recognition that their "marriages" were not valid before God. Matthew's "exception" needs to be taken in context too; look at the conclusion the disciples drew from Jesus' words, "If such is the case of a man with his wife, it is not expedient to marry." The bond between husband and wife is *so unalterable*, and marriage therefore requires *so much work*, that the disciples concluded it was better to just never take the plunge! Jesus reminded them however that it is only by God's grace, that a husband and wife can live out the marriage covenant. Now what sense would that exchange between the disciples and Jesus make if the marriage could be voided simply by one of the spouses cheating? It wouldn't. No, Jesus' prohibition of divorce and remarriage, recorded in *Mark*, was an absolute prohibition and our English translations of *Matthew* faulty.

"Porneia" and this issue of the *invalidity* of certain marriages does bring up another topic however, what the Catholic Church calls an annulment – the recognition that the Sacrament of Marriage never took place. Taking its cue from Jesus, the Church distinguishes between sacramental and legal marriages. Two Christians could profess vows to one another, but if one of them interiorly had no intention of remaining faithful or of being open to children, then God did not unite the two If one of the spouses were emotionally or physically coerced into marriage the same would be true. Without an investigation into the particulars, the Catholic Church operates under the assumption that a marriage between baptized Christians, Catholic or not, is sacramental. Before someone could "remarry" in the Catholic Church he/she would have to go through a process of showing why the first marriage was not a sacrament. The Church would then issue an annulment, a statement that the first marriage may have been binding legally, but not sacramentally.

A Word to Victims of Divorce

I've seen divorce up close, and I know how tragic it can be. I also know that, like all tragedy, God is capable of taking it and using it to mold us into the image of His Son. "If God is for us, who can be against us?... In all these things we are more than conquerors through him who loved us" (Romans 8:31,37). Just as the Cross was the moment when Jesus' lifetime of Love for the Father, and for us, was brought to its greatest height ("Father forgive them, for they know not what they do...into Your hands I commit My spirit), so too can be these periods in our own lives: "Now for a little while you may have to suffer various trials, so that the genuiness of your faith, more precious than gold which though perishable is tested by fire, may redound to praise and glory and honor at the revelation of Jesus Christ" (1 Peter 1:6-7). How will we react to the trial? Will we break under its weight, or will we call out to God, again and again, for the strength to act as Jesus would? Kindness in response to another's kindness is easy; what about keeping an even-head and responding charitably when your soon-to-be-ex is shouting at you? To desire the best for someone else when he or she is making declarations of love is one thing, but to continue to desire good for them after they have betrayed and rejected you, is quite another. I'm not telling you to be a doormat; sometimes the most loving thing to do will be to take a hard, unyielding stand on an issue. At other times you will need to hold back and allow them to experience the difficult circumstances of the "new life" they've chosen for themselves (in the hope that it will wake them up to the wrongness of their decision).

The cross of an unwanted divorce calls for tremendous virtue, heroic virtue. It does not mean that you are a failure. Sure, you could have been a better wife or husband in some ways— that's true for everyone, it's a tough vocation! You asked your spouse again and again to work this out, to begin the healing process, but instead of embracing his or her own cross and working through their period of unhappiness and disillusionment, they "ran." Don't you do the same. Allow Jesus, the Faithful Spouse, to mold you. No one knows the pain of betrayal by a loved one better than Him. But He was not crippled by it; He did not, does not, cease to love and desire good for us when we, His spouse, are unfaithful. "If we are faithless, he remains faithful – for he cannot deny himself" (2 Timothy 2:13.) He continues to desire our good and a return to union – even if it has to be through a period of chastisement.

So if you are a Christian, who has been divorced by your spouse, by all means look into the annulment process. If it is found that your marriage was not sacramental, continue to grow in Christ and remain open to the possibility that God wants to bring you into a sacramental marriage with one of His children. If, through the annulment process, you find that your marriage was in fact a sacrament; then call out to God for the grace to live Jesus' tenacious, forgiving, challenging Love in your unique situation. Go on with your life, but continue to pray for your spouse's conversion and return to the grace of matrimony. Whether your spouse opens himself or herself to the Lord or not though, God is going to mold you into the image of His Son – He didn't want this divorce any more than you did, but He'll sure make use of it to deepen your holiness.

Finding My Bride

When I went away to college I started trading letters with one of my female friends from the youth group. She was incredibly intuitive; she really seemed to get me. I started looking forward to getting together with her on breaks. A couple of months and we had a long-distance romance going. After three more years of distance I finished school, moved back to St. Louis and was finally able to begin life with my bride.

I write these words nine years and two beautiful children later, and can personally testify to the fact that God works through wives and husbands, fathers and mothers, in sickness and in health, both when rich and when poor. My wife has manifested Christ Jesus to me, and God has made our love life-giving! But I'm getting a little ahead of myself, let me back up.

Chapter 10 – College: Friendships Inside and "Outside" the Church

Even though college meant being away from the girl I loved, it was an amazing experience. And the reason for that, pure and simple, were the friends I made and the lessons God taught me through them.

We usually don't think of dorm assignments being providential, but they were. I found myself surrounded by a great bunch of guys: funny, loyal, self-deprecating, adventurous, compassionate. We ate together, hit clubs, went to concerts; we even found time to study. And we talked about God – Catholics, Baptist, Presbyterian, non-denominational Christian, Jew, and agnostic. We shared, we asked questions, and some of us even prayed and studied Scripture together. Our little group came to be known as the Tribe, but to me they were brothers.

Incarnational Spirituality

I made a point of visiting many different campus ministries, but the Newman [Catholic] Student Center was where I plugged in. Initially I helped with an outreach to high school youth. By the spring of freshman year a small charismatic prayer group formed; I was a member throughout my time at school.

The thread that seemed to run throughout my spiritual reading at the time, including my reading of the Old Testament prophets, was the Incarnation. I refer not so much to the Son of God's conception in the womb of Mary as to what it set in motion - the enfleshing of the Son within you and me, within His Body, the Church.

I began to ponder the "mystery" of the Church. I started to notice things in Scripture I had not before:

> "[The Father] has put all things under [Christ's] feet and has made him the head over all things for the church, which is his body, *the fullness of him who fills all in all*" (Ephesians 1:22-23).

> [Jesus'] gifts were that some should be apostles, some prophets, some evangelists, some pastors and teachers, for the equipment of the saints, for the work of ministry, for building up the body of Christ, until we all attain to the unity of the faith and of the knowledge of the Son of

God, to mature manhood, to *the measure of the stature of the fullness of Christ* (Ephesians 4:11-13).

What? In God's eternal plan the Church is "the fullness" of Christ? If it wasn't Scripture, I would have called it blasphemy. But yes, the God Who is Love has always intended to enmesh us in the Person of His Son – for humanity to form one great Mystical Person with Jesus as its Head. The Father's heart is set upon Jesus *and His Church*, Jesus *and His Bride* – the two are inseparable.

This truth was hammered into the Apostle Paul from the beginning. When Jesus knocked him from his horse, He didn't ask Paul why he was persecuting the Church but, "why do you persecute *me*?" (Acts 9:4). The thought reached a crescendo in Paul's *First Letter to the Corinthians*, "you are the body of Christ, and individually members of it"(1 Cor.12:27); and allowed him to reach out in hope when disciples fell short, "if we are faithless, [Jesus] remains faithful - for he cannot deny himself" (2 Timothy 2:13). The Gospel could be summed up as "this mystery, *which is Christ in you*, the hope of glory" (Colossians 1:27).

As we have seen, Jesus' ascension was not the end of His earthly ministry but a change in *mode* (Acts 1:1). Instead of speaking to the world with the lips He received from Mary, He speaks through ours. He uses our feet to seek the lost, our hands to meet needs and communicate healing. We are His physical presence; that is why He could tell the Apostles "He who hears you hears me" (Luke 10:16). That is why, when the early Church faced a crisis, Peter, the Apostles, and presbyters could gather in council, pray, debate, and then pronounce, "It is the decision of the Holy Spirit, and ours too…" (Acts 15:28). Jesus told them, "He who receives you receives me, and he who receives me receives him who sent me" (Matt 10:40); "he who believes in me will also do the works that I do; and greater works than these will he do, because I go to the Father…and He will give you…the Spirit of truth" (John 14:12,16-17).

The Church of Christ Jesus, frail human beings animated by the Spirit of God, is central to the Father's plan for giving life to the world. Hadn't that been the case in my own life? What had Jesus given me that He had not used members of His Church to deliver? He brought me to baptism through my parents; gave me the books of Scripture through countless authors and editors; fed me in the Eucharist and healed my sin through the ministry of His priests; taught me through youth ministers and writers. Even the experience of seeing Him weep for me was joined to those words from my dad. "The Word became flesh and dwelt among us" (John 1:14); the Word *continues to become flesh* and dwell among us!

Again, recall how Jesus described the final judgment. The criteria is simple, and the point unmistakable:

> I was hungry and you gave me food, I was thirsty and you gave me drink, I was a stranger and you welcomed me, I was naked and you clothed me, I was sick and you visited me, I was in prison and you came to me... Truly, I say to you, as you did it to one of the least of these my brethren, you did it to me... [and] as you did it not to one of the least of these, you did it not to me" (Matthew 25:35-36, 40, 45).

For we Christians Heaven and eternal life are synonymous for union with Jesus. Look at the curve the Lord throws us though by making the men and women who surround us His "skin." The acts of love - or of rejection - we show to others *are shown to Him*. If I neglect Christ when He is in need, if I ignore Him out of self-centeredness, if I lash out at Him in frustration – if I mistreat Him *in His Church* then what good are my pious sentiments? This is the union Jesus has with His People. We are parts of His Body, and because of this, part of each other.

Healing the Breaks

This is what makes the divisions in Christianity such a scandal. Almost from the beginning, sin impinged on the Body's unity:

> I appeal to you, brethren, by the name of our Lord Jesus Christ, that all of you agree and that there be no dissensions among you, but that you be united in the same mind and the same judgment. For it has been reported to me...that there is quarreling among you...What I mean is that each of you says, "I belong to Paul," or "I belong to Apollos," or "I belong to Cephas," or "I belong to Christ." Is Christ divided? Was Paul crucified for you? (1 Corinthians 1: 10-13).

We could easily substitute the names of other Christian leaders and groups: "I follow Luther;" "I'm with Calvin;" "I think John Wesley had it right;" "I belong to the Baptist church;" "I'm a Roman Catholic;" "I'm with the Disciples of Christ."

Nothing could be more foreign to the heart of Christ Jesus. His prayer the night before He died was:

> [Father], I do not pray for [my apostles] only, but also for those who [will] believe in me through their word, that they may all be one; *even as thou, Father, art in me, and I in thee*, that they also may be in us, so that the world may believe that thou has sent me. The glory which thou hast given me I have given to them, that they may be one even as we are one, I in them and thou in me, that they may become perfectly one, so that the world may know that thou has sent me and hast loved them as thou hast loved me. (John 17: 20-23).

The unity of the Trinity - that is Jesus' prayer for the Church. It is a gift for the Church herself, but it is also meant to shine forth and attract the rest of the world. That is what drove the Apostle Paul to write:

> [Be] eager to maintain the unity of the Spirit in the bond of peace. There is one body and one Spirit, just as you were called to the one hope that belongs to your call, one Lord, one faith, one baptism, one God and Father of us all. . .
>
> [Jesus'] gifts were that some should be apostles, some prophets, some evangelists, some pastors and teachers, for the equipment of the saints, for the work of ministry, for building up the body of Christ, until we all attain to the unity of the faith and of the knowledge of the Son of God, to mature manhood, to *the measure of the stature of the fullness of Christ*...from whom the whole body, joined and knit together by every joint with which it is supplied, *when each part is working properly*, makes bodily growth and upbuilds itself in love (Ephesians 4: 3-6; 15-16).

So long as we are a broken Body, Christ does not "come to full stature." His mission is impeded and the world kept at a distance.

How to achieve the reunification of the thousands of Christian groups in the world is completely beyond me. It has to be the action of the Spirit, God Himself. And praise God that that is what we have been seeing these past 50 years! Just as in the early Church, so too today, the ordained shepherds, the successors to Peter and the Apostles, have gathered in council,

Vatican Council II. They debated, prayed, and discerned the Spirit's lead (Acts 15:28). One the Spirit's words to the Catholic Church concerned His thirst for unity:

> The restoration of unity among all Christians is one of the principal concerns of the Second Vatican Council. Christ the Lord founded one Church and one Church only[159]… But in subsequent centuries much more serious dissensions made their appearance and quite large communities came to be separated from full communion with the Catholic Church – for which, often enough, men of both sides were to blame (Decree on Ecumenism, 1,3). [160]

The Catholic Church walks the fine line of confessing that it is the continuation of the Church which Jesus "commissioned Peter to shepherd…governed by the successor of Peter and the Bishops in communion with him," while acknowledging that "many elements of sanctification and truth are found outside its visible structure."[161]

> The Church recognizes that in many ways she is linked with those who, being baptized, are honored with the name of Christian, though they do not profess the faith in its entirety or do not preserve unity of communion with the successor of Peter. For there are many who honor Sacred Scripture, taking it as a norm of belief and a pattern of life, and who show a sincere zeal…They are consecrated by baptism, in which they are united with Christ. They also recognize and accept other sacraments within their own Churches or ecclesiastical communities…They also share with us in prayer and other spiritual benefits. Likewise we can say that in some real way they are joined with us in the Holy Spirit, for to them too He gives His gifts and graces whereby

---

[159] The Catholic Church teaches that Christ founded *only one Church*. When the Apostles established local groups of believers, or churches, they were understood "as local units of the one, universal Church of Jesus Christ." The Apostle Paul wrote to "'the church *in* Philippi,' or 'the church *in* Corinth' to underscore that they were local expressions of the one, universal (or 'catholic) Church of Christ," Schreck, Allen, *Catholic and Christian* (Ann Arbor, Michigan: Servant Publications, 1989), p.56.
[160] < http://www.vatican.va/archive/hist_councils/ii_vatican_council/documents/vat-ii_decree_19641121_unitatis-redintegratio_en.html>
[161] < http://www.vatican.va/archive/hist_councils/ii_vatican_council/documents/vat-ii_const_19641121_lumen-gentium_en.html>

> He is operative among them with His sanctifying power.. (*Dogmatic Constitution on the Church*, 15).[162]
>
> The Sacred Council exhorts all the Catholic faithful to recognize the signs of the times and to take an active and intelligent part in the work of ecumenism…Catholics, in their ecumenical work, must assuredly be concerned for their separated brethren, praying for them…making the first approaches toward them…Nor should we forget that anything wrought by the grace of the Holy Spirit in the hearts of our separated brethren can be a help to our own edification. Whatever is truly Christian is never contrary to what genuinely belongs to the faith; indeed, it can always bring a deeper realization of the mystery of Christ and the Church. (*Decree on Ecumenism*, 4).[163]

This movement of the Spirit has already borne great fruits - the Lutheran World Federation and the Roman Catholic Church's *Joint Declaration on Justification* (1999) to name but one.

Not being a part of the international scene however, I asked the Spirit to use me right there on campus. I tried to hold every Christian I knew on an equal footing - visiting various campus ministries and getting to know the people there. Sometimes I spent Sunday mornings with a couple of guys from "the Tribe," church-hopping – worshiping with our Baptist, Methodist, Presbyterian, and Lutheran brothers and sisters. I was surprised by how closely the order of the ceremony mirrored the Mass, especially among the Missouri Synod Lutherans. It made sense though: from an historical standpoint the denominations I visited could be traced back through the branches of Reformation history to the Catholic. Not only did I visit other denominations, but my friends would also join me for Mass. In addition to my involvement at the Catholic student center (Newman), I joined my buddies for a Bible study sponsored by the Baptist Student Union.

The guys in the Tribe could say anything to each other; but when beginning to interact with most other Christians, I tried to keep the sharing on common ground. We talked about God's activity in our lives – answers to

---

[162] < http://www.vatican.va/archive/hist_councils/ii_vatican_council/documents/vat-ii_const_19641121_lumen-gentium_en.html>.
[163] < http://www.vatican.va/archive/hist_councils/ii_vatican_council/documents/vat-ii_decree_19641121_unitatis-redintegratio_en.html>

prayer, the changes He had worked (or was trying to work) in our outlook and behavior, evangelism. As we grew to know each other better though, we were able to talk about the points where we differed – respectfully, calmly. I will never forget when one young woman shared how, until getting to know me, she'd "never realized that a Catholic could be a Christian." I was happy to be able to open her eyes but sad to find out she had Catholics *within her own family*.

I felt good about this grass-roots type of ecumenism. If there is to be formal reconciliation, there have to be personal reconciliations, concrete manifestations of our family bond. Christian friends and neighbors need to see in each other what God sees in them. Our bonds of friendship can grow into bonds of prayer and facilitate the mutual understanding needed among denominations.

The Mystery Deepens...

As I said before, the Tribe wasn't made up of only Christians. I experienced brotherhood – the sharing of work, play, successes, and even deep pain – with men who did not recognize Jesus as the Way to the Father. And yet, they loved me. I mean *really* loved me; I could have asked them for anything, and if it was even remotely in their power, they would have come through. I found this kind of love exceptional, even among Christians. I could not explain it except to wonder if the God Who *is Love* had somehow come into their lives too. In loving me, hadn't they loved Jesus "in the least of His brothers" (Matt.25:35-45)? Could Jesus have somehow joined them to Himself without their even knowing it?

Yan was a member of the Tribe I felt especially close to. He had grown up as a Ukrainian Jew under Soviet rule and knew religious persecution first hand. He had immigrated to New York at age twelve and lived in a Hassidic[164] neighborhood for a time. Investigating his Jewish heritage meant a great deal to him, and lucky for me, he let me share it with him. I was invited to Rosh Hashanah (New Year) and Passover and was able to help him start a chapter of Hillel on our campus, a group for Jewish students. We even studied some of *Exodus* together.

---

[164] Strict, Orthodox Judaism.

We discussed Jesus quite a bit too. For Yan the thought of becoming a Christian was impossible though; in his mind it would be a betrayal of all the men and women who died *as Jews* in the Holocaust and then under Soviet persecution. That said, you can imagine how shocked I was one Sunday morning when, after finishing breakfast, he joined me for Mass. For me to celebrate Jewish feasts was one thing (because Jesus and His first disciples celebrated them, I considered them part of my heritage); but for my friend to attend Mass (mind you, he didn't join in the prayers) was an amazing show of his affection for me. It has been fun over the years, hearing subtle shifts in the way he speaks of the Christian, and in particular the Catholic, Faith. I can tell that while he doesn't agree with it, he respects it. He will kid me, "Any religion that thinks a Jewish man is God can't be all bad."

There was another member of the Tribe who made me do a lot of thinking. He was the one guy that initially I did not see myself becoming close to because of the stories he told and some of the remarks he made. (Which, given the words and innuendos that have/do come out of my mouth, was extremely hypocritical.) It didn't take me long to find out the size of his heart though: loyal, trusting, generous, hard-working, thoughtful. His friendship is one of the most valued of my entire life. He was not committed to a particular faith, but when you got him into a serious conversation he would let slip these spiritual jewels. I didn't think he had reached a firm decision as to who Jesus was; but there was an obvious depth to him and that, coupled with his treatment of others, compelled me to think that God was already at work in his soul. He seemed interiorly oriented toward loving Jesus "in the least of his brothers and sisters." The question had to be asked – what if he never came to an explicit recognition of Jesus as God the Son?[165]

...and the Circle Widens (the Salvation of Non-Christians)
The message of the New Testament seemed crystal clear: union with Jesus is the only way to overcome the damage of sin and attain union with the Father. "I am the way, and the truth, and the life; no one comes to the Father, but by me" (John 14:6).

---

[165] In time he did; both he and his wife call the Catholic Church home.

The Apostle Peter taught that, "there is salvation in no one else, for there is no other name under heaven given among men by which we must be saved" (Acts 4:12). Jesus had sent Peter and the Apostles with the mission, "Go into the whole world and proclaim the good news to all creation. The man who believes in it and accepts baptism will be saved; the man who refuses will be condemned" (Mark 16:15-16, NIV). So wouldn't all non-Christians stand condemned? There are Christians who answer "yes," and stop right there.

I, and many other Christians, however, have reached a different conclusion. The above passages cannot be treated superficially; they require a great deal of consideration. Take the last for instance, "the man who refuses [baptism] will be condemned" (Mk.16:16, NIV). First, what does it mean to "refuse" baptism? Wouldn't a true refusal necessitate an understanding of what was being offered - being convinced as to the truth of the Gospel, the need for baptism, *and then* refusing it? Second, what about the hundreds of millions throughout history, both before and after the coming of Jesus, who have lived and died without hearing His name? God loved them and brought them into being; surely He provided a way for them to participate in the salvation Jesus brings. What about the mentally handicapped who are unable to comprehend the Gospel or give adult consent to baptism? What about those who have never given the Gospel a fair hearing because of the evil perpetrated by those calling themselves Christian? Surely God, the God Who *is Love*, will look at all these with eyes of compassion, for He "desires all men to be saved and to come to the knowledge of the truth" (1 Timothy 2:4). I believe Scripture and Tradition give us sufficient reason to hope, but it will require patience of us if we wish to hear them speak.

We begin in the Old Testament, where we find examples of individuals outside the People of God, outside the usual channel of blessing, who were nonetheless pleasing to the Lord.[166] In *Genesis* we find Melchizedek, the king-priest of Salem, who blessed Abraham and offered a thanksgiving sacrifice of bread and wine on his behalf (12:18-20). Speaking of this event, Scripture says, "it is beyond dispute that the inferior is blessed by the supe-

---

[166] For this reminder I owe thanks to Depuis, Jacques, *Toward a Christian Theology of Religious Pluralism* (Maryknoll, New York: Orbis Books, 1997), pp. 36-37.

rior" (Hebrews 7:7). Melchizedek – greater than Abraham! Then there is the character of Job, the man tested through suffering. Even though he was not descended from Abraham or living under the Mosaic covenant, God boasted that "there is none like him on the earth, a blameless and upright man, who fears God and turns away from evil" (Job 1:8).[167]

Then in the very first chapters of the New Testament we encounter the Magi, the astrologers who followed the light of a star to the Christ-child. "Did not their religion kneel before Christ, as it were, in their persons, recognizing itself as provisional...as proceeding toward Christ?"[168]

The Apostle Paul made statements that cry out for consideration. When speaking to the people of Athens, Greece, he built upon their *already-existing* religious impulses:

> I note that in every way you are very religious. For as I passed along and observed the objects of your worship, I found also an altar with this inscription, "To an unknown god." What therefore you worship as unknown, this I proclaim to you. The God who made the world and everything in it, being Lord of heaven and earth, does not live in shrines made by man, nor is he served by human hands, as though he needed anything, since he himself gives to all men life and breath and everything. And he made from one every nation of men to live on all the face of the earth, *having determined allotted periods and the boundaries of their habitation, that they should seek God, in the hope that they might feel after him and find him.* Yet he is not far from each one of us, for
>
> "In him we live and move and have our being;"
> as even *some of your poets* have said,
> "For we are indeed his offspring."

And then, moving from this already-existing foundation of nature and culture (note the quotation of the poets Epimenides and Aratus).[169] Paul chal-

---

[167] The majority of Scripture scholars view the *Book of Job* as an extended parable, not history. That doesn't impact the point made here, however – the character of Job is that of a non-Israelite who is nonetheless a friend of God.
[168] Ratzinger, Joseph, *Truth and Tolerance: Christian Belief and World Religions.* (San Francisco: Ignatius Press, 2003), p.20.
[169] Ibid, pp.49-50.

lenged them to give up the distortions in their belief and come further into the truth:

> Being then God's offspring, we ought not to think that the Deity is like gold, or silver, or stone, a representation by the art and imagination of man. The times of ignorance God overlooked, but now he commands all men everywhere to repent, because he has fixed a day on which he will judge the world in righteousness by a man whom he has appointed, and of this he has given assurance to all men by raising him from the dead (Acts 17:22-31).

We find parallels to Paul's thought in Athens expressed in his *Letter to the Romans*. First, that nature serves as part of God's revelation, "what can be known about God is plain to them [the Gentiles, pagans], because God has shown it to them. Ever since the creation of the world his invisible nature, namely his eternal power and deity, has been clearly perceived in the things that have been made (Romans 1:19-20). And second, an echo of the idea that the Gentiles were to "seek God, in the hope that they might feel after him and find him":

> When Gentiles who do not have the law keep it as by instinct, these men although without the law serve as a law for themselves. They show that the demands of the law are written in their hearts. Their conscience bears witness together with that law, and their thoughts will accuse or defend them on the day when, in accordance with the gospel I preach, God will pass judgment on the secrets of men through Christ Jesus (Romans 2:14-15).

The prologue in the *Gospel of John* forms a nice complement to Paul's thought. John tells us that, "in the beginning was the Word [*Logos* in Greek], and the Word was with God, and the Word was God... all things were made through him" (John 1:1,3). The Word is "the true light that enlightens *every* man" (John 1:9). John's expression, inspired by the Spirit, formed a bridge between Jewish and Greek thought. For the Jew, God's powerful word had brought all things into being (Genesis 1). The Greeks, beginning with Heraclitus in the sixth century B.C., "asserted that the world is governed by a firelike Logos, a divine force that produces the order and pattern discernible in the flux of nature;" human reason was thought to "partake of the divine Logos."[170] John's prologue shows God the Son as the Divine Word-Logos through whom the Father first created man and woman in the image of the Trinity, *as well as the light continuing to shine on their intellect*, so that as Paul said, they can "seek God, in the hope that they might feel after him and find him!"

Paul and John's insights were not lost on the early Church. Some of its brightest minds, Justin Martyr and Cyril of Alexandria, picked up these threads. Justin, already quoted when we discussed the *Book of Revelation*, wrote (c.160 A.D.):

> We have been taught that Christ is the first begotten of God, and have previously testified that he is the Logos of which every race of humans partakes. Those who have lived in accordance with the Logos are Christians, even though they were called godless, such as, among the Greeks Socrates and Heraclitus and others like them…so also those who lived contrary to the Logos were ungracious and enemies to Christ (*First Apology* XLVI, 1-4).[171]

The Letter to the Hebrews tells us that, "without faith, it is impossible to please [God]. For whoever would draw near to God must believe that he exists and that he rewards those who seek him" (11:6). This was the faith operative among the Gentiles – *implicit faith*. In living by what light they had received, they *implicitly* embraced Christ. And if they had implicity embraced Christ, then they implicitly shared in the grace of Baptism as well! Justin went on to teach:

> In moral philosophy the Stoics have established right principles, and the poets too have expounded such, because the seed of the Word was implanted in the whole human race (*Second Apology* VIII,1).[172]

> But it is one thing to possess a seed, and a likeness proportioned to one's capacity, and quite another to possess the reality itself, both the

---

[170] Brumbaugh, Robert S., available at < http://mb-soft.com/believe/text/logos.htm>
[171] Quoted in Dupuis, Jacques, *Toward a Christian Theology of Religious Pluralism* (Maryknoll, NY: Orbis, 1997), p.58.
[172] Ibid.

partaking and the imitation of which are the results of grace which comes from him (*Second Apology* XIII, 4-6).[173]

Clement of Alexandria, one of the great Egyptian teachers of Christianity, wrote in agreement with Justin, but went even further by recognizing preparations for the Gospel among Hindus and Buddhists:

> Before the advent of the Lord, philosophy was necessary to the Greeks for righteousness…For this was a schoolmaster to bring the "Hellenic mind," as the Law of the Hebrews, to Christ. Philosophy, therefore, was a preparation, paving the way for him who is perfected in Christ…The way of truth is therefore one. But into it, as into a perennial river, streams flow from all sides. (*Strom.*I,5,1-3)[174]

> The Indian gymnosophists are also in the number, and the other non-Greek philosophers. And of these there are two classes, some of them called Sarmanae, and others Brahmins…Some, too, of the Indians obey the precepts of Buddha, whom, on account of his extraordinary sanctity, they have raised to divine honour (*Strom.* I, 15).[175]

Coming to such conclusions did nothing, however, to diminish the absolute centrality and preeminence of the Gospel:

> Our doctrine surpasses all human teaching, because we have the Word in his entirety in Christ, who has been manifested for us, body, reason and soul. All right principles that philosophers and lawgivers have discovered and expressed they owe to whatever of the Word they have found and contemplated in part. They reason why they have contradicted each other is that they have not known the entire Word, which is Christ (Justin's *Second Apology* X, 1-3).

All that we have looked at so far in the Old and New Testaments and the Tradition of the early Church has dealt with preparations for the Gospel – that those outside God's covenant people Israel were still provided for, still given a means of salvation. Did this still hold once the Word became flesh, once the fullness of truth had come?

---

[173] Ibid, p.59.
[174] Ibid, p.67.
[175] Ibid, p.68.

A variety of factors led the Catholic Church to answer "yes" - probably the greatest being the discovery of the Americas.[176] Millions of people had lived and died there since the coming of Christ. Chronologically Christ had entered *the world*, but the Church had not yet carried Him to *their* world. The American natives could not be charged with the sin of rejecting Christ, and all that we have seen from Scripture convinces us that God desired their salvation. Implicit faith, and the grace flowing from it, must have somehow been available to them too.

Events connected with the evangelization of the New World called the Church to even deeper insights. The conquistadors, among the first Christians the natives met, proved horrible ambassadors for Christ. Their treatment of the natives did nothing to recommend the Gospel. It caused theologians to recognize that the natives were "put under no fresh obligation [to believe] by a simple declaration of [the Faith], for such announcement is no proof or incentive to belief...It does not appear that the Christian religion has been preached to them with sufficient propriety and piety that they are bound to acquiesce in it."[177] That insight paved the way for the next by the Flemish theologian Albert Pigge.

Pigge, writing in 1542, began to ask what factors could render someone "invincibly ignorant" of the Gospel? What factors may make someone unable to hear even a convincing and loving presentation of the Christian Faith?

> One cannot doubt that in so great a multitude of those who follow the doctrine of Mohammed, being imbued with this by their parents from infancy, there are some who know and revere God, as the cause of all things, and the rewarder of the good and the wicked [Hebrews 11:6], and who commend to him their salvation, which they hope from him, and they keep the law of nature written in their hearts [Romans 2:14-16], and they submit their wills to the divine will. What is to be thought of such people?

---

[176] Sullivan, Francis A., *Salvation Outside the Church? The History of the Catholic Response* (Maqwah, New York: Paulist Press, 1992), p.69.
[177] Francisco de Vitoria (died 1546), as quoted in Sullivan, Francis A., *Salvation Outside the Church? The History of the Catholic Response* (Maqwah, New York: Paulist Press, 1992), p.72.

> I grant that the Moslems have heard the name of Christ. But they have been so educated that they think our faith is false and mistaken, while the faith in which they have been educated is the true faith, and they believe that God commands them to hold that faith. For it is thus that they have been instructed by their parents and elders, to whom natural reason prescribes that the young and simple be submissive, unless or until divine illumination teaches them otherwise. And so they feel it would be wrong, indeed, that they would be damned if they doubted...They do not know anything about divine revelation; they have not seen signs or miracles that would prove their religion false, nor have they heard them in such a way that they would be truly obliged to believe those who told them of such things...Therefore, erroneous faith does not condemn, provided the error has a reasonable excuse and that they are invincibly ignorant of the true faith.[178]

I am obviously abbreviating centuries of reflection, but I hope the Church's thought-process is discernable. We live at a time when the Spirit has deigned to authoritatively clarify the whole matter – to gather the bishops, together with the Successor of Peter , to pray, debate, and then teach- "It is the decision of the Holy Spirit, and ours too…" (Acts 15:28, NIV):

> Nor is God far distant from those who in shadows and images seek the unknown God, for it is He who gives to all men life and breath and all things [Acts 17:25-28], and as Saviour wills that all men be saved [1 Timothy 2:4]. Those also can attain to salvation who through no fault of their own do not know the Gospel of Christ or His Church, yet sincerely seek God and *moved by grace* strive by their deeds to do His will as it is known to them through the dictates of conscience. Nor does Divine Providence deny the helps necessary for salvation to those who, without blame on their part, have not yet arrived at an explicit knowledge of God and *with His grace* strive to live a good life. Whatever good or truth is found amongst them is looked upon by the Church as a preparation for the Gospel. She knows that it is given

---

[178] Quoted in Sullivan, Francis A., *Salvation Outside the Church? The History of the Catholic Response* (Maqwah, New Jersey: Paulist Press, 1992), pp.80-81.

by Him who enlightens all men so that they may finally have life (*Dogmatic Constitution on the Church*, 16).[179]

Notice that it is the grace of God, the grace that flows only from union with Christ Jesus, that brings one to salvation:

> Pressing upon the Christian to be sure, are the need and the duty to battle against evil through manifold tribulations and even to suffer death. But, linked with the paschal mystery and patterned on the dying Christ, he will hasten forward to resurrection in the strength which comes from hope.
>
> All this holds true not only for Christians, but for all men of good will in whose hearts grace works in an unseen way. For, since Christ died for all men, and since the ultimate vocation of man is in fact one, and divine, we ought to believe that the Holy Spirit in a manner known only to God offers to every man the possibility of being associated with this paschal mystery. (*Pastoral Constitution on the Church in the Modern World*, 22).[180]

Anyone who has entered into the mystery of Jesus' passage to the Father has to be related to the Church as well:

> Those who have not yet received the Gospel are related in various ways to the people of God. In the first place we must recall the people to whom the testament and the promises were given and from whom Christ was born according to the flesh [Romans 9:4-5].On account of their fathers this people remains most dear to God, for God does not repent of the gifts He makes nor of the calls He issues [Romans 11:27-29]; But the plan of salvation also includes those who acknowledge the Creator. In the first place amongst these there are the Mohamedans, who, professing to hold the faith of Abraham, along with us adore the

---

[179] <http://www.vatican.va/archive/hist_councils/ii_vatican_council/documents/vat-ii_const_19641121_lumen-gentium_en.html>
[180] <http://www.vatican.va/archive/hist_councils/ii_vatican_council/documents/vat-ii_cons_19651207_gaudium-et-spes_en.html>

one and merciful God, who on the last day will judge mankind (*Dogmatic Constitution on the Church*, 16).[181]

Vatican II then went on to note positive elements found in Hinduism[182], Buddhism[183], and even tribal religions,[184] stating that, "The Catholic Church rejects nothing that is true and holy in these religions. She regards with sincere reverence those ways of conduct and of life, those precepts and teachings which, though differing in many aspects from the ones she holds and sets forth, nonetheless often reflect a ray of that Truth which enlightens all men."[185]

That there be no confusion though, as to the absolute centrality of Christ Jesus, the council fathers' very next words were:

> Indeed, [the Church] proclaims, and ever must proclaim Christ "the way, the truth, and the life" (John 14:6), in whom men may find the fullness of religious life, in whom God has reconciled all things to Himself [2 Corinthians 5:18-19]. The Church, therefore, exhorts her sons, that through dialogue and collaboration with the followers of other religions, carried out with prudence and love and in witness to the Christian faith and life, they recognize, preserve and promote the

---

[181] <http://www.vatican.va/archive/hist_councils/ii_vatican_council/documents/vat-ii_const_19641121_lumen-gentium_en.html>

[182] "Thus in Hinduism, men contemplate the divine mystery and express it through an inexhaustible abundance of myths and through searching philosophical inquiry. They seek freedom from the anguish of our human condition either through ascetical practices or profound meditation or a flight to God with love and trust" (*Declaration on the Relation of the Church to Non-Christian Religions*, 2).
<http://www.vatican.va/archive/hist_councils/ii_vatican_council/documents/vat-ii_decl_19651028_nostra-aetate_en.html>

[183] "Buddhism, in its various forms, realizes the radical insufficiency of this changeable world; it teaches a way by which men, in a devout and confident spirit, may be able either to acquire the state of perfect liberation, or attain, by their own efforts or through higher help, supreme illumination" (*Declaration on the Relation of the Church to Non-Christian Religions*).

[184] "From ancient times down to the present, there is found among various peoples a certain perception of that hidden power which hovers over the course of things and over the events of human history; at times some indeed have come to the recognition of a Supreme Being, or even of a Father. This perception and recognition penetrates their lives with a profound religious sense" (*Declaration on the Relation of the Church to Non-Christian Religions*, 2).

[185] Ibid.

good things, spiritual and moral, as well as the socio-cultural values found among these men *(Declaration on the Relation of the Church to Non-Christian Religions*, 2).[186]

Perhaps the greatest Catholic meditation on this subject since Vatican II was Pope John Paul II's encyclical letter, *Redemptoris Missio (Mission of the Redeemer)*. I must quote one portion at length:

> Thus the Spirit, who "blows where he wills" (cf. Jn 3:8), who "was already at work in the world before Christ was glorified," and who "has filled the world...holds all things together [and] knows what is said" (Wisdom 1:7), leads us to broaden our vision in order to ponder his activity in every time and place. I have repeatedly called this fact to mind, and it has guided me in my meetings with a wide variety of peoples. The Church's relationship with other religions is dictated by a twofold respect: "Respect for man in his quest for answers to the deepest questions of his life, and respect for the action of the Spirit in man." Excluding any mistaken interpretation, the interreligious meeting held in Assisi [Italy] was meant to confirm my conviction that *"every authentic prayer is prompted by the Holy Spirit, who is mysteriously present in every human heart."*
>
> This is the same Spirit who was at work in the beginning of the Incarnation and in the life, death and resurrection of Jesus, and who is at work in the Church...*Whatever the Spirit brings about in human hearts and in the history of peoples, in cultures and religions serves as a preparation for the Gospel* and can only be understood in reference to Christ, the Word who took flesh "by the power of the Spirit" so that as perfectly human he would save all human beings and sum up all things...
>
> Our own time, with humanity on the move and in continual search, *demands a resurgence of the Church's missionary activity.* The horizons and possibilities for mission are growing ever wider, and we Christians are

---

[186] Ibid.

called to an apostolic courage based upon trust in the Spirit. *He is the principal agent of mission! (Redemptoris Missio, 29)*[187]

Since the Incarnation God the Son reaches out to humanity not just as the Word, but as *the Word made flesh,* the God-man Christ Jesus. He told Pontius Pilate, "For this I was born, and for this I came into the world, to bear witness to the truth" (John 18:37). And so *explicit faith* remains the goal because in the fullness of revelation there is true knowledge of the Divine Beloved and the fullness of means to grow in intimacy with Him even now – through word and sacrament in the midst of God's People on earth. Jesus reaches out to every human being – Jew, Moslem, Buddhist, Hindu, Taoist, agnostic, atheist, etc., etc. – to sharpen their view of reality, to tell them that "no eye has seen, nor ear heard, nor the heart of man conceived what God has prepared for those who love him" (1 Cor.2:9).

One Negative Encounter

In all the ecumenical moments I was given, the only truly negative encounter I had was with a speaker giving an evangelism conference at one of the campus ministries. In the course of sharing stories it became clear that he had misgivings about the salvation of Catholics. He spoke about one acquaintance as, "Catholic, *but a born-again Catholic.*" A couple more remarks like that and I knew we needed to speak.

After introducing myself I shared that I could not help but feel that some of his remarks cast Catholics in a poor light. He assured me that it had not been his intent. I brought up the example of needing to qualify someone as a "born-again Catholic," yet not making such a qualification when referring to believers of his own denomination. He noted that a much higher percentage of his denomination had "come to know Jesus as personal Lord and Savior." I questioned how he could state something so factually: "First, Catholics rarely use the phrase 'born again.' And second, Catholics are the largest denomination in the United States. If you run into a greater number of lax or mediocre Catholics it could simply be because there's so many more of us; it proves nothing about your group being more intimate with the Lord."

---

[187] <http://www.vatican.va/holy_father/john_paul_ii/encyclicals/documetns/hf_jp-ii_enc-07121999>

He didn't mince words after that. He wanted to know what role I saw "the Church" having in my faith life. I shared the conviction I had been coming to, that the Church acted as Christ's presence - His voice and hands in the world. He shot it down categorically; the Church was not a mystical extension of Christ and my saying so "put the Church in the place of Christ. God speaks His Word to us in Scripture, not through the intermediary of the Church."

Before I could get in a word he was already onto the papacy, how Catholics had misunderstood Jesus' words to the Apostle Simon (Peter) in *Matthew 16*. He assured me that if I were to study Jesus' words in Greek, the language of the New Testament, I would have to abandon the Catholic position. He elaborated: After Simon had confessed Jesus as "the Christ, the Son of the living God," the Lord said, "you are Peter [*Petros* in Greek, meaning "pebble"], and on this rock [*petra*, Greek for "massive stone"] I will build my church" (Matthew 16:17-18; NIV). The gentleman explained that Simon-Peter was not designated by Jesus as "the Rock" on which the Church would be built, the first Pope; the truth was exactly the opposite! Simon the man was a *Petros*, an insignificant little pebble. His confession that Jesus was "the Messiah, the Son of the Living God," on the other hand, was the *Petra*, or "Rock" upon which the Church would rise. He challenged me to study the Greek for myself.

Admittedly, this was news to me; but surely a Catholic had noticed it in the course of two thousand years. The only thing I could say at the time was, "So to truly understand the New Testament, I need to read it in Greek – a completely foreign language? Personally, I don't know any Christians who read Greek; and I don't believe that God expects us to all go out and learn it either. It seems to me that most Christians are forced to look to someone else to interpret the Bible for them. I believe that illustrates a point I was trying to make earlier: human beings, the Church, are called to act as God's voice in the world, even to the point of taking the written word and making it intelligible to the masses."

I must have made him angry because his next comment was, "You're visiting this campus ministry for one of three reasons: 1) You're looking to make converts to Catholicism, 2) You are thinking of converting to this denomination, or 3) You think the people here are swell and enjoy hanging around them." I assured him that there was a fourth reason, "God's children meet here, and wherever God's children are, I feel at home. I'm not trying to win converts to Catholicism, simply to pray and get to know my brothers and sisters."

Academics and the Incarnation

Because of a friend from Church – there is the Church's action in my life again, I took an introductory course in Communication Disorders as an elective. I found it fascinating – stuttering, language disorders, autism, sign language, etc. I took a few more electives in the discipline; a year later it was my major. As pulled as I felt toward studying theology, when I prayed, pursuing a career as a speech-language pathologist was where I felt the peace. I still find myself torn between the two sometimes, teaching the Faith in my parish while working full-time in an elementary school; but I believe I went down the path God wanted. Part of believing that the Lord wants to be present and minister to each person means being willing to "get down in the trenches" and use the gifts He has given.

Chapter 11 - Loose Ends Finally Tied

During my Junior year of college the charismatic prayer group at the Newman Center saw a growth spurt. Four new regulars joined us. One of them, Todd Reitmeyer, had just transferred in to pursue a Masters in counseling. It became clear, early on, that we did not see eye-to-eye on some issues. He stuck me as "legalistic," a stickler for Church discipline: any rule that the Church laid down, well, that's just the way it was. His manner wasn't what you would call subtle either.[188] When he began talking up the book *Catholicism & Fundamentalism*, offering to lend out his copy, I was too biased to take him up on it. As you will see though, God had another plan.

When I returned to St. Louis for spring break I helped my old youth minister, Paul, give a retreat to eighth graders preparing for Confirmation. I remember one of the more thoughtful retreatants coming up at the end of the day to ask a few pointed questions. One of them must have been about the papacy because I can distinctly recall Paul saying, "Starting with John Paul II we can follow an unbroken trail of successors straight back to the Apostle Peter. I've got some literature on it if you'd like to check it out." I had heard that claim before, but never from Paul's lips; and while the existence of the papacy in the Middle Ages was common knowledge, I had never actually *seen* the historical proof for it from the earliest days of the Church.

As Paul and I drove home together he told me about some exciting audiocassettes by a Presbyterian minister who had converted to Catholicism, Scott Hahn. Paul described him as brilliant: at the age of twenty-six he had been offered a position as dean of a seminary. He turned it down, however, because his intense study of Scripture was pointing him toward the Catholic Church. Since his conversion, in debates with evangelical theologians, he had reportedly been dazzling his opponents with the biblical basis for the Catholic faith. Because of my love for Scripture, and my conviction that it contained Catholic doctrine, you can understand why I was

---

[188] Pleae don't think me uncharitable. Todd and I became good friends; and I know he would say the same about himself during that period. In 2003, Todd became Fr. Todd. Just three short years later he was called Home by the Lord. You can read the incredibly inspirational account of his final days at
<http://www.catholic.org/featured/headline.php?ID=3452&page=1>

anxious to hear this guy for myself. Paul offered to loan me Hahn's conversion story as well as a tape on the papacy entitled, *The Pope: Holy Father*.

Hahn did not disappoint. He was sincere, passionate, and more knowledgeable than any speaker I had heard. At the beginning of Hahn's story he had held strong anti-Catholic convictions: the Catholic Church had introduced corruptions, piling purely human traditions onto the teachings of Scripture. His conversion was a detective story; the Holy Spirit led him, through Scripture, to recognize one Catholic belief after another. His teaching on the relationship of Scripture, Tradition, and the teaching authority of the Church was amazing.

In retrospect I can see that the Holy Spirit had been leading me down this path for some time. Up until that point my justification for believing that God speaks through Tradition, as well as Scripture, was dismissed by evangelical brothers and sisters I talked with: "The Bible doesn't *clearly* say that;" "Traditions might be helpful, but they're *never* binding or authoritative in the way the Bible is." And yet, there were verses like *1 Timothy 3:15*, "the church of the living God [is] the pillar and bulwark of the truth," demonstrating exactly what my evangelical friends had asked for. (We will explore this more in depth in the next chapter.)

And the tape on the papacy – what a God-send! The very first thing he addressed was *Matthew 16:17-19*'s usage of *Petros* and *petra*. Hahn demonstrated beyond a shadow of a doubt that Jesus did designate Simon-Peter as the Rock on which His Church would be built, and here was the real beauty – Hahn used *Protestant* biblical scholars to do it.[189]

In both of the tapes I listened to, Hahn recommend books for further study. The first was *Catholicism & Fundamentalism* by Karl Keating, the same book Todd had recommended. It turned out that Karl Keating was the head of a Catholic apologetics organization, Catholic Answers (I had never heard of someone doing *Catholic* apologetics). When I spoke to Todd he was more than happy to loan me the book. He was already familiar with Hahn and expressed surprise that I would agree with Hahn's strong views on papal authority. I clarified that I had no difficulty believing that the Pope

---

[189] Not that these scholars would have followed the Catholic Church in its convictions about the papacy. They did, however, agree with the Catholic Church's traditional interpretation that Peter was the Rock on which Christ built His Church.

spoke authoritatively on matters of doctrine and morality, but that the jury was still out concerning matters of discipline (canon law, fasting, the obligation to attend Mass on Sundays and holy days, etc.).

Catholicism & Fundamentalism proved to be biblical, historical, and logical. The book had been written in response to the many objections raised by fundamentalist Christians to the Catholic Church and her doctrines. Keating had chapters such as *Tradition versus "Traditions of Men," Development of Doctrine, Fanciful Histories of Catholicism, Salvation, Peter and the Papacy, The Eucharist, Marian Beliefs,* and *The Inquisition*. I devoured the book, finishing it with an incredible sense of awe at being part of the Catholic Church.

The most important thing it did was introduce me to the Fathers of the Church, the leaders who immediately followed the Apostles, and shepherded the Church through the early centuries of persecution. I had heard the charge that the Catholic Church introduced her distinctive doctrines beginning in the 400's and proceeding up into the Middle Ages. But there was Keating quoting not just the New Testament, but the acknowledged leaders of the Church in 110, 150, and 180 A.D. – and they were articulating Catholic dogma clearly and unambiguously! How much closer could we get to the Apostles? If you refer back to my discussion of the Sacrament of Reconciliation and purgatory you will see that I could not resist incorporating their testimony.

I made it my goal the summer after junior year to study Scott Hahn and Karl Keating's claims more in-depth. I purchased almost every book I had heard Hahn recommend, as well as a number recommended by Catholic Answers. Among them were Stanley Jaki's *And On This Rock* and *The Keys of the Kingdom*, Jacque Maritain's *On The Church of Christ*, Frank J. Sheed's *Theology for Beginners*, Rev. Henry Graham's *Where We Got the Bible*, and the first of William Jurgen's three volume set *The Faith of the Early Fathers*.

As a result of my study I came to a new vision of the Catholic Church. I saw her as the spokesperson for God's entire family. I finally came to accept her authority in matters of *discipline* (it had only been seven years coming). If Christ had appointed human shepherds for me, and I was now thoroughly convinced that He had, then I would honor their directives out of love and respect for Him – just as I did my mom and dad's when growing up, even when we disagreed. Before, I could not understand what observances like fasting or attending Mass on specific holy days had to do with life as a Christian. What I finally saw was that it is all about living as a family! There is freedom in Christ Jesus – great freedom. We are freed from the darkness of unreality; we are given the power to overcome our addictions and fears. But with that freedom comes the responsibility of living as God's children. We have family obligations – obligations to gather in celebration and to pray and fast for one another, the obligation to listen to those God has called to servant leadership: "Obey your leaders and submit to them; for they are keeping watch over your souls, as men who will have to give account. Let them do this joyfully, and not sadly, for that would be of no advantage to you" (Hebrews 13:17).

It is not my intention to offend Protestant brothers and sisters by what I share; I am absolutely convinced that the truths and grace I have found within the Catholic Church are intended for *every* child of God. My goal for the next chapter is to introduce you to the Church that I believe, in the eyes of God, every Christian is already joined to. I pray that the Holy Spirit might use this humble effort to crack open the full deposit of "the faith delivered once for all to the saints" (Jude 3).

Chapter 12 – The Church & The Word of God
But when the time had fully come, God sent forth his Son, born of a woman...The Word became flesh and made his dwelling among us" (Galatians 4:4; John 1:14).

When our Lord Jesus came, He did so not only to redeem us through His life of obedient love, but also to *teach* us – to reveal the Trinitarian Life of God and instruct us how to enter into that Life and live it out in this world. As Christians we affirm that He was (and is) the greatest teacher the world has ever known. I stand by that.

I can see where one might dispute it though. I mean, if the Lord Jesus was such a great teacher then why is it that we Christians cannot agree on the meaning of His words or the content of His doctrine? For example, one group of Christians will teach that baptism is simply an outward sign of the Christian's interior, saving faith. Another group will teach that the physical act of baptism is necessary for salvation. Those who confess the need for baptism are divided amongst themselves as to whether the baptized need to be fully immersed or if pouring and sprinkling of water are equally valid. Further, can infants be baptized, or must children wait until they have "reached the age of reason?" Now add to this all the other points on which denominations and individuals disagree. Surely the Son of God was capable of making His will on such matters known – and surely through the Holy Spirit He was able to mold the Apostles into capable teachers of others. If we in the twentieth century cannot agree on Christ's doctrine then I have to believe that the fault, or deficiency, lies not with Christ but with us.

"How much easier it would have been if Jesus would have just sat down and written a catechism!" we may lament. And yet, the Lord did not leave us a single word in writing. I am not upset with Him over it, though; He has been in my life long enough for me to understand that He is Wisdom. If He chose not to write then, rest assured, He had good reason.

As God, Jesus knew what the future held for those who believed in Him. He was keenly aware that there would be doctrinal disputes, arguments, heresy. I have to trust that He wouldn't leave His people to fend for themselves – individuals striving to make sense of it all through the passage of years, with our limited intellects, and still under-developed spiritual ears. The One Who said, "for this reason I was born, and for this I came into the world, to testify to the truth" (John 18:37, NIV), *would have* found a way, would have provided for His Beloved's future. We have already said that He did not write a book. Well, then what did He do? Let's look at Jesus' public ministry.

Kingdom of the Word

The proclamation of the Kingdom of God was the heart of Jesus' message. When the Angel Gabriel announced His birth to Mary he had said that, "the Lord God will give to him the throne of his father David, and he will reign over the house of Jacob for ever; and of his kingdom there will be no end" (Luke 1:32-33). The gospels tell us that the initial theme of His preaching was "the kingdom of God is at hand; repent, and believe the good news" (Mark 1:15). Jesus was the prophesied King – and His Kingdom was about to be inaugurated. As we saw in Chapter 3, it would be the fulfillment of the Kingdoms of David and Solomon – not just a national kingdom but a global one, the "Israel of God" (Galatians 6:16), the Church.[190] His Kingdom was not to be solely a "spiritual" kingdom, an in-

---

[190] There are those who would wish to deny this identification of the "Kingdom" with the "Church." The Church, for them, is a social body of believers moving through time. The Kingdom, on the other hand, is that perfect reign of Christ occurring in heaven and breaking through to earth only at the end of history. I maintain, however, that such a distinction ignores the way Jesus used the terms Church and Kingdom interchangeably in Matthew 16:18-19 as well as how He spoke of His Kingdom containing sinners (see Matthew 13:47-48; 13:24-30; 25:1-12), something which would make no sense if the Kingdom refers only to the heavenly, or end-time, reign of Christ. That the Church on earth contains sinners is a foregone conclusion.

I believe that the answer lies in seeing the Church on earth as transitional, the Kingdom awaiting its full-flowering. It *is* the Kingdom already present *but in seed form*. Those of us who belong to it are full citizens, but our citizenship is forfeitable. It's only those in heaven who enjoy the Kingdom in its fullness and are assured that they have won the fight against sin.

Perhaps someone may object, "But Christ said to Pilate, 'My kingship is not of this world' (John 18:36)." That verse does not invalidate what has been said thus far. Jesus' words can be understood by looking just a chapter earlier in John's Gospel. The Lord, when praying for the Apostles, said "I do not pray that thou shouldst take them *out* of the world, but that thou shouldst keep them from the evil one. *They are not of the world, even as I am not of the world*" (John 17:15-16). If Jesus and the Apostles can be *in* the world but not *of* the world then the same can be said of the Kingdom; it is physically present but its origins and mode of existence are not of this world system.

visible brotherhood of the faithful. The Lord gave it a definite, visible structure.

We are told that after a night of prayer Jesus called forth Twelve from His crowd of disciples and designated them as Apostles (Luke 6:12-13). The magnitude of such an action should not be lost on anyone familiar with the Old Testament. God's people under the Old Covenant were descended from the Twelve Sons of Jacob. In establishing this new "Israel of God" Jesus selected twelve new foundations (Ephesians 2:20; Revelations 21:14)[191] for God's covenant people.[192] They were to act as shepherds to their brothers and sisters (John 21:15-17) – and we know the length to which Jesus expected shepherds to go, "The good shepherd lays down his life for the sheep" (John 10:11). When Jesus first called them as ministers they could not have known that their Master would ascend to heaven only three years later, that He was training them for the role they would exercise after His departure. They were told how "the rulers of the Gentiles lord it over them," and how "It shall not be so among you; but whoever would be great among you must be your servant, and whoever would be first among you must be your slave" (Matthew 20:25-27).

In short, this was to be a Kingdom unlike *any* the world had ever seen. And this is because besides being a Kingdom, it was to be a Family – the very Family of God. Because of the saving action Jesus was to perform, a fallen race would have the chance to become sons and daughters of God. That is why our Lord taught His disciples to pray "Abba," or "Daddy," and that after His resurrection He could send Mary Magdalene to the Apostles with the message "I am ascending to *my* Father and *your* Father" (John 20:17). The unity between God and each of His children was so real that He said, "they shall all know me, from the least of them to the greatest"

---

[191] *Ephesians 2:19-20*, "you are fellow citizens with the saints and members of the household of God, built upon the foundation of the apostles and prophets;"
Revelation 21:12-14, "[The wall of the New Jerusalem had] twelve gates, and at the gates twelve angels, and on the gates the names of the twelve tribes of the sons of Israel...and the wall of the city had twelve foundations, and on them the twelve names of the twelve apostles of the Lamb. "
[192] That Jesus was establishing a new Israel is also demonstrated by how, after choosing the Twelve, He chose seventy (many Bible manuscripts have seventy-two) other disciples whom He empowered to spread the word about Him and heal the sick. This parallels the Old Testament account of God bestowing "the spirit" upon seventy elders Moses had gathered to assist in serving the people (Numbers 11:16-25), as well as upon two additional elders of the Lord's choosing (v.26-30).

(Jeremiah 31:34). Jesus declared that each child of the Kingdom was to be "the light of the world" (Matt. 5:14). *The Book of Revelation* calls the new community a "kingdom, priests to his God and Father" (1:6). The Family of God, the Kingdom of God; it is one and the same. Jesus was incorporating the Apostles into His Own mission – He the eldest brother molding them into "older brothers" to assist in the nurturing of the Family once He returned to the Father's right hand. I shared earlier my conviction that the Church was to act as Christ's visible and physical presence in the world; what I now realize is that the shepherds whom Christ raised up are meant to represent Christ in a uniquely visible way *within the Church* - as uniquely ordained servants to the rest of us.

This is not to say that they weren't granted authority. It would have been impossible to carry out their mission as shepherds had they not. Imagine a parent trying to guide a child into adulthood without being granted authority by the Lord unto that end. Jesus had told those He sent, "He who hears you hears *me*, and he who rejects you rejects me" (Luke 10:16). I find it interesting that the early Christians looked to the Apostles not just as older brothers but as *father figures* (2 Corinthians 6:13).

In His Kingdom upon earth Jesus knew that His people wouldn't always act like angels. It wasn't without reason that He taught us to pray, "Your Kingdom come...on earth as it is in heaven!" In Jesus' parables He warned the Apostles that His Kingdom on earth would contain both the virtuous and the wicked. His Church would be like a net containing both good and bad fish (Matthew 13:47-48), a field containing both wheat and cockle (Matthew 13:24-30), ten virgins – five with oil in their lamps and five without (Matthew 25:1-12). Thus, the Twelve were given authority to declare actions allowable or disallowable for members of the community, "Truly, I say to you, whatever you bind on earth shall be bound in heaven, and whatever you loose on earth shall be loosed in heaven" (Matthew 18:18). The same terminology was used by the rabbis of Jesus' day, and referred to their authority to declare this or that action as allowable under, or in violation of, divine law.[193] This power of "binding and loosing" would have been understood by the first Christians as applying to even purely dis-

---

[193] Jaki, Stanley, *And on This Rock: Witness of One Land and Two Covenants* (Manassas, Virginia: Trinity Communications, 1987), p.43.

ciplinary measures (like when to fast, etc.); after all, Jesus had said *"whatever you bind..."*

Jesus empowered the Twelve to help the erring members of the Church. They were instructed that when one brother had wronged another, and the offender refused to repent, the matter was to be referred "to the Church." "If he refuses to listen *even to the church*, let him be to you as a Gentile and a tax collector" (Matthew 18:17). In other words, it would be time for "tough love" from the shepherds. St. Paul referred to this action of putting someone outside the Church as "delivering [him] to Satan for the destruction of his flesh, that his spirit may be saved in the day of the Lord Jesus." Paul's hope was that exclusion from the Body would force the offender to recognize the danger unrepentant serious sin posed, and elicit a change (See 1 Corinthians 5:4-5). As we saw in our discussion of Reconciliation, Jesus had entrusted the Apostles with an enormous responsibility: "If you forgive the sins of any, they are forgiven; if you retain the sins of any, they are retained" (John 20:23).

A Shepherd to the Shepherds

Among the Twelve the Lord chose Simon (Peter) to hold a special position. After Christ's resurrection and ascension he would be a shepherd to the shepherds. Simon was marked for the position after his profession of faith at Caesarea Philippi, "You are the Christ, the Son of the Living God" in the face of the other Apostles' silence. What Jesus said to Simon at that time bears careful examination. We will look at *Matthew 16:17-19*, in sections, beginning with:

> Blessed are you Simon Bar Jonah! For flesh and blood has not revealed this to you, but my Father who is in heaven. And I tell you, you are Peter [Petros in Greek] and on this rock [petra in Greek] I will build my church, and the powers of death shall not prevail against it.

I have already noted an objection to the Catholic understanding of this verse (that Simon-Peter is the rock on whom Christ's Church is built) by a visiting campus minister. When looked at by some of the best Protestant biblical scholars in the world, however, his objection doesn't hold water.[194]

---

[194]Scott Hahn presents the findings of Herman Ridderbos, R.T. France, W.F. Albright, Gerhard Maier, and Donald Carson in his audiocassette *Holy Father: The Pope* (St. Joseph's

The reason for Matthew's Gospel, in Greek, using two different words (Petros and petra) is surprisingly simple. Anyone who studied French or Spanish in high school will undoubtedly remember that these languages have masculine and feminine nouns; you can tell which gender a given word is by checking the word ending. The same holds true in Greek. "Petra," or "massive rock," is a feminine noun and thus has a feminine ending. It would have been improper to give the name to Simon; when applied to him the ending had to be changed, and thus we see "Petros" instead of "petra." Now "Petros" just happened to be an already existing word, which in ancient Greek poetry was used to denote "pebble." By the time of Jesus, however, "Petros" had lost this restrictive meaning and could be used interchangeably with "petra." to denote a "massive rock."[195]

Thus far I have been discussing Jesus' words as found in the Greek of *Matthew's Gospel*. We have to remember, though, that *Jesus would not have spoken those words in Greek*. The everyday speech of a Palestinian Jew was Aramaic. (Hebrew was spoken but reserved for religious ceremony.) Jesus' use of Aramaic is attested to in the gospels. We hear it in the *Our Father* —

Communications), the transcript of which is available at <http://www.star.ucl.ac.uk/~vgg/rc/aplgtc/hahn/m4/pp.html>.

A more in-depth look at the scholarship on Jesus' words to Simon, can be found in Butler, Scott; Norman Dalgren, & David Hess (Eds.), *Jesus, Peter & the Keys: A Scriptural Handbook on the Papacy* (Santa Barbara, California: Queenship Publishing Company, 1997) For example:

> Gerhard Kittel's *Theological Dictionary of the New Testament* (1968) is cited, "*Petros* himself is the *petra*, not just his faith or his confession…The idea of the Reformers that He is referring to the faith of Peter is quite inconceivable" (p.31);
> Craig Blomberg, a Baptist scholar and Professor of New Testament at Denver Seminary says, "Peter's name (*Petros*) and the word 'rock' (*petra*) makes sense only if Peter is the rock and if Jesus is about to explain the significance of this identification" (p.32);
> R.T. France, a renowned Anglican scholar, in his *The Gospel According to Matthew* (1985) wrote that, "The feminine word for rock, petra, is necessarily changed to the masculine petros (stone) to give a man's name, but the word-play is unmistakable (and in Aramaic would be even more so, as the same form kepha would occur in both places)…it is to Peter, not to his confession, that the rock metaphor is applied. And it is of course a matter of historic fact that Peter was the acknowledged leader of the group of disciples, and of the developing church in its early years" (p.36).

[195] James Akin in *Surprised By Truth*. Patrick Madrid ed. Basilica Press, San Diego. p.68

"Abba" is Aramaic, not Hebrew or Greek. *Matthew* and *Mark* record the Jesus' cry from the cross in Aramaic, "Eli, Eli, lema sabachthani" (Matthew 27:46). So when Jesus made His statement to Simon He would not have used the Greek word "Petros," but the Aramaic "Kepha;" and "Kepha" can *only mean* "massive stone."

I can say this with certainty because of how the rest of the New Testament bears this out. We see Simon referred to not just as Peter (Petros), but as *Cephas* – the Aramaic *Kepha* spelled with the Greek alphabet.[196] *John's Gospel* shows this clearly: "So you are Simon the son of John? You shall be called Cephas (which means Peter)" (1:42). Paul always referred to Simon as "Cephas" (see 1 Corinthians 1:12, 3:22, 9:5, and Galatians 2:9, 11, 14).

Now all these linguistic gymnastics are only meant to bring out the true meaning of Jesus' words to Simon. He promised a weak, rash man that he would be transformed by grace into the unique foundation of His Church. Some believers still have difficulty accepting this, objecting that Christ is the *true* Rock (1 Corinthians 10:4). And to this objection Simon-Peter, the current pope, and the Catholic Church would all answer "Amen!" Simon could become the rock on whom the Church is built *only because Christ is the Rock on whom Simon-Peter stands.* Simon being allowed to share in Christ's "Rockness" is not without precedent: We human beings are allowed to share in God's act of creating new lives; our participation does not mean that we supplant Him as *the* Creator. If I am a good teacher it is only because of the One Teacher (Matthew 23:10); if someone is wise it is because of the One Who *is* Wisdom. And if Simon became a Rock (Kepha/ Cephas/ Peter) for the Church, it is only because Christ made him so. To recognize someone as a parent, or wise, or a good teacher, is not a denial of God the Father or Christ's fullness and neither is calling Peter the Rock. We are only echoing the Lord; He was the One Who renamed Simon!

Turning back to our passage, we hear Jesus promise, "and on this rock I will build my church." Notice that it is Christ Who builds the Church, the Kingdom. Peter plays a part. The Apostles play a part; every Christian plays a part. But ultimately the growth of the Church is a supernatural process

---

[196] The technical term for this is *transliteration*.

carried out by the Lord Jesus Himself.[197] And "the powers of death [also translated "gates of Hades"] shall not prevail against it" (16:18). Some interpret this to mean that the Church will not be overcome by any of Satan's lies or deceptions; that is fine but it only captures half of the truth. It actually says that Christ's Church, and the Gospel it is entrusted with, will overcome Satan. The Church is the one thing on earth that we can count on being here until the end of time; we have the Master's guarantee.

That said we can turn our attention to the second half of Jesus' statement, "I will give you the keys of the kingdom of heaven, and whatever you bind on earth shall be bound in heaven, and whatever you loose on earth shall be loosed in heaven" (16:19). First, notice how the words "Church" and "kingdom" were interchangeable in Jesus' mind. Second, we hear of the power of "binding and loosing." The quotation cited earlier, in which Jesus bestowed this authority upon all the Apostles, actually occurred two chapters later in Matthew's Gospel (18:18). Peter alone shared this responsibility for a time. Something unique also stands out about the Master's bestowal upon Peter; Jesus granted him alone "the keys of the kingdom." That phrase has to be contended with if we are to understand Peter's function in the Church, and by extension that of the popes.

The Jewish mind, hearing those words in the first century, would have immediately been transported back to the Kingdoms of Judah and Israel. The Lord was using a phrase, an image, from those governments. The Protestant scholars, W.F. Albright and C.S. Mann, wrote "[Isaiah 22] undoubtedly lies behind this saying. The keys are the symbol of authority and Roland DeVaux rightly sees here the same authority as that vested in the vizier, the master of the house, the chamberlain of the royal household in ancient Israel. Eliakim is spoken of as having the same authority in Isaiah."[198] Albright and Mann contend that Jesus' wording reflects that of *Isaiah 22*, where the Lord addressed the man serving as the vizier, or Master of the Palace in the Kingdom of Judah: the Lord would remove him from

---

[197] *1 Corinthians 3:7-9*, "So neither he who plants nor he who waters is anything, but only God who gives the growth. He who plants and he who waters are equal, and each shall receive his wages according to his labor. For we are God's fellow workers, you are God's field, God's building."
[198] Albright, William F., & C.S. Mann (Eds.), *Matthew (Anchor Bible)*. (New York: Doubleday, 1971), p.196. Cited by Scott Hahn in his audiocassette, *The Pope: Holy Father*, St. Joseph Communications.

office and install Eliakim, a man who would exercise authority as the Lord wished:

> In that day I will call my servant Eliakim the son of Hilkiah, and I will clothe him with your robe, and will bind your girdle on him, and will commit your authority to his hand; and he shall be a father [pope in Italian] to the house of Judah. And I will place on his shoulder *the key of the house of David; he shall open, and none shall shut; and he shall shut, and none shall open.* And I will fasten him like a peg in a sure place, and he will become a throne of honor to his father's house. And they will hang on him the whole weight of his father's house... (Isaiah 22:21-23; emphasis and information within brackets added).

Fortunate for us, theologian Stanley Jaki has done the legwork in investigating what role the vizier, or Master of the Palace, played in ancient Israel:

> By the time of Isaiah the office of the master of the palace was three centuries old and the highest of the royal administration which Solomon organized in full. . . Solomon set up the office in imitation of the office of the Pharaoh's vizier. . .in Egypt as well as in Judah and Israel the master of the palace was the second in command after the king. . . the master of the palace of the king of Israel headed the list of royal officials (2 King 18:18) and he alone appears with the king (1 King 18:3). The importance of the title is particularly apparent when [Prince] Jotham assumes it in his capacity of regent of the kingdom during the final illness of his father King Azariah (2 Kings 15:5).[199]

Given this Old Testament background we are in a much better position to appreciate Jesus' words. He, the One Who came to sit upon the throne of David and Solomon's kingdom, revived the office of the Master of the Palace – appointing Simon-Peter to it. Peter was to be the King's *chief* minister, and his authority so far-reaching that he could override the policies of other ministers, such was the symbolism of the keys of the kingdom. It would be meaningless to speak of the authority of other ministers to bind and loose apart from their unity with Peter. The purpose was not to make Peter some type of dictator in regard to the other Apostles; they were

---

[199] Jaki, Stanley, *The Keys of the Kingdom: A Tools Witness to Truth* (Franciscan Hearld Press, 1987), p.27-28.

brothers charged with the mission of representing Christ to the world. In Christ's Kingdom the greatest serves the rest. In the Kingdom here on earth this service would involve speaking the final word when matters are in dispute, thus maintaining the unity of the Body. This service would be especially important when those disputing were fellow shepherds.

Jesus' declaration that "whatever you bind on earth shall be bound in heaven," cannot mean that God was bound to rearrange spiritual and temporal realities to coincide with whatever Peter arbitrarily decided. God is not manipulated. Peter was but the servant in Another's Kingdom; he spoke to the Church and the world on behalf of the King. Jesus' declaration only makes sense if we recognize a corresponding action on God's part – that should Peter ever attempt to teach something false, God would intervene to prevent him from doing so.

The last piece we need to consider is also implicit in Jesus' statement to Peter. I have already said that Jesus revived the office of the vizier and that Simon would hold it (once the Holy Spirit had been breathed upon him). Yet, Peter's sojourn on earth would come to an end; the Kingdom (or Church's) survival on earth, on the other hand, was guaranteed by our Lord until the end of time. Because of that fact we should expect there to be *successors* to Peter, others to hold the much needed keys of service.

Lets now turn our gaze to the Upper Room, the place where Peter would receive the Holy Spirit (John 20:22-23; Acts 1:13, 2:1-4). I don't wish to jump immediately to the day of Pentecost but to peer into this room some fifty-four days earlier, during the Last Supper. The Lord's time in the world was short and He spent His final night preparing the Apostles for the intense days that lay ahead. He gave them the Eucharist, the means of continually uniting their lives and ours with the power of His death, resurrection, and ascension.[200] He also spoke of the Spirit's coming: "I will pray the Father, and he will give you another Counselor, to be with you forever, even the Spirit of Truth. . .the Holy Spirit whom the Father will send in my name, he will teach you all things, and bring to your remembrance all that I

---

[200] As I noted earlier in the text, Dr. Brant Pitre makes an excellent observation: In offering His Body and Blood under the appearances of bread and wine, Jesus fulfills the messianic prophecy of Psalm 110:4, "You are a *priest* forever, after the manner of Melchizedek." In commanding the Apostles to "do this in memory of Me," He was inserting them into *His own priestly ministry*.

have said to you. . .he will guide you into all the truth" (John 14:16-17, 26; 16:13).

Truth – proclaiming the Truth of Christ – is one of the chief reasons for lavishing the Spirit upon the Apostles.[201] Teaching and living the Truth is *the* business of the Kingdom, the Church; and Christ, by His divine power, guarantees she will succeed. Paul the Apostle, moved by the Holy Spirit, wrote of "the household [or family] of God, which is the church of the living God, *the* pillar and bulwark of truth" (1 Timothy 3:15). That is the Church's identity. To fulfill that role she would need something very special from God: a divine protection from teaching error. Without that protection the Church could not be what the Apostle Paul claimed. This hearkens back to Jesus' words to Peter about the Church not being overcome by Satan, but instead doing the overcoming. For that purpose the Apostles were promised, at the Last Supper, the charism of Truth. Peter, as the servant of the rest and the holder of the keys, would need to possess the charism of Truth, or infallibility, in a preeminent way. Being granted the "final word" on questions concerning Revelation and morality within the Church logically necessitates it.[202]

Jesus' words to Simon-Peter at the Last Supper brought his role into stark relief. Jesus warned the man who would be Rock, "Simon, Simon, behold, Satan demanded to have you [singular], that he might sift you [plural] like wheat, but I have prayed for you [singular] that your faith may not fail; and when you have turned again, strengthen your brethren" (Luke 22:31-32; information in brackets added). Satan is a creature of immense intelligence. To single out Simon for attack denotes his importance; take out the one who was to become Rock for the others, and the whole group would

---

[201] The other is God's love for them as sons, the same love He has for each of us.

[202] Some will dispute Peter's use of the charism of infallibility later in his life – saying that St. Paul had to correct him (Galatians 2). If we read Paul's account, however, we see that Paul wasn't calling Peter to repentance on a matter of error in formulating doctrine – the area which is protected by the gift of infallibility. Rather, Paul is calling Peter to repent because he had spoken God's Truth that Christians need not follow Jewish dietary law – but then refrained from taking non-Kosher meals with the Gentiles when the community was visited by Jewish converts who couldn't yet divorce themselves from that obligation. Peter's actions caused scandal – he had proclaimed that dietary laws didn't matter but then acted as if they did. There's no violation of infallibility there; Peter was rendered infallible in his *proclamation* of Christ's Truth – *he wasn't rendered impeccable in his living of the proclamation.*

fold. In response to the Lord's warning Simon pledged that he would follow the Lord even to prison and death. We know he did not though. Simon had to learn a lesson; his own strength and resolve were pitiful – he would deny the Lord three times. Only by hitting his knees in repentance, confessing his weakness and sin and receiving Jesus' strength, Jesus' Holy Spirit, could Simon become *Cephas*, Rock. (John 20:21-22).

Jesus officially installed Simon in his office of servant and shepherd to the entire flock on the shores of Lake Galilee. Before six others, four of whom Scripture clearly identifies as Apostles, the risen Jesus asked him "Simon, son of John, do you love me more than these?" Peter answered "Yes, Lord." "Feed my lambs." The exchange was repeated two more times, mirroring Simon's three denials (John 21:15-19). When that painful moment came to an end Christ's Rock foundation had been laid; He could now build His Church upon him.

It bears recalling what Jesus mandated the Apostles to do just prior to His ascension. His command was not to write the New Testament but to assist in the birthing of the Church, the Kingdom. "Go therefore and make disciples of all nations, *baptizing* them in the name of the Father and of the Son and of the Holy Spirit, *teaching* them to observe *all* that I have commanded you; and lo, I am with you always, to the close of the age" (Matthew 28:19-20). All that remained was to grant them the fire of Pentecost:

> he charged them not to depart from Jerusalem, but to wait for the promise of the Father, which, he said, "you heard from me, for John baptized with water, but before many days you shall be baptized with the Holy Spirit...you shall receive power when the Holy Spirit has come upon you; and you shall be my witnesses in Jerusalem and in all Judea and Samaria and to the ends of the earth. And when he had said this, as they were looking on, he was lifted up, and a cloud took him out of their sight (Acts 1:4-5, 8-9).

The Apostles did just as Jesus commanded. They returned to the Upper Room and spent nine days joined in prayer with Mary (Jesus' Mother and now theirs) and 107 other disciples.[203] During those nine days before

---

[203] The nine days of prayer proceeding Pentecost is mirrored today when Catholic Christians "pray a novena" – nine days of prayer for a particular intention.

Pentecost we find the first instance of apostolic succession, someone succeeding to the office of shepherd left vacant by the death of an Apostle:

> Peter stood up among the brethren (the company of persons was in all about a hundred and twenty), and said, "Brethren, the scripture had to be fulfilled, which the Holy Spirit spoke beforehand by the mouth of David, concerning Judas who was guide those who arrested Jesus. For he was numbered among us, and was allotted his share in this ministry…it is written in the book of Psalms,
>> 'Let his habitation become desolate, and let there be no one to live in it'[Ps.69:25]; and
>> 'His *office* let another take.' [Ps.109:8]
>
> So one of the men who have accompanied us during all the time that the Lord Jesus went in and out among us, beginning from the baptism of John until the day when he was taken up from us – one of these men must become with us a witness to his resurrection. And they put forward two, Joseph called Barsabbas, who was surnamed Justus, and Matthias. And they prayed and said, "Lord, who knowest the hearts of all men, show which of these two thou hast chosen to take the place in *this ministry and apostleship* from which Judas turned aside, to go to his own place." And they cast lots for them, and the lot fell on Matthias; and he was *enrolled* with the eleven apostles (Acts 1:15-26).

On the day of Pentecost the Church, the Kingdom, was inaugurated in power. The Spirit of God was unleashed upon the Church in a new way. In that single day three thousand people accepted baptism and were born into the Family, also receiving the gift of the Spirit. I believe that in our own day, through the various renewal movements the Holy Spirit has raised up, we are witnessing something of what the gift of the Spirit meant in the day-to-day life of the first Christians. That they saw themselves as a family is witnessed to by how they conducted themselves:

> They devoted themselves to the apostles' teaching and fellowship, to the breaking of bread and the prayers. . . And all those who believed were together and had all things in common; and they sold their possessions and goods and distributed them to all, as any had need. And day by day, attending the temple, and breaking bread in their homes,

they partook of food with glad and generous hearts, praising God and having favor with all the people" (Acts 2:42, 44-47).

The Shepherds Ordain Others

It did not take long for circumstances to teach the Twelve that they would need help in shepherding the flock. (Circumstance is often one of the Lord's greatest teachers.) The Church, though still limited to Judea at that point, was growing by leaps and bounds. The Twelve could not personally see to the bodily needs of dependent members of the community. So that they could "concentrate on prayer and the ministry of the word" (Acts 6:4) the office of deacon was created. Seven men were chosen and ordained by the Apostles via prayer and the laying on of hands (Acts 6:6). Reading *Acts of the Apostles* it quickly becomes evident that the deacons were also given a share in the Twelve's ministry of teaching; the deacon Philip was the Holy Spirit's instrument in bringing the faith to the Samaritans, and Stephen was so outspoken that he became the Church's first martyr.

His martyrdom marked the beginning of the Church's first great persecution. Saul of Tarsus, known to most of us as Paul, would play a large part in it. As Christians left Jerusalem for safer areas they spread the faith as they went. The Kingdom was extending itself beyond Judea; the Holy Spirit soon arranged for Peter to welcome the first Gentiles into the Family of the Church. The Jewish Christians, raised to consider the Gentiles as no better than swine, had such a difficult time with this that had the Holy Spirit used anyone but the key-bearer they may have been unable to acquiesce (See Acts 11). Once the Lord Jesus brought Paul to the light of faith the Church's boundaries would grow to include almost the whole of the Roman Empire. The reality of all this expansion was that the Twelve needed to ordain still others to share in their ministry, ones who would assume more of the Apostles' functions than the deacons had.

Thus we begin to hear of presbyters (Greek for "elders") and bishops (literally "overseers"). The terms seem to have been used almost interchangeably in Paul's epistles. Both Peter and Paul referred to them as shepherds of God's flock (Acts 20:28; 1 Peter 5:1). As such they shared in the authority of the Apostles, "you that are younger be subject to the elders" (1 Peter 5:5). "Obey your leaders and submit to them; for they are keeping watch over your souls, as men who will have to give account. Let them do this joyfully, and not sadly, for that would be of no advantage to you" (Hebrews 13:17). Paul wrote to his fellow minister Titus, "This is why I left you in Crete, that you might appoint elders in every town as I directed you. . .a bishop, as God's steward, must be blameless. . .he must hold firm to the sure word as taught, so that he may be able to give instruction in sound doctrine and also to confute those who contradict it" (Titus 1:5, 7, 9). "[A bishop] must manage his own household well, keeping his children submissive and respectful in every way; for if a man does not know how to manage his own household, how can he care for God's church?" (1 Timothy 3:4-5). During the Council of Jerusalem, when it was being discerned whether the Gentile converts needed to be circumcised or take on other elements of Jewish ceremonial law, the decision was reached by the Apostles *in union with* the elders (Acts 15:6). The letter drafted and sent to the Gentile believers in Antioch, Syria, and Celicia began,

> The brethren, *both the apostles and the elders*, to the brethren who are of the Gentiles. . .Since *we* have heard that some persons [from Jerusalem] have troubled you with words, unsettling your minds, although we gave them no instructions, it has seemed good to us *in assembly* to choose men and send them to you with our beloved Barnabas and Paul...For it has seemed good *to the Holy Spirit and to us* to lay no greater burden than these necessary things" (Acts 15:23-25).

The bishops/elders (elders = presbyters in Greek) were entrusted with other aspects of the Apostles' ministry as well. They received the ministry of anointing and praying for healing, a prayer whose efficacy obtained pardon for sin. The Apostles could not be present to each branch of the Church; others had to be appointed to their ministry of "binding and loosing" from sin, "Is any among you sick? Let him call for the elders of the church, and let them pray over him, anointing him with oil in the name of the Lord; and the prayer of faith will save the sick man, and the Lord will raise him up; and if he has committed sins, he will be forgiven" (James 5:14-15). The bishops/elders were also empowered to ordain others to their ministry; when Paul wrote to the young bishop Timothy he encouraged him, "Do not neglect the gift you have, which was given you by prophetic utterance *when the elders laid their hands upon you*" (1 Timothy 4:14). This marks the second time we have heard of a rite of ordination, the first being in connection with the deacons. That the bishops/elders also presided at the Eucharist during New Testament times is a foregone conclusion considering the solemnity of the act and the way they shared in the other unique elements of apostolic ministry.

Even with the appointment of bishops/presbyters and deacons the Apostles continued to feel a personal love and responsibility for the entire Church. Paul, the thirteenth Apostle if you will, made a point of communicating through letters to various branches of the Church – admonishing, praising, and correcting them. Peter and John also wrote letters to the young flock. The Apostles' letters clearly were not written to set out the faith in a systematic way (as a catechism, or book of doctrine, would) but to address the situations being immediately encountered by the Church. That their letters contain statements of belief is obvious, but an orderly and systematic presentation of belief was not their goal; that had already been accomplished through their preaching and that of the bishops and deacons. Peter and John – and Matthew if we include his gospel – were the only members of the Twelve whose writings have come down to us (the epistles of James and Jude were not penned by Apostles but by relatives of the Lord Jesus who came to faith after the resurrection). Not even the gospels were written to be full accounts of Christ's life and teaching; John made this clear when ending his gospel, "Now Jesus did many other signs in the presence of his disciples, which are not written in this book. . . But there are also many other things which Jesus did; were every one of them to be written, I suppose that the world itself could not contain the books that would be written" (John 20:30; 21:25).

But again, Jesus Himself had not penned a book. Had He done so it still would have been liable to misinterpretation. Nor are we told that He commanded any of His Apostles to do so prior to His ascension. They were sent to preach, teach, baptize, shepherd, bind and loose. When writing allowed them to address a distant part of the Church the Holy Spirit inspired their message, just as He did when they taught their flocks face-to-face. But writing was not the primary way the Spirit made the Gospel known in the world; it was through the members of the Church, Christ's Mystical Body. For that reason He raised up apostles, prophets, evangelists, pastors and teachers to build up the body of Christ (Ephesians 4:11).

THE CHURCH & THE WORD OF GOD

Rather than commit every nuance of the Faith to writing the Apostles followed the model given them by the Master. As Paul taught the bishop Timothy, "what you have heard from me before many witnesses entrust to faithful men who will be able to teach others" (2 Timothy 2:2). The faith was deposited by Christ within the Church, and the Apostles were made its guardians. They in turn, guided by the Holy Spirit, ordained others to share in that service to the Body. Their teaching was authoritative, whether verbal or written, "So then, bretheren, stand firm and hold to *the traditions* which you were taught by us, *either by word of mouth or by letter*" (2 Thessalonians 2:15). This Tradition is not something created by men. By Tradition (with a capital "T") I am not referring to customs such as fasting on certain days, styles of dress, the Mass being said in Latin, etc. No, by Tradition I am mean the Truths taught us by the God-Man and His Apostles, elements of the Gospel. That it cannot be corrupted is a guarantee made by our Savior to Peter and the Eleven.

Nowhere in the New Testament are we taught that Scripture and Tradition are to exist as two separate entities. To truly possess the full word of Christ we are going to have to give ear to both; only the two together make up the Word of God. If someone were to examine the correspondence between members of my family, the Kapler's, do you think they could reconstruct our life as a family? Only very imperfectly. There have to be a hundred unwritten rules about how we relate to one another. If someone wanted to really know us then they would need to hang around the house, pull up a chair for dinner, learn the old family stories (which are so familiar to all of us that we wouldn't think to lay them out in our correspondence with each other). In short you have to have the family tradition to understand what it is to be a Kapler, possibly to even understand things we write to each other, comments made in passing, etc.

The same is true for the Family of the Church. The knowledge and experience which comes to us from the Church is infinitely more important than the experience of being a Kapler; it involves the fullness of blessings God wishes us to have in this world and our eternal well being in the next. Besides needing the Family Traditions and the Family Writings (the Scripture), the Church constantly needs authoritative interpretation of these two sources in the face of ever-new challenges and deceptions. This is the function of the popes and bishops; if we want to know what the Tradition of the Church is, how to understand a difficult passage of Scripture, then we need only seek out their authoritative teaching. This is the method the Lord gave us of keeping the Truth intact, and I am not about to debate Him on its merits.

Allow me to come at this issue of Tradition, Scripture, and the teaching authority of the Church from a different angle, that of a speech-language pathologist. One of the first things I learned about language was that the *context*, or setting, in which a message is spoken and received greatly affects its meaning. For example, if a friend walked up to you and said, "Well, it looks like you're having a great day!" the events of your day will affect how you understand it – if you are grinning from ear to ear when it is said then you understand that he is just making an observation, possibly implying that he wants to know why you are so happy. If that same friend says that to you after you have walked into work ten minutes late and then spilled coffee on your boss, then you understand his words as sarcasm. Now let's pretend that when your friend says that to you in the second example you are so disheveled that you think he is serious – that you really do look like you are having a good day. You don't understand how he could think that. What do you do? You say, "What do you mean? Do you see that stain on Mr. Smith's suit? I am having a horrible day!" Your friend would probably answer, "Hey, I was just trying to lighten your spirits, kid around with you. I can tell it's a tough morning." The technical term for clearing up these misunderstandings, or breakdowns in communication, is "conversational repair." It is something that most of us make use of everyday in conversation – we are not sure we have understood a friend correctly so we say, "Now let me make sure I have got this right. . ."

Now if context and conversational repair are necessary for correctly understanding daily human interactions then I would definitely expect to need them when it comes to understanding a message as important as the Gospel. What I mean by this is that the Truth of Christ comes to us in the language of men and women, words open to misunderstanding, and therefore we need to know context to understand them properly - and we have to have an opportunity to question the speaker to make sure we have got it right. God gifted us with language; He knows what we need to use it effectively. For that reason Christ gave us not only the Scripture but Tradition (context)[204] and His duly appointed spokeswoman the Church (who can answer our questions).

A good example of the interplay between these three elements can be found by looking back at the chapter on the Sacrament of Reconciliation. The Apostle John wrote, "If we confess our sins, he is faithful and just, and will forgive our sins and cleanse us from all unrighteousness"(1 John 1:9). I have heard several of my fundamentalist brothers and sisters quote this passage as a proof that confession of sins to a presbyter, or priest, is unbiblical; our confession should be made "directly to God." But in making that claim they are taking the passage out of its context. John said simply that if we acknowledge our sins the Lord can be counted on to forgive them; he did not stipulate if we should do that through private prayer, or for grave sins, make confession through God's ordained representative. A person raised in a Protestant home, or who first learned the faith from Protestant brothers and sisters, upon hearing this passage, will probably make an automatic mental adjustment and add "directly to God" to the passage. One raised as a Catholic will probably hear it and automatically makes the adjustment, "directly to God *through His ordained representative, the priest.*" Realizing that only one of these meanings can be objectively correct[205] we have to ask what the original context of John's statement was. If we consult *John 20:23* and *James 5:15-16* we find that confession of sin, grave sin, was not just a matter for private prayer; it called for the ministry of the ordained shepherds – the apostles or bishops/presbyters. We also have the historical witness from the first three centuries of the Church that there was a public rite of confession – made to God, through the presbyter, in front of the entire Church congregation. So when we consider *1 John 1:19* within the larger context of both the New Testament and the early post-apostolic Church we see that John is not calling confession through the presbyters unbiblical. If someone continues to debate this, however, they can seek out the teaching of Peter's successor on the matter; he too confirms that confession through a presbyter is the normal means of remitting serious sin.

---

[204] Tradition is not only a matter of giving context; some elements of the Christian belief come down to us only through Tradition.
[205] This is assuming we're talking about mortal sin; venial sin can be remitted through private prayer *or* confession through a minister.

I confess that the Bible is the inspired, inerrant Word of God. Yet what I have realized is that if we misunderstand that Word it does not profit us in the way God intends. If we neglect Tradition and the teaching of those whom Christ protects from error (the Popes and the Pope and Bishops gathered in Councils[206]) then we are going to miss out on part of the message.

Where Does the Bible say "The Bible Alone"?

I know that there are brothers and sisters who will continue to insist that the Bible, and the Bible alone, should be the Christian's sole authority. There are certain passages of Scripture that they appeal to in making this claim; if they are correct then that introduces a contradiction as we have already seen numerous passages referring to Tradition and Church as authoritative. As a brother, concerned with Family unity, I wish to examine the passages that are put forward as support for a "Bible only" hypothesis, explaining why I am convinced that they do not teach this.

The most frequently cited verse is *2 Timothy 3:16*, "All scripture is inspired by God and profitable for teaching, for reproof, for correction, and for training in righteousness, that the man of God may be complete, equipped for every good work." Before saying anything else I have to point out that the Apostle Paul said "all Scripture" is profitable for this purpose; he did not say that "only Scripture" was profitable. The next thing I wish to point out is that Paul was writing this letter to one of the early Church's bishops," his "son in faith" Timothy. It is a personal correspondence from an older shepherd and teacher to a younger. Understanding that, let's read the verse in context:

> …evil men and imposters will go on from bad to worse, deceivers and deceived. But as for you, continue in what you have learned and believed, *knowing from who you learned it*…and how from your childhood *you have known the sacred writings* which are able to instruct you for salvation through faith in Christ Jesus. All scripture is inspired by God and profitable for **teaching, for reproof, for correction, and for training in righteousness,** that the man of God may be complete, equipped

---

[206] These are known as Ecumenical Councils. Taking the Council of Jerusalem (Acts 15) as our starting point, the popes and bishops have met in this way 21 other times.

for every good work. I charge you in the presence of God and of Christ Jesus who is to judge the living and the dead, and by his appearing and his kingdom: **preach the word**, be urgent in season and out of season, **convince, rebuke, and exhort, be unfailing in patience and teaching** (2 Timothy 3:13 – 4:2).

Read in context, I believe that *2 Timothy 3:16* is Paul's instruction to Timothy on how to be an effective preacher. First, Timothy needs to be faithful to what he learned from his Christian teachers. Likewise, he should make use of the Old Testament; therefore, Apostolic Tradition and Scripture are both extolled in this passage.

Allow me to advance an interpretation at this point – my own, not that of the Pope or bishops: Could it be that it is *the bishop Timothy's teaching*, itself nourished by Scripture, which will make his flock "complete, equipped for every good work"? I say this because of the repetition of the concepts (see portions in bold) where Paul charges him to *preach* both in season and out of season. If my line of thought is wrong here it is really of no consequence.

There is another reason why *2 Timothy 3:16* will not support my more fundamentalist brothers' and sisters' interpretation. If you disregard all I have written so far you still have to contend with the major glitch pointed out by Cardinal John Henry Newman:

> The Apostle here refers to the Scriptures, which Timothy was taught in his infancy. Now, a good part of the New Testament was not written in his boyhood: some of the Catholic Epistles[207] were not written even when St. Paul wrote this, and none of the Books of the New Testament were then placed on the canon of the Scripture books. He refers, then, to the Scriptures of the Old Testament, and if the argument from this passage proved anything, *it would prove too much*, viz., that *the Scriptures of the New Testament were not necessary for a rule of faith*.[208]

In fact, the full twenty-seven books of the *New* Testament would not be placed on the canon of Scripture for three hundred years. We will examine

---

[207] This refers to the epistles written by Peter, John, James, and Jude; these works were not addressed to specific communities as Paul's were, but to the Church universal (catholic).
[208] Found in Keating's *Catholicism & Fundamentalism*, p.136; originally in Newman's *On The Inspiration of Scripture*, p.131.

208 THE GOD WHO IS LOVE

the development of the canon, or authoritative list of New Testament books, shortly.

Some believers have tried to buttress a belief in the "Bible alone" from the last chapter of *The Book of Revelation*, the book found at the end of the New Testament. Allow me to italicize portions of the verses in question to illustrate why it does not teach what my well-intentioned brothers and sisters claim:

> I warn every one who hears the words of the prophecy of *this book*: if any one adds to them, God will add to him *the plagues described* in *this book*, and if any one takes away from the words of *the book* of *this prophecy*, God will take away his share in the tree of life and in the holy city, which are described in *this book* (Revelation 22:18-19).

Because the book is found at the end of the New Testament it is claimed that this verse should be applied to the whole Bible – anything added to the words of the Bible such as Tradition or Church teaching is therefore deserving of a curse. That is making a huge leap! John repeatedly said *"this* book," The Book of Revelation. He was telling people not to make additions to *this* particular book. The mention of the plagues should settle it for us.

If that is not enough, though, there is that fact that *The Book of Revelation*, or *The Apocalypse*, was one of the last books to be recognized as belonging to the New Testament. For a large number of Christians these words would not have been found at the end of the Bible up until the late-fourth or early-fifth century. Beside this there is also an Old Testament corollary to John's warning. Moses had instructed the Israelites, "And now, O Israel, give heed to the statutes and the ordinances which I teach you, and do them...You shall not add to what I command you, nor take from it" (Deuteronomy 4:1-2). If that verse is to be taken the way some take *Revelation 22:18-19* then the Old Testament should have ended after the first five books. But Moses was speaking about a particular body of teaching that was not to be tampered with – the Law, and his listeners knew it.

In defense of "the Bible alone" hypothesis some have pointed to the example of the Bereans given in *Acts 17:11-12*. It reads "Now these Jews [of Beroea] were more noble than those in Thessalonica, for they received the word with all eagerness, *examining the scriptures daily to see if these things [that*

Paul taught] were so. Many of them therefore believed." To understand this passage it would be helpful to go back a few verses in *Acts* to see how the Thessalonians, with whom the Bereans are contrasted, reacted to the Gospel:

> [Paul and Silas] came to Thessalonica where there was a synagogue of the Jews. And Paul went in, as his custom was, and for three Sabbath weeks he *argued with them from the scriptures, explaining and proving that it was necessary for the Christ to suffer and to rise from the dead*, and saying, "This Jesus, whom I proclaim to you, is the Christ." And some of them were persuaded. . .[But others] were jealous, and taking some wicked fellows of the rabble, they gathered a crowd, [and] set the city in an uproar (Acts 17:1-3, 5).

Paul was speaking to a Jewish audience, trying to show them that Jesus had fulfilled the Old Testament prophecies of the Messiah. Much more so than the Thessalonians, the Bereans took Paul up on the challenge and poured over those prophecies for themselves, comparing them with the Gospel Paul preached. A similar explanation holds for Jesus' words to the Jewish leaders in *John 5:39*, "You search the scriptures, because you think that in them you have eternal life; and it is they that bear witness to me." Jesus is simply directing them back to the Old Testament which prophesied His life and ministry. These passages have nothing to do with teaching that the Bible was meant to stand alone, apart from Tradition and the teaching authority of the Church.

When we separate Sacred Scripture from Sacred Tradition and the teaching of the Church's shepherds we run into trouble. We are left with our own fallible interpretation of Scripture. If we turn away from the mechanisms which Jesus and the Holy Spirit have put in place to keep us in His Truth that is the result. I think that is the best explanation for why so many people are reading the Scripture and sincerely praying to the Holy Spirit for understanding but coming up with contradictory interpretations: One says that baptism is merely a symbol, another that it is a necessity for salvation; one that only baptism by immersion is legitimate and another that pouring and sprinkling are just as valid. One person teaches that salvation cannot be lost, another that it can through serious sin. The Holy Spirit has provided a means through the confusion, if only we take it – if we but listen

210   THE GOD WHO IS LOVE

to the shepherds He has established for us, those who have the same guarantee of Truth as that given to Peter and the Apostles.[209]

Successors to the Apostles

Is there *really* evidence that the authority of the Apostles, and the guarantee that their teaching would be that of the Holy Spirit, was passed onto others, to continue in the Church until the end of time? I think we have already reviewed the biblical portion of it:

- Jesus revived the office of the Master of the Palace and made Peter its first occupant.
- *Peter moved that another fill the office left vacant by Judas.*
- The Apostles raised up bishops (overseers), or presbyters (elders), as well as deacons and gave them a share in their ministry.
- The decision reached by the Council of Jerusalem was said to be not only that of the Apostles but the presbyters (elders).
- The presbyters shared in the Apostles' authority to absolve sins.
- The apostles charged the flock with being obedient to the guidance of the presbyters.
- We know from the Apostle Paul that the bishops/presbyters were to pass on their offices to others: "what you have heard from me before many witnesses entrust to faithful men who will be able to teach others" (2 Timothy 2:2).

We need to look at history and see whom some of the "faithful men," or bishops, were. You see, after the deaths of the Apostles, one presbyter (elder) in a given community was raised above the others, becoming a bishop or "overseer," establishing the role of bishop as we know it in the Church today. That such was the Apostles' will is witnessed to by the silence in which this transition occurred; the first Christians would have been

---

[209] I get an eerie feeling when I read the Apostle Peter's *Second Epistle* and recall how misunderstandings of the Apostle Paul's letters have led to so many divisions within Christianity. *2 Peter 3:15-16* reads, "Consider that our Lord's patience is directed toward salvation. Paul, our beloved brother, wrote you this in the spirit of wisdom that is his, dealing with these matters as he does in all his letters. There are certain passages in them hard to understand. The ignorant and the unstable distort them (just as they do the rest of Scripture) to their own ruin . . ."

in an uproar if it was some unsanctioned innovation. In addition to this, there is also the historical record which claims this was Christ's will. For most of my life my thinking on the Church leaped from the period of the New Testament straight to today, with a short layover in the Middle Ages and the period of the Reformation. There is so much more that can be known though. Chiefly I am referring to the writings of the Church Fathers, those whom God used to guide the Church through her darkest days, as well as the "Apostolic Fathers" – those who lived closest in time to the Apostles, some of them actually having known and been instructed by the Apostles. I had never been given any instruction about these men, and sadly I find this to be the case for the majority of today's Christians – even ministers.

The first person we will look at is Clement of Rome. He was the bishop of that city, quite a responsibility as both Peter and Paul shepherded there before being martyred.[210] What is important for us to realize is that this man held the keys of the Kingdom; when Peter was martyred in Rome the bishop of that city succeeded to his office. In approximately 80 A.D. Clement, the third to succeed to Peter's ministry, wrote a letter to the Church in Corinth. The Corinthians were in rebellion against their presbyters. He reminded them of the Church-order established by Christ:

> The Apostles received the gospel for us from the Lord Jesus Christ...they went forth in the complete assurance of the word of God, preaching the good news that the Kingdom of God is coming. Through countryside and city they preached; and they appointed their

---

[210] The early Church amply attests to Peter and Paul's martyrdom in Rome. The following quotations are from Jurgens, William A., *The Faith of the Early Fathers*, Volume 1(Collegeville, Minnesota: The Liturgical Press, 1970):
Ignatius, Bishop of Antioch, wrote to the Roman Church in 110 A.D., "Not as Peter and Paul did, do I command you," p.22.
In a letter from Dionysius, Bishop of Corinth, to Soter, Bishop of Rome, in 170 A.D. the former said, "You have also, by your very admonition, brought together the planting that was made by Peter and Paul at Rome," p.45.
Tertullian, in c.200 A.D. wrote, "But if you are near to Italy, you have Rome...where Peter endured a passion like that of the Lord, where Paul was crowned in a death like John [the Baptist's]" p.122

> earliest converts, testing them by the spirit, to be the bishops and deacons of future believers (*Letter to the Corinthians* 42:1-4).[211]
>
> Our Apostles knew through our Lord Jesus Christ that there would be strife for the office of bishop. For this reason, therefore, having received perfect foreknowledge, they appointed those who have already been mentioned, and afterwards added the further provision that, if they should die, other approved men should succeed to their ministry. As for these, then, who were appointed by them, or who were afterwards appointed by other illustrious men with the consent of the whole Church…we consider it unjust that they be removed from the ministry. Our sin will not be small if we eject from the episcopate those who blamelessly and holily have offered its Sacrifices (*Letter to the Corinthians* 44:1-3).[212]

Clement, as a bishop, was the successor to the Apostle's authority within the Church. As the Bishop of Rome he was the successor to one Apostle in particular – Peter, Christ's chief steward and wielder of the keys. When the time came for Peter to leave this world someone had to assume his office; all of Christian history says that it was the Bishop of Rome. We will come to the outright statements soon enough. For the present we find sufficient testimony in Clement's words to the Corinthians,

> Shameful, beloved, extremely shameful, and unworthy of your training in Christ, is the report that on account of one or two persons the well-established and ancient Church of the Corinthians is in revolt against the presbyters (47:6).[213]
>
> You, therefore, who laid the foundation of the rebellion, submit to the presbyters and be chastened to repentance, bending your knees in a spirit of humility. (57:1)[214]
>
> Accept our counsel and you will have nothing to regret. (58:2)[215]

---

[211] Ibid, p.10
[212] Ibid
[213] Ibid, p.11
[214] Ibid
[215] Ibid

> If anyone disobeys the things which have been said by Him through us, let them know that *they will involve themselves in transgression and in no small danger* (59:1).[216]

Clement was using the keys to restore unity to the Family. It was apparently well within his rights to do so: The Apostle John was still alive at the time and would surely have intervened if the Church in Rome had overstepped its bounds. But instead of this, history tells us that the Corinthians repented. Eighty years later Dionysius, the Bishop of Corinth, wrote to Soter, then Bishop of Rome, telling him how Clement's letter was still read aloud during Sunday worship. That means that the Corinthians would have read it right alongside Scripture! Clement's words carried a lot of force in the minds of the early Christians.

Another Apostolic Father from whom we have correspondence is Ignatius, the Bishop of Antioch. He wrote his letters while being transported from Antioch to Rome (where he would be fed to the lions in 110 A.D.). Ignatius had actually heard the Apostle John proclaim the faith. What was Ignatius' understanding of the Church? If this man did not understand the faith then *none* of *us* should feel safe.

> I cried out while I was in your midst, I spoke with a loud voice, the voice of God: *"Give heed to the bishop and the presbytery and the deacons."* Some suspected me of saying this because I had previous knowledge of the divisions which certain persons had caused; but He for whom I am in chains is my witness that I had no knowledge of this from any human being. It was the Spirit who kept preaching these words: *"Do nothing without the bishop,* keep your body as the temple of God, love unity, *flee from divisions,* be imitators of Jesus Christ, as He was imitator of the Father" (*Letter to the Philadelphians* 7:1).[217]

> Indeed, when you submit to the bishop as you would to Jesus Christ, it is clear to me that you are living not in the manner of men but as Jesus Christ, who died for us, that through faith in His death you might escape dying. It is necessary, therefore, and such is your practice, – that you do nothing without the bishop, and that you be subject also to the

---

[216] Ibid
[217] Ibid, p.23

presbytery, as to the Apostles of Jesus Christ our hope, in whom we shall be found, if we live in Him. It is necessary also that the deacons, the dispensers of the mysteries of Jesus Christ, be in every way pleasing to all men (*Letter to the Trallians* 2:1-3).[218]

Wherever the bishop appears, let all the people be there; just as wherever Jesus Christ is, there is the Catholic Church (*Letter to the Smyrnaeans* 8:2).[219]

Ignatius' *Letter to the Church in Rome* bears witness to the position of leadership that part of the Body held for all Christians:

To the church beloved and enlightened after the love of Jesus Christ, our God, by the will of Him that willed everything which is; to the church which *holds the presidency* in the place of the country of the Romans...who are filled with the grace of God without wavering, and who *are filtered clear of every foreign stain*. You have envied no one; but *others you have taught*. I desire only that *what you have enjoined in your instructions may remain in force* (1:1, 3:1).

For me this is an acknowledgement of the purity and force of Rome's teaching – an implicit acknowledgement of its' bishop's office as Rock and key-bearer of Christ's Church.[220]

In those early centuries Satan came against the Church with everything he had. One of his chief weapons was religious deception – trying to mingle falsehood with Truth. The Gnostics were a diverse and pesky group for the Church; they claimed to possess secret teachings of the Apostles, a wisdom

---

[218] Ibid, p.20

[219] Ibid, p.25. This is the first written record we have of Christ' Church being called the Catholic Church. The date was approximately 110 A.D. It's interesting that it would come from a citizen of Antioch; that is the city in which the name "Christian" was first used (Acts 11:26).
The term "Catholic Church" spread very quickly. By 155 A.D. *The Martyrdom of Polycarp*, a Christian classic, was addressed to "all the diocese of the holy and Catholic Church, in every place" (*The Faith of the Early Fathers*, Vol.1, p.30). The earliest list of books to be included in the New Testament, *The Muratorian Fragment* (155 - 200 A.D.), speaks of "one church spread abroad through the whole world ...the Catholic Church" (*The Faith of Early Fathers*, Vol.1, p.108).

[220] For a discussion of what it means for the Pope to speak *ex cathedra*, or "from the chair [of Peter]," please refer back to Chapter 8, p.145.

not known to the masses. To combat them, and the myriad of other splinter groups, the Church called her children to hold fast to the Rock Christ established. Irenaeus, the Bishop of Lyons (France), in his masterly *Against the Heresies,* put forward the Bishops of Rome from Peter to the time of the work's composition (c.189 A.D.):

> Since it is too long to enumerate in such a volume as this the succession of all the Churches, we shall confound all those who, in whatever manner, whether through self-satisfaction or vainglory, or through blindness and wicked opinion assemble other than where it is proper, by pointing out here the successions of the bishops of the greatest and most ancient church known to all, founded and organized at Rome by the two most glorious Apostles, Peter and Paul, that Church which has the tradition of the faith which comes down to us after having been announced to men by the Apostles. *For with this Church, because of its superior origin, all churches must agree, that is, all the faithful in the whole of the world; and it is in her that the faithful everywhere have maintained the Apostolic tradition.*
>
> The Blessed Apostles [Peter and Paul] having founded and built up the church [of Rome], they handed over the office of the episcopate to Linus. Paul makes mention of this Linus in the Epistle to Timothy. To him succeeded Anencletus; and after him, in the third place from the Apostles, Clement was chosen for the episcopate. He had seen the Blessed Apostles and was acquainted with them. It might be said that he still heard the echoes of the preaching of the Apostles, and had their traditions before his eyes. And not only he, for there were many still remaining who had been instructed by the Apostles.
>
> . . .To this Clement, Evaristus succeeded; and Alexander succeeded Evaristus. Then, sixth after the Apostles, Sixtus was appointed; after him, Telesphorus, who also was gloriously martyred. Then Hyginus; after him, Pius; and after him, Anicetus. Soter succeeded Anicetus, and now, in the twelfth place after the Apostles, the lot of the episcopate

has fallen to Eleutherus. *In this order, and by the teaching of the Apostles handed down in the Church, the preaching of the truth has come down to us* (Book III, 3:2-3).[221]

Irenaeus had many other things to say about apostolic succession and Sacred Tradition.

> Polycarp, however, was instructed not only by the Apostles, and conversed with many who had seen Christ, but was also appointed bishop of the Church in Smyrna, by the Apostles in Asia. I saw him in my early youth; for he tarried a long time, and when quite old he departed this life in a glorious and most noble martyrdom. He always taught those things which he had learned from the Apostles, and which the Church had handed down, and which are true. To these things all the Churches in Asia bear witness, as do also the successors of Polycarp even to the present time (Book III, 3:4).[222]

> If there should be a dispute over some kind of question, ought we not have recourse to the most ancient Churches in which the Apostles were familiar, and draw from them what is clear and certain in regard to that question? (Book III, 4:1).[223]

> It is necessary to obey those who are presbyters in the Church, those who, as we have shown, have succession from the Apostles; those who have received, with the succession of the episcopate, the sure charism of truth according to the good pleasure of the Father. But the rest, who have no part in the primitive succession and assemble wheresoever they will, must be held in suspicion (Book IV, 26:2)[224]

Tertullian, a Roman lawyer who converted to the Faith (you may recall quotations from him in my discussions of Reconciliation and purgatory) also wrote extensively against the heretical sects. In 198 A.D. he wrote, "At the outset I propose this: that there is something specific and definite estab-

---

[221] Ibid, p.90
[222] Ibid
[223] Ibid, p.91
[224] Ibid, p.96

lished by Christ. . .proof will be shown that we [the Catholic Church] are what Christ established."[225]

The quotations are numerous but in the interest of finishing this book I will refer to only three more Fathers of the Church. The first, St. Clement of Alexandria, was the head of the school of catechumens in Alexandria, Egypt. In 202 A.D. he wrote:

> From what has been said, then, it seems clear to me that the true Church, that which is really ancient, is one: and in it are enrolled those who, in accord with a design, are just. . .We say, therefore, that in substance, in concept, in origin and in eminence, the ancient and Catholic Church is alone. . .[226]

St. Cyprian of Carthage was a dynamic leader of the Church during the persecutions of the Emporer Decius. He was the first African bishop to die as a martyr. In 250 A.D. he wrote:

> Our Lord, whose commands we ought to fear and observe, says in the Gospel, by way of assigning the episcopal dignity and setting the plan of His Church: "I say to you that you are Peter, and upon this rock I will build My Church, and the gates of hell will not overcome it. And to you I will give the keys of the kingdom of heaven: and whatever things you bind on earth will be bound also in heaven"

> From that time the ordination of bishops and plan of the Church flows on through the changes of time and successions; for the Church is founded upon the bishops, and every act of the Church is controlled by the same rulers. . .This has indeed been established by divine law.[227]

In 350 A.D. St. Cyril of Jerusalem, said:

> [The Church] is called Catholic then, because it extends over the whole world, from end to end of the earth; and because it teaches universally and infallibly each and every doctrine which must come to the knowledge of men, concerning things visible and invisible, heavenly and earthly; and because it brings every race of men into subjection to god-

---

[225] *The Demurrer Against the Heretics*, Ibid, p.119
[226] *Stromateis*. Ibid, p.185
[227] *Letter Without Heading, of Cyprian to the Lapsed*, Ibid, p.229

liness, governors and governed, learned and unlearned; and because it universally treats and heals every class of sins, those committed with the soul and those with the body; and it possesses within itself every conceivable form of virtue, in deeds and in words and in the spiritual gifts of every description."[228]

The testimony of the Church Fathers is invaluable. These are the very men who withstood the persecutions and battled the great heresies (the Arian, Sabellian, Monothelite, Monophysite, and Nestorian). You couldn't find more orthodox Christians – and you couldn't find stronger advocates of apostolic succession, Sacred Tradition, the Sacrament of Reconciliation, the real presence of Christ in the Eucharist, the necessity of baptism, baptism of infants, purgatory, etc., etc. These beliefs are not needless additions to the Christian Faith; they were present in the deposit of faith from the beginning. There is one more thing we Christians look to the authority and testimony of the Church Fathers for – what books are to be included in the New Testament.

Witnessing to the Bible

Throughout my walk with the Lord the Bible has played such a key role, *the* key role. I think the frequency with which I have referenced it in presenting my beliefs bears this out. The one question which I had never asked myself, though – and which I had never heard any other Christian ask – was "Why do I believe that these books, and these books alone, are the inspired, inerrant written Word of God?" Please don't confuse the issue by making the quick response, "There is plenty of archeological evidence to support the Bible." I am not questioning the historical reliability of the books of the Bible. We could go to any bookstore and find stacks of books that would pass muster as historically reliable, but we wouldn't automatically rank these as as "inspired," literally "God-breathed." I ask you the reader to let the question really sink in, "Why is the New Testament made up of only these 27 books?" None of the believers I have asked to consider this question have had a ready response. The inspiration of the Bible is an assumption which most of us accepted when we made our profession of faith in Christ. When I really wrestled with the question of why these indi-

---

[228] *Catechetical Lectures*, Ibid, p.359

vidual books were included in the Bible, however, to the exclusion of dozens of others, I found only one answer that was historically and intellectually satisfying. Let's walk through it together.

The Apostles and those intimately associated in their ministry left us writings; that is the starting point for our consideration. Early on, these writings were considered Scripture, on par with the Old Testament; in Peter's *Second Epistle* he referred to Paul's letters as such (3:5-6). The difficulty which arose, however, was that there were many letters in circulation which claimed to be from Paul – not to mention twenty or so gospels and multiple accounts of the Apostles' ministries. Which should be gathered together to form the New Testament? The Church did not seem to be in a race to answer the question; she existed for *centuries* without the unified collection of books we today call the New Testament.

A man by the name of Marcion seems to be the first to volunteer a response. His book of Scripture excluded the Old Testament; he saw no relation between the God described there and the Father of Jesus. To support his particular take on the Gospel he proposed a Scripture canon consisting of a retooled version of Luke's Gospel and ten of Paul's epistles.[229] When the Church caught wind of what Marcion had proposed she was outraged. Various bishops spoke out against him. One of them, our friend Irenaus of Lyons (whom I have already quoted from), was quite firm that *Luke's Gospel* did not stand alone, and especially not in the mutilated form that Marcion presented it. Around 185 A.D. he wrote, "It is not possible that the Gospels can be either greater or fewer in number than they are. Just as there are four regions of the world in which we live and four universal winds. . .He has given us a four-fold gospel embracing one spirit."[230]

Marcion made an assertion and the Church weighed it, deciding that his beliefs were inconsistent with the deposit of faith. His idea of grouping together the Christian texts which were held to be inspired, however, may have gotten the Church thinking along those lines. Several scholars assert this based upon the fact that it is only after Marcion that we begin seeing other attempts at producing a New Testament canon. Below is a chart I

---

[229] Farmer, William R. and Denis M. Farkasfalvy, *The Formation of the New Testament Canon: An Ecumenical Approach*, (New York: Paulist Press, 1983).
[230] *Against the Heresies*. Book Three, Ibid, p.91.

have compiled of the New Testament's development. What you will undoubtedly notice is that the canon was slimmer in its initial stages; many documents which we now accept were in doubt by certain quarters of the Church. While all of the documents had been in existence since the time of the Apostles, we have to remember that some documents may have taken time to reach distant areas – each document would have had to be recopied by hand and then walked to its destination. With that type of transmission going on, the history and tradition backing various documents would have suffered in some locales. If we consider the matter fairly we couldn't expect the bishops, the repositories for the deposit of faith, in different areas to be aware how many epistles Peter or John had written – initially the bishops were probably only familiar with the writings that had been sent to their communities or the ones closest to them. The Church had to begin a process of gaining knowledge on the claims attached to these books, and then its shepherds use the charism of truth to recognize which books were actually the words of the Holy Spirit.

Key

The final column indicates whether the author proposed a New Testament Canon or was simply commenting on the books in question.

"+" indicates an addition to today's New Testament

"−" indicates that this book was not yet recognized

Year	Author	Location	Work in which information is found	Canon or Comments
155 – 200 A.D.	Unknown	Unknown, possibly Rome	*The Muratorian Fragment*	*Canon* + Wisdom + Apocalypse of Peter − Hebrews − James − 1 Peter − 3 John − 2 Peter
190 – 210 A.D.	St. Clement, director of the school of catechumens	Alexandria, Egypt	*Sketches*	*Canon* + Epistle of Barnabas + Apocalypse of Peter
226 – 232 A.D.	Origen	Probably Alexandria	*Commentaries on John*	Comment: Calls 2 Peter's authenticity "doubtful"

Year	Author	Location	Work in which information is found	Canon or Comments
300 – 325 A.D.	Eusebius Pamphilus, Bishop of Caesarea	Palestine	*History of the Church*, Book III	Comment Labels as "disputed" James, Jude, 2 Peter, 2 John, 3 John. Labels as "spurious" Acts of Paul, The Shepherd, Apocalypse of Peter, Epistle of Barnabas, Didache, and *Apocalypse of John* (Revelation)
343 – 381 A.D.	Council of Laodicea (Note, local council, NOT Ecumenical Council, and therefore NOT an infallible statement)	Phrygia, Asia Minor	*Canons* [or Rulings] *of Laodicea*	*Canon* –Apocalypse of John (Book of Revelation)
350 A.D	St. Cyril, Bishop of Jerusalem	Palestine	*Catechetical Lectures*	*Canon* –Apocalypse of John (Book of Revelation)
367 A.D.	St. Athanasius, Bishop of Alexandria	Alexandria, Egypt	*Thirty-Ninth Festal Letter*	**CURRENT CANON**

Date	Person/Body	Location	Work	Comment
380 A.D.	St. Ampholichius of Iconium, Bishop	Iconium (Present day Turkey)	*Iambic Letter to Seleucus*	"Of the Catholic epistles, some say seven need by accepted, others only three: one of James, one of Peter, one of John, – or three of John and with them two of Peter, – the seventh that of Jude. the Apocalypse of John some accept, but most will call it spurious. . ."
382 A.D.	St. Damasus I, Pope	Rome, Italy	*The Decrees of Damasus*[231]	*CURRENT CANON*
383 – 389 A.D.	St. Gregory of Nazianz, Bishop	Arianz, Eastern Asia Minor	*Collected Poems*	*Canon* – Apocalypse of John
393 A.D.	Council of Hippo	Hippo, Africa	*Canons of the Council of Hippo*	*CURRENT CANON*

---

[231] *The Decree of Damasus* appears to have originally been part of the Decrees of the Council of Rome (a local council, not an Ecumenical). As such it is not considered an infallible statement. Remember, to be considered infallible the Pope must speak a) from his office as the successor of Peter, b) teach on a matter of faith or morals, c) with the clear intention that what he says be considered binding upon *all* Christians. Because of the Pope's role within the Church I believe that everything he teaches should be given consideration by a Christian, but only those things which are taught in the above manner are considered infallible.

Year	Author	Location	Work in which information is found	Canon or Comments
397 A.D.	St. Augustine, Bishop of Hippo	Hippo, Africa	*Christian Instruction*	*CURRENT CANON*
405 A.D.	Innocent I, Pope	Rome, Italy	*Letter to Exsuperius,* (Bishop of Toulouse)[232]	*CURRENT CANON*
419 A.D.	Council of Carthage -local council, presided over by St. Augustine (because its minutes were approved by the Pope, however, most Christians appear to have felt bound by its decision on the canon)	Carthage, Africa	*Canons of the Council of Carthage*	*CURRENT CANON*

[232] Again, a letter from the pope to another bishop does not constitute an infallible statement of belief.

Even though the Popes' statements cited here cannot be construed as infallible statements, it should not escape our notice that the New Testament canon affirmed by the Successor of Peter is the one which has come down to us. The Church would eventually issue an infallible statement, at the Council of Trent in 1546.

The impetus for the Church to do so at that time was the new questioning of the Canon begun by the Reformation. Seven books of the Old Testament had already been discarded by the Reformers[233] and Luther had begun speaking of certain New Testament books as being of lesser value – placing *Hebrews, James, Jude,* and *The Book of Revelation* at the end of his 1522 translation of the New Testament. *The Epistle of James*, for example, was described by Luther as "an epistle of straw." "It is flatly against St. Paul and all the rest of Scripture in ascribing justification to works [2:24]…this epistle is not the work of any apostle."[234] Of *The Book of Revelation* he wrote, "I can in no way detect that the Holy Spirit produced it…let everyone think of it as his own spirit leads him. My spirit cannot accommodate itself to this book…I stick to the books which present Christ to me clearly and purely."[235] Thanks be to God that the thought of the other Reformers prevailed and these books were retained on an equal footing with the rest of the New Testament. It was this doubt, however, that impelled the Catholic Church, at the Council of Trent, to infallibly declare which books were canonical.

If a Christian today holds these twenty-seven books, and only these twenty-seven, as comprising the New Testament then they implicitly affirm two things. First, that Tradition is authoritative; without it we could not verify the origin of these books. Second, that there is a legitimate development of doctrine. The development of the New Testament canon is a classic example: a question faced the Church concerning the Deposit of Faith she was entrusted with, she looked inside herself and with the guidance of the Holy Spirit formulated a response. This response provided the Body of

---

[233] For a discussion of the Old Testament "Apocrypha" or "Deutero-canonicals" please turn to Appendix IV.
[234] Luther, Martin, *Luther's Works*, Volume 35 (St. Louis: Concordia, 1965), p.396.
[235] Ibid, p. 398-399.

Christ with greater knowledge of the Deposit.[236] It was not an addition to the faith but a penetration into what was always there, not an invention but an organic growth.[237] You cannot confess the New Testament canon as binding and at the same time deny the Catholic Church's Tradition or teaching authority. Apart from the Catholic Church's authoritative testimony the most that historical Protestantism – even with its immense love of God's written Word – can claim for the Bible is that it is "a *fallible* collection of infallible books."[238]

---

[236] The Catholic Church, by her witness to the canon, did not make the books of the New Testament Scripture. From the day they were written they were the inspired Word of God. What the Church did was to give authoritative testimony as to what constituted the Word of God. That was the mission Christ entrusted to the Apostles, and it is the mission of the Church to this day.

[237] All Christians have implicitly accepted this principle of development. An example is the Christian opposition to slavery. Neither Jesus, nor the Apostles after Him, made any move to overturn the practice of slavery. (In fact, the Apostle Paul even counseled slaves to be obedient to their masters [Ephesians 6:5; Colossians 3:22]) While Roman and Jewish slaves seemed to receive better treatment than American slaves, there was still that offensive notion of one human being owning another. How can we Christians today feel justified in our condemnation of this practice when Jesus and the Apostles didn't oppose it? Are we tacking on purely human opinions to the doctrine and morality of Jesus?

I maintain that we're not; that the current stance is simply the full-flowering of that which was always implicit in the Gospel. Jesus gave the command *"Love your neighbor as yourself,"* qualifying that *all* human beings are neighbor to each other (Luke 10:25-37). He told us that we each should love each other so completely that we would be willing to lay down our lives for each other. In the Apostle Paul's *Epistle to Philemon* he asked pardon for the runaway slave, Onesimus. Philemon was challenged to look upon Onesimus not just as a servant but as a brother in the Lord. Paul also reminded us that in Christ there is neither "Jew nor Greek, there is neither slave nor free, there is neither male nor female; for you are all one in Christ Jesus" (Galatians 3:28); *all human beings have equal dignity in the eyes of God.*

It took 1800 years, but Christians finally applied these principles to the issue of slavery. If it's true that all men have the same dignity, and if we must love our neighbors as we would want to be loved by them, then there is no justification for slavery. We cannot claim a person as a possession; their dignity before God forbids it, and we would never desire to be someone else's possession. These principles were always implicit within the Gospel – just not taken to their logical end until much later.

[238] Sproul, R.C., *Now That's A Good Question!* (Wheaton, Illinois: Tyndale Publishers, Inc., 1996), p.82, emphasis added.

I do not mean to be uncharitable, but I think there is a great deal of contradiction there. In what sense can Christians say these books are the very Word of God, with claims on our lives, if there's no authoritative word on what makes up the Bible, no true "table of contents" if you will? If you are a Christian who holds there are no infallible statements outside of the Bible, however, then that is the quandary you are left with. The only historical and fully logical reason I can find to accept these twenty-seven books (or any other belief for that matter) is that it is witnessed to by the Church founded by Christ – authenticated by her whom Christ protects from teaching error.[239]

Studying the development of the New Testament canon has brought me back to my point of departure. Was the Church somehow deprived of the fullness of God's Word during the three hundred years it took for all twenty-seven books to gain recognition? Of course not! Christ deposited His Truth with His Church; we might call the Church the Kingdom *of the Word*. A large chunk, although not the totality, of that Truth was crystallized in the writings that became the New Testament. But before the Word even found expression in writing it already existed fully within the Church. When it did find expression in writing it was through members of the Church. God never meant for "the Book" to make the Church's teaching or Sacred Tradition obsolete. If He had He surely would have had the printing press

---

[239] Some people will contend that the Catholic Church has contradicted herself in what she demands of the faithful, thus proving that her doctrine does not undergo organic development but is invented or erased as the Church deems necessary. Two examples I've heard cited are: "In the 1950's the Church said it was a sin to eat meat on any Friday, but now its not;" "The Mass use to have to be said in Latin but now it's said in the language of the people." The mistake which both of these examples illustrate is confusing *doctrine* and *discipline*. In the 1950's the shepherds of the Church requested that we abstain from meat on Fridays as a means of fasting, an aid in recalling how Christ had suffered for us on Good Friday as well as a chance to practice self-discipline. When the shepherds found that people were missing the point of the Friday fast, however, they no longer required it, but instead asked the people to practice some other means of self-denial. The Church never claimed that eating meat on Fridays was a sin; the sin would have been in disobeying the shepherds a loving Father had appointed for us (just as it would be a sin for us to sneak into the kitchen and eat the cake mom had specifically told us to hold off on until after dinner). There's no sin in eating cake, nor in eating meat; but there is a sin of disobedience. Disciplinary rules will change according to the time and place in which we live – the Faith does not.

invented before the fifteenth century.[240] He also would have seen to it that more than just the upper-crust of society were taught to read prior to last century.

Truth is trinitarian. The One God exists as a three-fold, reciprocal relationship of Love; and the fullness of His Truth is guaranteed to us *through the reciprocal relationship* existing between Scripture, Tradition, and the teaching office of the Church.[241]

But What About the Middle Ages?

It is common knowledge that the Popes during the Middle Ages were not angels. Several of them lived lives of debauchery. Does that debunk the claim that they possessed the charism of infallibility? Not in the least. It is a scandal, and it damaged the witness of the Church; but it does *not* damage the integrity of The Faith. Each Christian reading this can demonstrate the truth of what I am saying for him or herself. We need only think of our own sinfulness, and the many ways in which we have failed to live as Christ commands. Do our sins cause Christ's Gospel to be any less true? No, not one iota. When we proclaim that Gospel we may sometimes be hypocritical, but what we proclaim is not falsified. Caiaphas, the high priest who along with Pilate condemned Jesus to death, was used by the Holy Spirit to utter prophecy (John 11:49-52). Christ, with perfect foreknowledge, chose Judas to be one of His Twelve Apostles. Why? Maybe to prepare us for when the successors of the Apostles, especially Peter's Successors, would fall from grace. Judas' betrayal did nothing to diminish the *office* of apostle. Likewise, the personal sinfulness of someone in Peter's office does not diminish the authority nor function of the key-bearer. When we think about atrocities such as the later Crusades and the Inquisitions we have to keep this in mind; they were monstrous, horrendous actions; but they were not

---

[240] Before the invention of the printing press, "A new Bible would cost a community about as much as a new church building. Books in the Middle Ages were done on parchment or on vellum (made from the skins of young sheep or cattle) and lettered, guilded, or illuminated by hand. A whole Bible took maybe four hundred animals and years of work by a score of scribes and artists," Johnson, Kevin Orlin, *Why Do Cahtolics Do That?* (Ballantine Books, 1995), p.25.

[241] This teaching office, held by the pope and bishops, is also known as the Magisterium. Thanks to Fr. John Corapi for pointing out the trinitarian parallel.

instances of the Popes making proclamations as to what constitutes the deposit of faith.

Sometimes we have to look at the men sitting in Peter's Chair as a delinquent parent. We respect them not because of their actions, but solely because of their relation to us (through the Blood of Christ) and the position of authority which God the Father has allowed them to assume. An Old Testament image of this is the relationship between David and King Saul.

Saul was the first King of Israel. His reign started out well, but he eventually fell into disobedience to the Lord's command. Scripture tells us that because of this, even while Saul reigned, the prophet Samuel was sent by the Lord to secretly anoint a young shepherd, David, as the future king. David eventually killed Goliath, became very close to King Saul and his family, and distinguished himself as a warrior. When David's popularity in Israel grew greater than even Saul's, however, the reigning king became jealous and began plotting David's death. When David caught wind of Saul's intent he went into hiding. Saul pursued him into the desert. What I want to draw your attention to was David's reaction: two times the Lord delivered King Saul's life into David's hands, but David responded, "The LORD forbid that I should do this thing to my lord, the LORD's anointed, to put forth my hand against him, seeing he is the LORD's anointed" (1 Samuel 24:6); "who can lay hands on the LORD's anointed, and be guiltless? As the Lord lives, the Lord will smite him" (1 Samuel 26:9-10). It was not the man Saul whom David honored but the *office* which the Lord God had established. Far from being a simpleton, David is the only man whom Scripture calls a man after God's Own Heart (1 Samuel 13:14). Our attitude in dealing with sinful bishops and Popes must be the same as David's.

The way God uses sinful human beings to convey His Revelation is one of the truly great surprises in salvation history. It may seem like a tremendous risk on God's part; perhaps it is simply a commentary on the power of His grace and the Word which He has entrusted to His Church. There is an Old Testament story that gives me a humble chuckle. The Lord "opened the mouth of [an] ass," a donkey, and gave it the power of speech (Numbers 22:28). I have to laugh at how many other asses He has bestowed the power of speech upon to further the Gospel; I can only hope that when my life comes to an end I will find myself ranked among them.

Chapter 13 - Who Are My Brothers and Sisters?

So with the strong convictions I reached regarding the Catholic Church, do I now have less affection for other Christians? Absolutely not, they are my brothers and sisters; and as I stated earlier, that is the position of the Catholic Church. I have no less admiration or affection for them then I did when Jesus first touched me through the writings of Billy Graham and Dennis Bennett – or the experience of worship I had at Grace World Outreach. I find the image of the family ideal for considering the relationship between different Christian groups.

My siblings, Andy and Amanda, and I have the same set of parents. You could say that our parents' life adheres in us; any DNA test would show that we came from the same source. Now if my teenage sister was to strike out on her own – tell dad that she appreciated his advice over the years but could handle things on her own now; moved out of the house; stopped coming over for Sunday dinner; heck, even changed her last name – none of this would change the objective, biological fact that she is my sister. We would still have the same "life" of our parents within us. In fact, I bet she would unconsciously use a lot of Kapler phrases, mannerisms, and traditions. Oh, she may choose never to speak to my brother or I again; and yet, in a very real sense she could never be completely rid of us – our blood ties and common upbringing ensure it. We will always be family. What is true of the Kapler family (at least in this regard) is also true of God's Family, the Church.

There is only one Family of God, stretching from heaven down to earth. The heavenly branch of the Family is in perfect unity; the earthly has obviously not been as fortunate. What is common to *every* member of the Family is that we have the same Life of God adhering in our souls; each of us has been born from the same "imperishable seed" (1 Peter 1:23). People of every "tribe and tongue and people and nation"(Rev. 5:9) are welcome in this Family, and for that reason it took the name "Catholic," or universal. The Founder of the Family, enthroned in Heaven, has raised up the Pope as a visible source of unity - an older brother if you will, to image the Father's love and care for us. It is Jesus' and the Father's will that we love him as an older brother and respect and obey him in Jesus' physical absence. If one of God's children, or a group of them, decide to "move out of the house" – no longer feel bound to the Pope's decisions in disciplinary matters or doctrinal pronouncements, abstain from the Eucharist, change their name from Catholic (to Lutheran, Calvinist, Anglican, Presbyterian, Baptist, Methodist, etc.) - that wouldn't change the objective fact that we still draw our life from the same Heavenly Father. You might say that we have the same "spiritual DNA;" maybe we can't confirm it in a laboratory, but I am sure angels and demons see the Family resemblance quite clearly. Nothing can erase this spiritual reality. And not only is there the connection on the level of the spirit, but so many who "moved out of the house" held onto a lot of the Family's outward "characteristics", or "habits" – the Bible, Sunday worship (for the most part), the early Ecumenical Councils' statements on the Trinity and Jesus' divine and human natures, baptism (albeit with different emphasis), and the order of worship (of many groups). There are other similarities,[242] but these are major ones which leap out at me.

Although my separated brothers and sisters may not agree, *I recognize them*, objectively/spiritually, as united to the Catholic Church. I believe that that is how the Lord Jesus views all of us. Oh the visible, or formal, unity may not be there – the same as if my sister cut off her ties with my parents and I - but the common origin and family characteristics remain.

Please don't think I am devaluing the ministries of my "separated" brothers and sisters. I believe my story is testimony to how the Lord Jesus is at work through people of all denominations to further His Kingdom. Just because ministers of other denominations were not ordained by successors of the Apostles does not negate their function or value within the Body of Christ. Jesus has called people to a variety of ministries (Ephesians 4:11). The call is not limited to the popes, bishops, or presbyters (priests) and deacons united with them. It is true that by their ordination they participate in Jesus' shepherding of the Church: presiding at the Eucharist, ab-

---

[242] Just an added tid-bit: A friend asked me why Catholics leave off the end of *The Lord's Prayer*, "For Thine is the kingdom, the power, and the glory now and forever." The answer is surprising. It's not that Catholics leave this off, it's that most other Christians add it on. The earliest biblical manuscripts do not have those words at the end of the prayer (Matthew 6:9-13; Luke 11:2-4). They have become forever linked to *The Lord's Prayer* though because they are the words which follow it *in the Mass*. At the time of the Reformation they were mistakenly retained by those separating from the Catholic Church as the ending to the prayer Jesus taught us.

solving sins, taking disciplinary measures, etc.; these are all tasks unique to their role within the Body.[243] There are other functions, however, which God calls not just popes, bishops, priests, and deacons to but *any* believer whom He chooses. God graces some people as organizers and administrators, some as prophets, others as evangelists and teachers. And it is these graces, or gifts, which I see at work among Protestant ministers as well as the laity of all denominations. We Christians, *all* of us together, form a "royal priesthood, a holy nation, God's own people, that [we] may declare the wonderful deeds of him who called [us] out of darkness into his marvelous light" (1 Peter 2:9). Each member of Christ's Body has a purpose, a ministry, and the corresponding gifts to accomplish it — the bishops have theirs, and I have mine; some are common to both of us and some to our individual roles within the Body.

My Protestant brothers and sisters are showing forth many graces which, though they exist within the Catholic Church, can often be neglected by her visible members: an intense study of Scripture; vitality in song and worship; intense personal prayer lives; a conviction that Truth is objective and calls for a change of life; and a passion to share the faith with others. God has definitely been building up the average Catholic in these areas over the past four decades, but Protestant groups — especially Evangelical and Pentecostal groups — seem to have a leg up on the rest of the Body. I have to wonder if the Father is working something out, challenging the whole Church to open ourselves to the power of the Holy Spirit. I learned something while reading Ralph Martin's *The Catholic Church at the End of an Age*[244] that really excited me.

Some of you may be familiar with a vision Pope Leo XIII was reported to have had at the end of the nineteenth century. As he was concluding Mass, the Lord Jesus revealed to him that the century which lay ahead, the twentieth century, would be a time when Satan would be allowed to tempt the Church as at no other period in her history. In response to this revelation the Pope did two things: 1) He composed a prayer asking for the inter-

---

[243] And frankly I'm not aware of any ministers in other denominations who claim to have the authority to absolve sins, or that the words they pray at the Lord's Supper bring about the change of the bread and wine into the Body and Blood of Christ.
[244] Martin, Ralph, The Catholic Church at the End of the Age, (San Francisco: *Ignatius Press*, 1994) p.31-32.

vention of Michael the Archangel on the Church's behalf, requesting that it be prayed after every Mass [a practice performed into the 1960's] and 2) He asked that on the first day of the twentieth century the entire Catholic Church pray for a fresh outpouring of the Holy Spirit on the Church. That date should stand out to my Pentecostal friends; it was the day that the modern Pentecostal, or charismatic, movement began in Topeka, Kansas. The first believers to experience it were the students of Charles Parham, a Methodist minister's, Bible school.[245]

I find that fascinating: it seems that God heard the prayers offered by the formal Catholic Church but poured out the new Pentecost upon those invisibly and unknowingly united to her. Sixty some years later, when Pope John XXIII asked the Catholic Church to again pray for a new Pentecost, the Pentecostal movement entered the Catholic Church, beginning with a group of college students in Pittsburgh, Pennsylvania.[246] And whom did these students learn about the "baptism in the Spirit" from? That is right, our "separated" brothers and sisters whom the Lord had been schooling in it for close to seven decades.[247] What *could* the Lord be up to?

I have a theory. Perhaps He was trying to show Catholics the beauty of our siblings of other denominations. Through them He would call many Catholics to delve into neglected treasures. The Pentecostal renewal, cutting across denominational lines, gave Catholics and Protestants the chance to worship together, pray with and for each other, study Scripture, even evangelize together.[248] For Protestant brothers and sisters this became a chance to recognize Catholics as authentic Christians, instead of members of a Church which had "long ago forsaken the Gospel of Christ's free grace." And perhaps, just perhaps, Protestants have glimpsed some of those treasures left behind at the time of the Reformation.

---

[245] Whalen, William J., *Separated Brethren*, (Huntington, Indiana: Our Sunday Visitor Press, 1979), p.111.
[246] The Charismatic Renewal was not the only movement that the Holy Spirit raised up – Cursillo, Marriage Encounter, Teens Encounter Christ – and *all* of this on the heels of that immense movement of the Holy Spirit known as Vatican Council II.
[247] To this day the Pentecostal movement is the fastest growing segment of Christianity.
[248] I am not trying to hold up the charismatic renewal as the example par excellence of ecumenical activity; it is but one among many over the last thirty years.

The lesson I have learned in my own life is one I believe applicable to the larger Body of Christ. You see, to live the Christian life in the way Jesus intended it is not enough to have the Spirit – that personal experience of God at work in our lives. Nor is it enough to be a member of Christ's Catholic Church, His Bride, as if it were an institution. To live the Christian life in all its fullness I am convinced that we have to have both – the Spirit *and* the Bride. To have just the Spirit is to deprive ourselves of the Family life that Christ sacrificed His Own bodily life to establish; and to have the Church without the Spirit is to have a lifeless corpse – an institution instead of a family, lifeless ritual instead of life-giving actions, legal rulings instead of shepherding.

What a reunified Christianity will look like I don't know. Protestant Christians need not fear that they would be the ones "doing all the changing." Cardinal Joseph Ratzinger, now Pope Benedict XVI, has been very candid in saying that renewal must constantly take place; Church structures which have outlived their usefulness should be discarded, cleared away so that the beauty of Christ and His Bride can shine forth.[249] The ancient ministries established by Jesus and His Apostles are legitimate and necessary for the Church's life, but the bureaucracy which has grown up around them (often necessary for functioning in this world) is definitely open to change. Catholics need to differentiate between that which is part of the Deposit of Faith, and that which can be changed so as to allow the Church to function effectively in a new age and social reality. I think Pope John Paul II had the boldest words on the matter. In his Encyclical Letter *That They May Be One: On Commitment to Ecumenism* he said,

> In this way the primacy exercised its office of unity. When addressing the Ecumenical Patriarch His Holiness Dimitrios I, I acknowledged my awareness that "for a great variety of reasons, and against the will of all concerned, what should have been a service sometimes manifested itself in a very different light. But ... it is out of a desire to obey the will of Christ truly that I recognize that as Bishop of Rome I am called to exercise that ministry ... I insistently pray the Holy Spirit to shine his light upon us, enlightening all the Pastors and theologians of

---

[249] Ratzinger, Joseph, *Called To Communion: Understanding the Church Today*. (San Francisco: Ignatius Press, 1996), p.142.

our Churches, that we may seek - together, of course - the forms in which this ministry may accomplish a service of love recognized by all concerned.[250]

As I said, what the "face" of the Church will look like after separated communities and ministers are fused with the ancient ministry of the Catholic bishops I cannot speculate. What I am absolutely sure of, however, is that the interior life of the Church would be of a beauty unknown since the early centuries – a blessing to both Catholic and "Protestant." Imagine the man and the woman in the pews' familiarity with the Scripture, their comfort at praying with and speaking to others. Imagine even further the unity, the clarity, that we would possess on what the Lord Jesus taught; think of the unified front this would present to the world. And what would it be like for everyone who calls upon the Lord Jesus to partake of the Eucharist together?

---

[250] John Paul II, *Ut Unam Sint [That All May Be One]* <http://www.vatican.va/holy_father/john_paul_ii/encyclicals/documents/hf_jp-ii_enc_25051995_ut-unum-sint_en.html>

Chapter 14 - The Eucharist: Christianity's Source and Summit

"The bread we break, is it not a participation in the body of Christ? Because there is one bread, we who are many are one body, for we all partake of the one bread" (1 Corinthians 10:16-17)

I remember my high school New Testament class, being absorbed by Mr. Burns' explanation of what Jesus did at the Last Supper. His perspective, that of a Jewish-Catholic, was insightful:

> While celebrating the Passover, Jesus took bread and said to the Apostles, "This is My body." He took a cup of wine and said, "This is My blood. Do this *in remembrance* of Me." Now people, "in remembrance" had a very special meaning for Jews. The Jewish word for "remembrance" is *zikkaron,* and a remembrance is "a ceremony in which a past event is rendered present so that believers can participate in it and reap its benefits."
>
> The Passover meal was already considered a remembrance, a *zikkaron,* of the Israelites' freedom from slavery in Egypt. The exodus was a one time historical event – but through the Passover meal every Jew born after that time also passed through the Exodus. They too had been set free! The *zikkaron,* the remembrance, the Passover meal made it present for them.
>
> People, this is what Jesus did at the Last Supper. He transformed the Passover meal, created a new *zikkaron* from it – the Eucharist! And every time we participate in this ceremony His Passover, His death and resurrection, are made present to us so that we can share in them and reap the benefit of eternal life! After the priest prays Jesus' words, "This is My body…This is My blood," you don't have bread and wine there anymore; it's Jesus! You don't fall on your knees in the kitchen when you walk by the *Wonder Bread.* People, we go down on our knees in church because that's not bread anymore, it's Jesus Himself!

It was this same conviction that led the bishops gathered at Vatican Council II (1964) to proclaim that the Eucharist is "the source and summit of the Christian life."[251] It has to be. It is *Jesus* – body, blood, soul and divinity, Jesus uniting *His Body the Church* in His Spirit-empowered gift of Self to the Father. The Eucharist, joined with the eternal moment of Cross-Resurrection-Ascension, is the sacrifice of the New Covenant.[252] The Eucharist, understood as such, brought the Church into being – just as it is the summit to which we strive to be configured.

I am reminded of the beautiful story the *Gospel of Luke* relates of Easter Day. Two disciples were traveling from Jerusalem to Emmaus – brokenhearted at the death of Jesus and bewildered at the report that He had been raised. Jesus approached but "their eyes were kept from recognizing him" (24:16). He began to instruct them how all that had taken place had been according to the plan of God. "And then beginning with Moses and all the prophets, he interpreted for them in all the Scriptures the things concerning himself..." When the disciples reached a place of lodging they prevailed upon Jesus to join them. "When he was at table with them, he took bread and blessed, and broke it, and gave it to them. *And their eyes were opened and they recognized him*; and he vanished out of their sight" (24:30-31). The two bolted back to Jerusalem to tell the Apostles "what had happened on the road, and *how he was known to them in the breaking of the bread*" (24:35). The Eucharist's power to reveal lies in the fact that it is not just summit, but *summation*. It ties everything together: the images under the Old Covenant, Christ's sacrifice, and the future of His Church.

Always in View

Very early in this work we looked at the centrality of sacrifice in Israel's relationship to God. The God of Love is not blood-thirsty; that is not what the animal sacrifices of the Old Testament were about. Blood was used because it was the symbol of life (Leviticus 17:11). The life-blood of the ani-

---

[251] Flannery, Austin, *Vatican Council II: The Conciliar and Post Conciliar Documents*, (Northport, New York: Costello Publishing Company, 1992), p 362.
[252] *Hebrews 9: 28* says that Christ was "offered once to bear the sins of many." And yet *Hebrews* goes on to tell us that it was "through the *eternal* spirit [that he] offered himself without blemish to God" (9:14). The effects of His sacrifice cut through time, stretching out to atone for sins in the past, present, and future. Scripture elsewhere calls Him "the Lamb slain from the creation of the world" (Revelation 13:8; NIV). In the Eucharist that eternal moment of redemption is made present in the here and now.

mal was poured out at the base of the altar of sacrifice. Part of the animal was then burned in offering to God, part of it held back to be eaten by the priests, and part taken home to the family making the offering (Leviticus 6-7). God and His People were being *united in the life of the sacrificial victim*. Communion, a family bond, was being reestablished after a lapse into sin, or in cases of thanksgiving and petition, reaffirmed and strengthened.

We see such a covenant meal celebrated at the two highest moments of Israel's history. When God and Israel entered into covenant at Mount Sinai we are told that Moses made a burnt offering of oxen, read the book of the covenant to the people, and threw the sacrificial blood on them and the altar saying, "Behold the blood of the covenant which the Lord has made with you in accordance with all these words." The culmination, however, was when Moses and the nation's seventy elders ascended Mount Sinai and "beheld God, and ate and drank" (Exodus 24:5-11).

The second covenant meal I want to discuss actually preceded the one eaten on Sinai by a period of months, the Passover:

> The Lord said to Moses and [his brother] Aaron in Egypt, "Tell the whole community of Israel that on the tenth day of the month each man is to take a lamb for his family, one for each household…The animals you choose must be year-old males without defect…they shall take some of the blood and put it on the sides and tops of the doorframes of the houses where they eat the lambs. That same night they are to eat the meat roasted over the fire…head, legs and inner parts…along with bitter herbs, and bread made without yeast…The blood will be a sign for you on the houses where you are; and when I see the blood, I will pass over you…This shall be for you a memorial day, and you shall keep it as a feast to the Lord; throughout your generations you shall observe it as an ordinance forever" (Exodus 12:1-3,5-10,13-14).

Now we can see various other images of the Eucharist in the Old Testament – the Israelites being fed in the desert with "bread from heaven" (Ex.16:1-16,35) and their thirst quenched by water flowing from a rock (Ex.17:3-6) each time they stopped to camp (1 Corinthians 10:4); the use of bread and wine in Israel's sacrifices (Exodus 29:38-42; Leviticus 23:18); Twelve loaves of unleavened bread were kept before the Temple's Holy of

Holies (Exodus 25:30; Leviticus 24:5-9); the Messiah would be a priest "after the order of Melchizedek" (Psalm 110:1-4), a priest who offered a thanksgiving ("eucharist" in Greek) sacrifice of bread and wine (Genesis 14:18-20); Elijah being sustained in the desert for forty days by bread and water from an angel (1 Kings 19:5-8) – but the Passover is undoubtedly the New Testament's favorite image.

The Time of Fulfillment

John's Gospel couldn't advance a chapter without John the Baptist thrusting his finger at Jesus, "Behold, the Lamb of God!" (John 1:36). We find it again at the Gospel's culmination, when Jesus is crucified. John points out that, like the Passover lamb, none of His bones were broken (John 19:33-34; Exodus 12:46). John surrounds this with other Passover imagery:[253] Jesus stood before Pilate at "about noon" (John 19:14), on the same day and at the same time the Passover lambs were sacrificed in the Temple; Jesus wore a seamless garment (John 19:23), just as the high priest; and He was given a drink via a sponge on a hyssop branch (John 19:29), the same type of branch used to spread the Passover lamb's blood on the doorposts of the Israelite homes (Exodus 12:22).

What comes between these two points in the Gospel is key to our study. We are told in *John 6:4* that the Feast of Passover was near. John wants Passover at the front of the reader's mind as he/she reads on. He recounts Jesus' miraculous multiplication of the loaves and fishes, and walking on water. "The miracle of the loaves proved that Jesus could do anything he wanted with bread. His walking on water proved that he could defy the laws of nature with his body."[254] With those two points established John presents Jesus' most controversial discourse.

The crowd, reminding Jesus of when Moses called down bread from heaven, asked for a sign. He answered, "it was not Moses who gave you bread from heaven; my Father gives you the true bread from heaven. For the bread of God is that which comes down from heaven, and gives life to

---

[253] Hahn, Scott, *A Father Who Keeps His Promises: God's Covenant Love in Scripture*. (Ann Arbor, Michigan: Servant Publications, 1998), p. 228.
[254] Shamon, Albert J.M., *Our Lady Says: Let Holy Mass Be Your Life*, (Milford, Ohio: The Riehle Foundation, 1989), p.2.

the world...*I am* the bread of life; he who comes to me shall not hunger, and he who believes in me shall never thirst" (6:32-33,35).

The crowd stirred; what did He mean He came from heaven? Jesus continued:

> "Do not murmur among yourselves. No one can come to me unless the Father who sent me draws him; and I will raise him up at the last day...Your fathers ate the manna in the wilderness, and they died. This is the bread which comes down from heaven, that a man may eat of it and not die. I am the living bread come down from heaven; if any one eats of this bread, he will live for ever; and *the bread which I shall give for the life of the world is my flesh*" (John 6: 43-44, 49-51).

Jesus had finally crossed the line. His Jewish listeners began to argue among themselves, saying, "How can he give us his flesh to eat?" The crowd thought He was speaking literally; and, like almost all cultures, the Jews considered cannibalism an abomination.

If they had misunderstood Him then Jesus would have, should have, paused right there and explained His language as figurative; but He didn't. His statements became even more explicit: "Truly, truly, I say to you, unless you *eat* ["phogein" in Greek, the usual verb for "eat"] the flesh of the Son of man and drink his blood, you have no life within you; he who *eats* ["trogein" in Greek, meaning "to munch or gnaw"] my flesh and drinks my blood has eternal life, and I will raise him up at the last day" (John 6:53-54; emphasis and information within brackets added). He pressed on, "For my flesh is *real food* and my blood is *real drink*. Whoever eats my flesh and drinks my blood remains in me, and I in him" (John 6:55-56, NIV). Talk about blunt – "gnaw on my flesh," "real food," "real drink."

The Passover and Temple sacrifices united God and His people in the life of the sacrificial victim. God's people had to take that life into themselves through a covenant meal. Jesus is saying that this continues under the New Covenant.[255] In *6:51* we hear Him say, "the bread which I shall give for the life of the world is my flesh." The bread is His flesh – we have to take Him into ourselves through a covenant meal. "If the flesh we eat for eternal life is meant in only a 'figurative way,' or 'spiritually speaking,' then

---

[255] In fact, in Christian hindsight we recognize that the sacrifices under the Old Covenant were meant to point ahead to the reality of the Eucharist!

so is the flesh of crucifixion! Jesus equated the two. Either they are both literal, or they are both figurative."[256] In the Eucharist we truly receive His flesh and blood. The Cross and Eucharist, the sacrifice and the covenant meal, are interconnected; together they form the New Covenant Passover.

Look at the reaction of Jesus disciples:

> Many of his disciples, when they heard it, said, "This is a hard saying; who can listen to it?" But Jesus, knowing in himself that his disciples murmured at it, said to them, "Do you take offense at this? *Then what if you were to see the Son of man ascending where he was before?* It is the spirit that gives life, the flesh is of no avail; the words that I have spoken to you are spirit and life"…After this many of his disciples drew back and no longer went about with him (John 6: 60-63, 66).

Jesus refused to recant - even at the cost of disciples. He did not explain away the difficulties; He called them to faith. They were supposed to be His disciples; if He was the One Who came forth from the Father, then shouldn't His word redefine their expectations? He didn't make it easy – didn't explain that He would give them His Body and Blood under the appearance of bread and wine. He was calling for unwavering faith, and a line had been drawn.

He turned to the Twelve Apostles, "Will you also go away?" (John 6:67). Either they took Him at His word or they could follow the departing crowd. Simon Peter spoke for them, "Lord, to whom shall we go? You have the words of eternal life; and we have believed, and have come to know, that you are the Holy One of God" (John 6: 68-69). Peter's words offer the only rationale for Eucharistic faith – Jesus' reality-defining word.

Witness to the Eucharist

The Apostle Paul testified to all we have noted thus far. His *First Letter to the Corinthians* proclaims, "Christ, our paschal [or passover] lamb, has been sacrificed. Let us, therefore, celebrate the festival" (1 Corinthians 5: 7-8). Because the Passover had been a *perpetual* ordinance for Israel (Ex.12:14), so too its fulfillment in the Eucharist. Paul reminded his readers, "I received from the Lord what I also delivered to you" (1 Corinthians

---

[256] Currie, David B., *Born Fundamentalist, Born Again Catholic*, (San Francisco: Ignatius Press, 1996), p.37.

11:23), that on the night before He died Jesus took bread and wine and said, "This *is* my body which is for you. Do this in remembrance of me… This cup *is* the new covenant in my blood. Do this, as often as you drink it, in remembrance of me" (1 Corinthians 11:23-25).[257] What Paul said next is inexplicable unless He understood Jesus to be speaking literally – that the bread and wine truly became His ascended Body and Blood so as to establish communion between believers and the Father:

> Whoever, therefore eats the bread or drinks the cup of the Lord in an unworthy manner will be guilty of profaning the body and blood of the Lord. Let a man examine himself, and so eat of the bread and drink of the cup. For *any one who eats and drinks without discerning the body eats and drinks judgment on himself.* That is why many of you are weak and ill, and some have *died* (1 Corinthians 11: 27-30).

A man isn't charged with murder for tearing up a photograph, a mere representation. To sin against the Lord's Body in such a way that sickness and death are suitable chastisements – it *must* be present.

Such an understanding underlies Paul's comments elsewhere in the letter. He asked the Corinthians to "Consider the practice of Israel; are not those who eat the sacrifices *partners in the altar*?" (10:18).[258] "The cup of blessing which we bless, is it not a *participation* in the blood of Christ? The bread which we break, is it not a *participation* in the body of Christ?" (10:16). If the Christian wants to share in the benefits of Christ's sacrifice then he/she must share in the covenant meal; it is the way communion is established – not just vertically but horizontally: "Because there is one bread, we who are many are one body, for we all partake of the one bread" (10:17). Jesus is the bread (John 6:35), and because we all share in Him we form one mystical Body. Because we have consumed His Body, we can be His Body.

---

[257] There were some forty different ways that Jesus could have said "is figuratively" in His native Aramaic; but Paul recorded Jesus using the same simple, blunt language that He had in the "Bread of Life" discourse in John 6. See Rumble, Leslie and Charles M. Carty, *Eucharistic Quizzes*, (Rockford, Illinois: Tan Books and Publishers Inc., 1976).
[258] We find the same insight reiterated in *The Epistle to the Hebrews*, "We have an altar from which those who serve the tabernacle [of the Jerusalem Temple] have no right to eat" (Hebrews 13:10; information within brackets added).

EUCHARIST: SOURCE AND SUMMIT

Gaining Clarity

It is difficult: *How* can the bread and wine become Jesus? The Catholic Church has used the term "transubstantiation," or "change of substance," to describe what happens when the priest speaks Christ's words, "This is My Body; This is My Blood." What on earth does "change of substance" mean? The Church is *not* saying that there is a discernible chemical change. If you looked at these substances under an electron microscope both before and after the prayer of consecration you would not see a difference. When the Church uses the term "substance," it simply means "that which gives something its *definitive identity*."

And a logical question would be, "If that's not molecules and chemical bonds then what is it?" And my answer is...I don't know. As the Creator, however, Jesus grasps matter much better than I. If He pronounced the bread and wine to be His Body and Blood then I have to believe He can make it so. Lets keep in mind, this is the same Person who said, "Let there be light...dry land...living creatures....man...woman" (Genesis 1-2). He showed Himself able to manipulate matter at will – multiplying the loaves, walking on water, even appearing and disappearing into thin air after His resurrection. And let's not forget that this is the Body and Blood formed in the womb of Mary without sexual intercourse – talk about turning the laws of nature upside down!

Why is it so hard to take Jesus at His word on the Eucharist? Is it because we cannot observe the change through our five senses or detect it with our most sensitive instruments? Our technology is finite – His power limitless! Christians believe that the eternal, omniscient, omnipotent God became a man – that is absolute nonsense to many. A God Who would demean Himself in this way; can we Christians honestly believe that He is above transforming bread and wine into His Body and Blood to nourish us? Jesus chose to be born in Bethlehem (the word means "House of Bread") and laid in a manger, a feeding trough for animals. "God chose what is foolish in the world to shame the wise" (1 Corinthians 1:27). The Eucharist sums up and focuses the foolishness of the Cross, the foolishness which ends in the glory of resurrection – for Christ and His Church!

The Catholic teaching on the Eucharist is nothing novel; it is simply the witness of the Church from her earliest moments – that when we receive the Eucharist, because it is Jesus Himself, we are united to Him in His Passover from this world to the Father.

Historical Witness

The first work that we will look at is the *Didache*, or *The Teaching of the Twelve Apostles*. As we have noted, written between 70 and 120 A.D., its testimony is invaluable: "On the Lord's Day of the Lord gather together, break bread and give thanks, after confessing your transgressions so that your *sacrifice* may be pure. (14:1)"[259]

Bishop Ignatius, the disciple of the Apostle John mentioned earlier, wrote in 110 A.D. that he desired "the Bread of God, which is the Flesh of Jesus Christ, Who was of the seed of David, and for drink, His Blood, which is love incorruptible."[260] He admonished the believers in Philadelphia, Asia Minor, to "use one Eucharist so that whatever you do, you do according to God: for there is one flesh of our Lord Jesus Christ, and one cup in the union of his blood; one altar as there is one bishop with the presbytery and the deacons."[261] To the Church in Smyrna Ignatius wrote:

> Take note of those who hold heterodox [or heretical] opinions on the grace of Jesus Christ which comes to us, and see how contrary their opinions are to the mind of God...They abstain from the Eucharist and from prayer, because they do not confess that *the Eucharist is the flesh of our Savior Jesus Christ, flesh which suffered for our sins and which the Father, in his goodness, raised up again.* They who deny the gift of God are perishing in their disputes.[262]

Justin the Martyr, one of the most important Christian apologists of the second century, wrote of the Eucharist in his *Apology to the Emperor Antoninus Pius*:

> For not as common bread nor as common drink do we receive these...the food which has been made into the Eucharist by the Eucharistic prayer set down by Him, and by the change by which our

---

[259] Ibid, p.4
[260] Ignatius of Antioch's *Letter to the Romans*, Ibid, p.22.
[261] Ignatius of Antioch's *Letter to the Philadelphians*, Ibid, p.22
[262] Ignatius of Antioch's *Letter to the Smyrnaeans*, Ibid, p.25

blood and flesh is nourished, is both the flesh and the blood of that incarnated Jesus.[263]

Irenaeus, the second bishop of Lyons, Gaul, picked up this theme of Calvary and the Eucharist being the fulfillment of the Old Testament sacrifices in the fourth book of his five volume *Against Heresies* (180-199 A.D.):

> Sacrifice as such has not been reprobated. There were sacrifices then, sacrifices among the people; and there are sacrifices now, sacrifices in the Church. Only the kind has been changed; for now the sacrifice is offered not by slaves but by free men (18:2).[264]

Belief in Jesus' Eucharistic presence was so firmly held that Irenaeus could use it to debate those denying His full divinity. Note what is taken for granted in his argument:

> If the Lord were from other than the Father how could He rightly take bread, which is of the same creation as our own, and confess it to be His Body, and affirm that the mixture in the cup is His Blood? (Bk.4, 33:2).[265]

Origen, the prolific writer of the second century, whom I mentioned while discussing the Sacrament of Reconciliation, witnessed to the universal belief in Jesus' presence:

> I wish to admonish you with examples from your religion. You are accustomed to take part in the divine mysteries, so you know how, when you have received the Body of the Lord, you reverently exercise every care lest a particle of it fall, and lest anything of the consecrated gift perish. You account yourselves guilty, and rightly do you so believe, if any of it be lost through negligence (*Homilies On Exodus*, 13:3, post 244 A.D.).[266]

> Formerly, in an obscure way, there was manna for food; now, however, in full view, there is the true food, the Flesh of the Word of God,

---

[263] Ibid, p.55
[264] Ibid, p.95
[265] Ibid, p.97
[266] Ibid, p.205-206

> as He Himself says: "My Flesh is truly food, and My Blood is truly drink" (*Homilies On Numbers*, 7:2; post 244 A.D.).[267]

Cyprian, Bishop of Carthage, Africa, offered this testimony concerning the Old Testament roots and continuing sacrificial character of the Sacrament:

> Also in the priest Melchizedek we see the Sacrament of the Sacrifice of the Lord prefigured, in accord with that to which the Divine Scriptures testify, where it says: "And Melchizedek, the King of Salem brought out bread and wine, for he was a priest of the Most High God; and he blessed Abraham" [Genesis 14:18-19]... And who is more a priest of the Most High God than our Lord Jesus Christ, who, when He offered sacrifice to God the Father, offered the very same which Melchizedek had offered, namely bread and wine, which is in fact His Body and Blood! (*Letter To A Certain Cecil*, 248-258 A.D.)[268]

> If Christ Jesus, our Lord and God, is Himself the High Priest of God the Father; and if He offered Himself as sacrifice to the Father; and if He commanded that this be done in commemoration of Himself - then certainly the priest, who imitates that which Christ did, truly functions in place of Christ (*Letter To A Certain Cecil*, 248-258 A.D.).[269]

Cyril, Bishop of Jerusalem, had a great deal to say of the Eucharist in the catechetical lectures he delivered circa 350 A.D. I will quote only a small portion:

> Do not, therefore, regard the Bread and Wine as simply that; for they are, according to the Master's declaration, the Body and Blood of Christ. Even though the senses suggest to you the other, let faith make you firm. Do not judge in this matter by taste, but be fully assured by the faith, not doubting that you have been deemed worthy of the Body and Blood of Christ (*Catechetical Discourses: Mystagogic* 4, 22:9).[270]

---

[267] Ibid, p.206
[268] Ibid, p.232
[269] Ibid, p.232-233
[270] Ibid, p.361

> In approaching...*make your left hand a throne for you the right, since you are about to receive into it a King.* And having hollowed your palm...partake being careful lest you lose anything of it. For whatever you might lose is clearly a loss to you from one of your own members. Tell me: if someone gave you some grains of gold, would you not hold them with all carefulness, lest you might lose something of them and thereby suffer a loss? Will you not, therefore, be much more careful in keeping watch over what is more precious than gold and gems, so that not a particle of it may escape you? (*Catechetical Discourses: Mystagogic* 5, 23:21).[271]

John Chrysostom, Bishop of Constantinople, writing sometime around 390 A.D., declared:

> Christ is present. The One who prepared that [Holy Thursday] table is the very One who now prepares this [altar] table. For it is not a man who makes the sacrificial gifts become the Body and Blood of Christ, but He that was crucified for us, Christ Himself. The priest stands there carrying out the action, but the power and the grace is of God. "This is My Body," he says. This statement transforms the gifts (*Homilies On The Treachery Of Judas*, 1:6).[272]

Theodore of Mopsuestia delivered this homily sometime before 428 A.D. to new converts:

> [In receiving the Eucharist] each of us takes a small portion, but we believe that in that small portion we receive all of Him. (*Catechetical Homily* 6)[273]

> When [Christ] gave the Bread *He did not say, "This is the symbol of My Body," but, "This is My Body."* In the same way when He gave the Cup *He did not say, "This is the symbol of My Blood," but, "This is My Blood"*; for He wanted us to look upon the [Eucharistic elements] after their reception of grace and the coming of the Holy Spirit not according to

---

[271] Ibid, p.366
[272] Jurgens, William A., *The Faith of the Early Fathers*, Volume 2 (Collegeville, Minnesota: The Liturgical Press, 1970), p.104
[273] Ibid, p.82

> their nature, but [that we should] receive them *as they are, the Body and Blood of our Lord (Catechetical Homily* 5).[274]

The final citations will come from Augustine of Hippo:

> He took flesh from the flesh of Mary. He walked here in the same flesh, and gave us *the same flesh to be eaten unto salvation.* But no one eats the flesh unless first he adores it. . .not only do we not sin by adoring, we do sin by not adoring (*Explanation of the Psalms*, 98:9; 392-418 A.D.).[275]

> Christ is both the Priest, offering Himself, and Himself the Victim. He willed that the sacramental sign of this should be the *daily sacrifice* of the Church, who, since the Church is His Body and He the Head, learns to offer herself through Him (*City of God*, 413-426 A.D.).[276]

> Christ was carried in His own hands, when, referring to His own Body, He said: "This is My Body." For He carried that Body in His hands (*Explanation of the Psalms*, 33: 1,10; 392-418 A.D.).[277]

Each of these shepherds I have quoted from is a witness from the time when Christ's Church was one. They bear witness to how the first generations of Christians, beginning with those who actually knew the Apostles, understood the Eucharist. Their testimonies bear witness to the reality of the indescribable gift God wishes to give His children – all of His children. It was between the institution of the Eucharist and the Crucifixion that Jesus offered His High-Priestly Prayer, "that they may all be one; even as thou, Father, art in me, and I in thee" (John 17:21).

Putting the Eucharist "in Context"

I have spoken of the Eucharist in terms of Jesus' presence and how it joins the believer to His sacrifice. What I have neglected, however, is to place the liturgy of the Eucharist within the larger liturgical action of the

---

[274] Ibid
[275] Jurgens, William A., *The Faith of the Early Fathers*, Volume 3 (Collegeville, Minnesota: The Liturgical Press, 1970), p.20
[276] Ibid, p.99
[277] Ibid, p.16

Mass. You see, the Church doesn't simply gather and then pray Jesus' words "This is My Body…This is My Blood." At Mass we are nourished not just by the Eucharist but by God's Word in Scripture. And not only are we nourished, but we are empowered to speak to God with "divine vocabulary" and to surrender ourselves as Jesus did! We began this chapter with the beautiful story of the disciples on the road to Emmaus, how Jesus approached them, explained the Scriptures, and celebrated the Eucharist. I maintain that He does so every Sunday.[278]

At Mass we are meant to feast on the Word. And so Jesus comes to us in a reading from the Old Testament, the praying of one of the Psalms, the proclamation of a New Testament epistle,[279] and most directly in a reading from one of the Gospels. Jesus is the center of Scripture – it was to Him that the whole Old Testament streamed and from Him that the New flows. "Every proclamation of the Word in the liturgy is a moment irreducibly new: the event of Christ (all the events of Scripture are the event of Christ) becomes…the event of the assembly that here and now hears this Word."[280] "It is God's intervention and offer of salvation in the here and now of a particular gathering of believers."[281] The priest comes forward, ordained through apostolic succession to assist the assembly understand and apply this Word.

Earlier I said that we are empowered to speak to God with a "divine vocabulary." What I meant was that at Mass the Church responds to the Lord in the words of Scripture. Because the assembly's prayer is either direct quotations or paraphrases of Scripture we see the written Word come to life in worship.[282]

When the Church moves from this "Liturgy of the Word" to that of the Eucharist we see an intensification of the Word becoming flesh, God's as well as ours. Through the Holy Spirit the bread and wine become His

---

[278] In truth everyday since Mass is celebrated daily.
[279] Or a reading from *Acts of the Apostles* or *Book of Revelation*.
[280] Driscoll, Jeremy, "The Word of God in the Liturgy of the New Covenant," *Letter & Spirit* 1 (2005), p.91.
[281] Ibid, p.87.
[282] I recommend studying a work such as Fr. Peter's Stravinskas' *The Bible and the Mass: Understanding the Scriptural Basis of the Liturgy* (Ann Arbor, Michigan: Servant Publications, 1989).

Body and Blood and our prayer is transformed from one of word to an act of participation in Jesus' Passover – His death, resurrection, and ascension. The Church prays, "Through Him, with Him, and in Him, in the unity of the Holy Spirit, all glory and honor is yours almighty Father forever and ever. Amen." With Jesus we give ourselves to the Father, in the Spirit – realizing the purpose of our creation.

The Flow of Worship

This divine drama occurs every time Mass is celebrated, albeit unbeknownst to a number of those present. Each Mass begins by asking Jesus for forgiveness. In the Holy Spirit we then turn to praise of the Father and the Son. We listen to the Lord's Word and a homily. We profess our Faith by reciting the Nicene Creed and intercede for needs. A monetary collection is taken up and the gifts of bread and wine brought to the altar. The Eucharistic prayer begins. The Father is asked to send the Holy Spirit upon the gifts of bread and wine, just as He did upon the Virgin Mary, so that they may become the Body and Blood of Jesus. As brothers and sisters of Christ we pray the "Our Father." And then addressing Jesus as the Lamb of God, we ask Him once again to take away sin before we proceed forward to join ourselves with Him in Holy Communion. After a time of private prayer we receive a final blessing.[283]

Mass has flowed in just this way for millennia. Look at Justin Martyr's description in 150 A.D.:

> On the day which is dedicated to the sun. . .the day on which Jesus Christ our Savior rose from the dead. . .all those who live in the cities or who dwell in the countryside gather in a common meeting, and for as long as there is time the Memoirs of the Apostles or the writings of the prophets are read. Then, when the reader has finished, the president verbally gives a warning and appeal for the imitation of these good examples.

---

[283] Which priest leads the celebration doesn't concern me much; I know the High Priest who stands behind and in him. Whether there is a choir, organ, guitar, or no music whatsoever - the greatest worship possible is already taking place. The Mass, in the final analysis, is not about the feelings we can work up in ourselves, nor is it about the external beauty of the ceremony. It is our being united with Jesus' perfect worship and obedience to the Father

Then we all rise together and offer prayers *in common and heartily for ourselves. . .and for all others everywhere, so that we may be accounted worthy, now that we have learned the truth, to be found keepers of the commandments, so that we may be saved with an eternal salvation. Having concluded we greet one another with a kiss*[284]. . . bread is brought forward along with wine and water, and the president likewise gives thanks to the best of his ability, and the people call out their assent, saying the Amen. Then there is the distribution to each and the participation in the Eucharistic elements, which also are sent with the deacons to those who are absent. Those who are wealthy and who wish to do so, contribute whatever they themselves care to give; and the collection is placed with the president, who aids orphans and the widows, and those who through sickness or any other cause are in need...*(Apology to the Emperor Antoninus Pius, Chp.67).*[285]

The Mass Does Not End

The Eucharist has transformed my sense of unity with other members of the Catholic Church. When I began my faith journey I felt a sense of belonging with believers who had responded to an "altar call," or had made a conscious decision to open their lives to the action of the Holy Spirit, or who talked about their faith openly. I didn't feel especially close to the people I attended Mass with; so few talked about their faith outside of the sanctuary – as if their relationship with God was restricted to that hour on Sunday morning.

What the Lord Jesus convicted me of, however, was that I had no right to judge anyone (with my limited knowledge of hearts and inner lives), nor to pick my brothers and sisters. If Jesus fed all of us with His Flesh and Blood then there was a bond between us stronger than anything I had ever known – and there is no "altar call" like going forward to receive Jesus in Communion.

---

[284] Material within asterik is inserted from Chapter 65 of Justin's *Apology to the Emporer Antoninus Pius* in Jurgens, William A., *The Faith of the Early Fathers*, Volume 1 (Collegeville, Minnesota: The Liturgical Press, 1970), p.55.
[285] Ibid, p.55-56.

When we leave Mass the Lord Jesus has filled us with Himself that we might share Him with others. This doesn't mean just in our "official" ministries of youth group, parish council, the shelter, or ministering to the "unbeliever." If we limit the ministry of Christ to these channels then we are falling way short of the mark. Our Lord wants to fill our personal lives, our homes and families, with His power and glory. We cannot forget that He is dwelling within the people we fight with over the television remote. The home and the relationships that occur there are the primary places that our Lord wants to redeem through us. How we treat our families - and our extended families – that has to be the true test of our Christianity: Is it a living reality or are we playing pious head games?

Consider the example given by Jesus. His life was spent fulfilling the Father's will perfectly. Not a second of it was wasted nor misplaced. Knowing this, isn't it funny that only nine percent of His life on earth was spent performing *public* ministry? It is true - for thirty of His thirty-three years He was a son in a family, went to school and work, and lived the daily grind! Wasted time? He was showing us what our priorities should be: to love our God and serve Him present in our loved ones, our work, our neighborhoods, our daily grind. If we aren't doing that then all the rest is well-meant but hollow. We have not allowed Jesus to penetrate our core and teach us to love.

Assimilating the Word of God and then living out the Life of Jesus is the work of the Church until the Lord returns for her. Even now the Eucharist is a participation in the God Who is Love, even now a participation in the world to come. As Joseph Ratzinger, our new Pope Benedict wrote, "The *parousia* [or Second Coming] is the highest intensification and fulfillment of the liturgy...every Eucharist is *parousia*, the Lord's coming."[286] It is no coincidence that the *Book of Revelation* describes the consummation of history as the *wedding feast of the Lamb* (Revelation 19:9; 21:1-5).

---

[286] Ratzinger, Joseph, *Eschatology* (Washington, DC: Catholic University of America Press, 1988), p.203, quoted in Hahn, Scott, *Letter and Spirit: From Written Text to Living Word in the Liturgy* (New York: Doubleday, 2005), p.116.

Chapter 15 - Parting Thoughts

I thought it best to end with a story – to talk about "getting down and dirty" in the Faith. Since graduating from college I have worked full-time as a school-based speech-language pathologist. About six years ago that gave me the opportunity to work in a summer program with high school students having severe to profound mental and physical handicaps.

I knew going in that I would be responsible for working on more than communication skills; like the rest of my colleagues on the team, I would be leading physical education activities, giving academic instruction, and even assisting with *toileting*. "Germ freak" that I am, that last element terrified me. I prayed that it would consist of no more than accompanying the students to the bathroom and offering reminders about washing their hands. God's answer, though, was a resounding "No!" That became crystal when I found myself in a bathroom stall with a half-naked young man in the midst of gastro-intestinal problems.

His name was Joshua. He was fifteen, but in regards to size looked much more like an eight year-old. He was only able to express himself with a handful of words. Luckily, he was able to alert us to his need for the bathroom. I held his hand to help give him balance as we left class. By the time we reached the restroom he was already disrobing; I raced to the stall and ushered him inside. When I heard him starting to play in the water though, I knew I was in trouble. In I went, helping Josh to sit down and encouraging him to "take care of business." Once he had, I realized that I would be the one "cleaning off" his backside. It was not a pretty job. Mind you this was happening in a high school restroom, and summer school students had started coming down to make their own pit-stops. So when Joshua looked up at me, eyes filled with gratitude for the help I was giving him, and the only words he could get out were, "I love you," I was a bit panicked. Talk about the three words you don't want to hear from another guy in a public restroom! And yet, by the look in his eyes, I knew they came from the depths of Joshua's soul; and that, in its own way, the moment was holy. I have to tell you though, it didn't seem to matter when I found myself back in that stall with Josh the very next day!

"Lord, what are you doing? Why am I the one in this situation?" And the thought came back to me, "If not you, then who?" And the connections began to form: My student's name was Joshua; and that was the English equivalent of the Hebrew *Y'shua*, and the Greek *Jesus*. And as Jesus had already brought to my attention so often, "as you did it to one of the least of these my brethren, you did it to me" (Matt.25:40). I was taken aback, "So Lord…I cleaned…Your…backside? This is a new one for me; I don't remember this in the lives of the saints." Then another realization enveloped me: "Mary and Joseph – *they* cleaned Your backside! When You were a baby, they cleaned You off!" I had no idea when I was in that stall with Joshua what company I had begrudgingly entered – the Queen of Heaven[287] and the Protector of the Universal Church![288]

The two people who knew, loved, and *served* Jesus the best during His time on earth were not those who preached grandiose sermons or wrote beautiful works of theology, but those who embraced Him in His need. Mary and Joseph, the Church's two greatest models of holiness…cleaned Jesus' backside. How can you and I think we are above doing the same? If we want to draw close to Jesus, to touch Jesus, then we have to embrace the full scandal of His incarnation. We have to recognize and receive Him in the Eucharist, and we have to touch Him and serve Him in His People.

I complete this work in the midst of one of the most difficult periods in my life. (There's probably another book there, but don't worry; I have no plans to subject you to it anytime soon.) I am more convinced than ever though, that God is madly in love with us. Amidst all of the difficulties, I have witnessed Him provide for my family at least a hundred times. Sometimes it wasn't until the very last second, but He provided nonetheless – through His People.

What I hope to have driven home through this book is that there is no conflict between creedal faith, or dogma, and a living, breathing relationship with God. Nor does there have to be this sharp distinction between a "personal" relationship with God and a "communal" one. All of these facets flow together and coalesce in the God Who *is Love*. As St. Irenaeus wrote

---

[287] Mary hold this title as the Mother of the King (consider *Revelation* 12:1-2).
[288] Joseph is esteemed as such because of the role he exercised within the Holy Family. Upon his entrance into glory he continued this role through his intense intercession for Jesus' Body, the Church.

so long ago, "Where the Church is there is the Spirit of God; and where the Spirit of God, there the Church and every grace." [289]

If you the reader are a Catholic then I invite you to dig into the treasure you possess. If you are a Christian from another background then I thank you, my brother, my sister, for your patience; and I invite you to pray and look into our common heritage more deeply. I haven't written this work with the intention of offending but of sharing the gifts I am convinced our Father intends for all. And if you the reader are not yet a Christian, then I offer my warmest thanks to you. My hope is that you will find the Spirit of God praying within you, praying with Christ's Bride the Church, "Come, Lord Jesus!" (Revelation 22:20)

---

[289] Jurgens, William A., *The Faith of the Early Fathers*, Volume 1 (Collegeville, Minnesota: The Liturgical Press, 1970), p.94.

Appendix I – The Rationality of Belief in God

> "For from the greatness and beauty of created things comes a corresponding perception of their Creator" (Wisdom 13:5).
>
> "Ever since the creation of the world [God's] invisible nature, namely, his eternal power and deity, has been clearly perceived in the things that have been made. So [men and women] are without excuse; for although they knew God they did not honor him as God or give thanks to him, but they became futile in their thinking and their senseless minds were darkened. Claiming to be wise, they became fools" (Romans 1:20-22).

It may just be me, but I've always had the impression that many people in our society see faith and reason as being opposed to each other – that the most reasonable among us are not people of faith and vice versa. Now I'm not sure where that impression came from, character portrayals in movies and books or interactions I've had with others. I wanted to take this brief space to explain the Christian conviction, especially as it has been expressed within Catholicism, that belief in God's existence is not opposed by modern science and is in fact eminently reasonable.[290]

Perhaps, as a preliminary to our discussion, we should dismiss the myth that "science" has somehow disproved the existence of God. Anyone who has perpetuated such a myth has done nothing more than demonstrate his/her misunderstanding of science's parameters. Polls show that 40% of professional scientists profess religious belief.[291]

I would hope that the other 60% profess agnosticism as opposed to atheism. I say this because atheism requires a huge act of faith, and a very

---

[290] The Catholic Church reaffirmed this at Vatican Council I (1870), "God, our Creator and Lord, can be known with certainty by the natural light of reason from created things." Ott, Ludwig, *Fundamentals of Catholic Dogma* (Rockford, Illinois: Tan Books and Publishers Inc., 1960), p.13

[291] Lovgren, Stefan, "Evolution and Religion Can Coexist Scientists Say," Oct.18, 2004 <http://news.nationalgeographic.com/news/2004/10/1018_041018_science_religion.html>

prideful one at that: "I *know* that there is no god." Now such a profession is a universal negative, something forever impossible to prove. It requires having access to all of the knowledge in the universe (scientific, historical, philosophical, psychological, artistic, etc.) and finding that nothing in it pointed to the existence of a Supreme Being. No human being has that amount of knowledge at their disposal, and given what cosmology has told us about the size of our own galaxy, not to mention the universe, I do not see how it could ever be realized. Atheism is a statement of *faith*.

"Science," on the other hand, or more exactly scientific method, is concerned with the process of arriving at a more precise picture of the *physical* world through observation, the posing of hypotheses, and the testing of those hypotheses through carefully controlled, unbiased, repeatable experimentation. By its very nature, science is unable to comment upon the existence of God – at least the God professed by Christians and Jews, Who has always been conceived of as "outside" of the physical universe. Just as an artist is distinct and of a different material than the paint or canvas he uses to create, so God can be present to the universe, and yet of a completely different nature or order of being.[292] Science is impotent to comment on such a Being. It cannot offer answers to the biggest questions we pose: Why? Why this instead of nothing? What is the meaning of life, of *my* life?

If science were our only source for arriving at knowledge it would seem we were at an impasse. But what of logic, human reason? Can it be of use to us in the absence of experimental data? Yes, philosophy has glimpsed a way – reasoning from humanity's common *experiential* data.

In this vein Thomas Aquinas, the 13th century theologian and philosopher, and one of the most brilliant minds to ever grace our planet, pointed to five "inferential proofs…inductions based on the facts of the sensible world and the first principles of reason."[293] The validity of his five "proofs,"

---

[292] The great exception being Christianity's doctrine of the Incarnation: God joined Himself to creation as a child in the womb of Mary of Nazareth.

[293] Farrell, Walter, *Companion to the Summa*, Volume 1 (New York: Sheed & Ward, 1938) © Dominicans, Province of St. Albert the Great. Work available at: <http://www.domcentral.org/farrell/companion/comp102.htm>

258 THE GOD WHO IS LOVE

or ways, (motion, causality, contingency, participation, and finality) remains even today. Allow me to comment on two of them:

Aquinas' second proof is that from causality. In our experience, nothing is responsible for its own existence. *Right now*, as you read this, your earthly existence is dependent upon a multitude of other things – your body, water, air, our planet's atmosphere, etc., etc. Our existence is "caused" by these things. Keep in mind that we are not projecting backward into the past but talking about a chain of causation existing at this present moment. Each of these things we've mentioned is being caused by other things in this very instant: the interaction of different elements, themselves caused by atomic forces, which are caused by subatomic forces, and so on. Existence is borrowed at each step in the chain. At some point though, the chain has to have a foundation, a ground of Existence from which everything else has borrowed - a Cause that is itself uncaused. If we deny this we are left with but one alternative: at the beginning of the chain there is nothing. But logically, if there is nothing at the beginning, then there should be nothing at the end (or at any point in between). We would have to jettison "cause" altogether – and then what *can* we humans claim to know? Cause and effect are the foundational principles of human knowledge. As Aquinas demonstrated, logically there must be a Cause, Itself uncaused, holding all things in existence.

Aquinas's fifth proof, from finality, draws our attention to "the fact of a constant *order* of cause to effect."[294] Aquinas does not ask us to know the reason for every occurrence in the universe. No, it is sufficient to look at the world of nature and observe that "the eye is constructed for the purpose of seeing, the ear for hearing, that a mosquito bites for purposes of nourishment, that the snakes fangs are weapons of defense, and so on."[295] A mosquito or snake does not make a conscious decision to reach that end, and yet there is a purpose for its action – nourishment, defense. Where did the *purpose* come from, the direction to *this end*? Not from the insect or reptile; it is simply there, part of its existence. Could it have come from outside of them? Isn't that the only alternative left to us? And purposeful direction is the work of intelligence, an Intelligence outside of them! Note, this is not

---

[294] Ibid, italics added.
[295] Ibid.

a denial of evolutionary theory – simply the observation that there is a purpose to these occurrences in nature and that purpose is the product of intellect.

Suppose you were stranded on a deserted island. You were out walking one day and discovered a personal computer (pretend you had never seen or heard of one before). It came complete with a keyboard, mouse, 17-inch color monitor, sound and graphics card, and an 800 MHz processor. After a few hours of investigation you discover some of its capabilities - sound production, memory, graphics, mathematical calculations, word processing. Would you conclude that such an object was the product of a cosmic accident, or would you recognize it as having a purpose, the product of intelligence? What is the logical conclusion as you look at the galaxy, solar system, the intricate web of life on Earth, your body, and the function of your brain? Can such *order* be the result of chaos, of a myriad of accidental forces? In our experience chaos breeds more chaos, not order. What is the most logical conclusion?

Aquinas' developed his proofs believing that one was unable to show that the universe had a beginning. (He himself believed that it did, but he held this as a tenet of faith as opposed to philosophy.) The Kalam Argument, on the other hand, reasons to God's existence from the conviction that the universe did have a beginning. The argument is quite straightforward: If something begins to exist, then it had a cause. Because the universe began to exist, it had to have a cause. This cause, outside the universe and thus outside of space-time, is what we refer to as God. (I told you it was straightforward!)

One can find him/herself at odds with Aquinas or the Kalam Argument. But as I have said, to do so requires a denial of cause and effect. Philosophy demonstrates the reasonableness of recognizing an Uncaused Cause, a Necessary Existence, an Intelligence which orders things toward an end. Some have called this the "God of the Philosophers." Belief in such a Being isn't illogical, doesn't stand in contradiction to science. Quite the opposite – reason and logic are the pillars of philosophic method, just as they are scientific method. In fact, the knowledge of the universe that has resulted from scientific investigation, while admitting that it remains subject to revision, coincides quite nicely with the philosophical thought we have glimpsed.[296]

Observations Yielded From Science

In 1927, astronomer Edwin Hubble discovered that other galaxies were rapidly rushing away from our own – evidence that the universe was in a state of constant expansion. A popular theory at the time, the Steady State Theory, had held that the universe was eternal. Given Hubble's observation however, a new theory arose in its place, one postulating that the universe burst forth from a singularity, a point of infinite density that physics is unable to comment upon. Prior to that there literally was nothing – no space, time, or matter. From that "explosion" the universe spread out in all directions and gradually formed galaxies, stars, planets, etc. It became known as the "Big Bang Theory," and in 1964, it received a very large confirmation.

Arno Penzia and Robert Wilson, two scientists working on communication satellites for Bell Laboratories, discovered low-level "noise" emanating from every direction in the sky.[297] Physicists immediately recognized it as the echo of the original explosion, the big bang, that set our universe in motion. They calculated it as occurring 15 billions years ago. As a result, by the 1970's the Big Bang Theory was accepted by the vast majority of scientists.

In 1992, the Big Bang Theory moved into the "beyond a reasonable doubt" category when NASA's COBE (Cosmic Background Explorer) satellite observatory registered "feeble remnants of light that originated early in the history of the universe…measurements also revealed tiny ripples in the light's intensity, representing "lumps" no more than 0.001 percent richer in matter than the space around them."[298] This was exactly what the Big

---

[296] You may want to consult the story of Antony Flew's conversion from atheism to the "god of the philosophers" recounted in Antony Flew & Roy Abraham Varghese's *There Is A God: How the World's Most Notorious Atheist Changed His Mind* (New York: HarperOne, 2008).
[297] Penzia and Wilson won the 1978 Nobel Prize in physics as a result.
[298] Crenson, Matt. Oct.3,2006, "Americans Win Nobel for Big-Bang Study."
<http://www.msnbc.msn.com/id/15113168/>

Big Bang Theory had predicted.[299] Given what was said above regarding the Kalam Argument, one can see the philosophical implications of recognizing a beginning to the universe.

With the Big Bang as their start, physicists began looking at how manipulation of different variables would have affected the formation of the universe. "Sometimes you ended up with the wrong kind of stars. In other cases, you ended up with no stars at all…No matter what alternative scenario you tried to cook up, the most miniscule changes in the fundamental constants completely eliminated the possibility of life."[300]

This led to an historic paper and presentation in 1973, entitled "Large Number Coincidences and the Anthropic Principle in Cosmology," by Brandon Carter, an astrophysicist and cosmologist from Cambridge University.

The Anthropic Principle stated that "all the seemingly arbitrary and unrelated constants in physics have one strange thing in common – these are *precisely* the values you need if you want to have a universe capable of producing *life*."[301] Cosmologist Hugh Ross assembled a list of twenty-five of these variables. I want to cite just four of them to flesh out in a bit more detail:

> Ratio of Protons to Electrons
> "…the precise number of electrons must exist. Unless the number of electrons is equivalent to the number of protons to an accuracy of one part in 10^{37}, or better, electromagnetic forces in the universe would have so overcome gravitational forces that galaxies, stars, and planets never would have formed…The following analogy might help: Cover the entire North American continent in dimes all the way up to the moon, a height of 239,000 miles…Next, pile dimes from here to the

---

[299] This finding won COBE's architects, George Smoot and John Mather, the 2006 Nobel Prize in physics.
[300] Glynn, Patrick, *God: The Evidence : The Reconciliation of Faith and Reason in a Postsecular World*, (Rocklin, CA: Prima Publishing, 1997), p.28
Patrick Glynn, Ph.D., is the Harvard-trained associate director and scholar in residence at George Washington University's Institute for Communication Policy Issues. *God: The Evidence* chronicles the cosmological, biological, psychological, and medical data that moved him from atheism to theism.
[301] Ibid, p.22

moon on a billion other continents the same size as North America. Paint one dime red and mix it into the billion piles of dimes...The odds that [you] will pick the red dime are one in 10^{37}. And this is only *one* of the parameters that is so delicately balanced to allow life to form."[302]

Mass Excess of the Neutron Over the Proton
"If the neutron were just another 0.1% more massive, so few neutrons would remain from the cooling off of the big bang that there would not be enough of them to make the nuclei of all the heavy elements essential for life...If the neutron were 0.1% less massive, protons would decay so readily into neutrons that all the stars in the universe would have rapidly collapsed into either neutron stars or black holes. Thus for life to be possible in the universe, the mass must be fine tuned to better than 0.1%."[303]

Balance of Matter to Antimatter
" In the formation of the universe, the balance of matter to antimatter had to be accurate to one part in ten billion for the universe to even arise.."[304]

Expansion Rate of the Universe
"There would have been no universe capable of sustaining life if the expansion rate of the Big Bang had been one billionth of a percent larger or smaller."[305]
"The universe has to know in advance what it is going to be before it knows how to start itself. For in accordance with the Big Bang Theory, for instance, at a time of 10^{-43} seconds the universe has to know how many types of neutrino there are going to be at a time of 1 second.

---

[302] Ross, Hugh, *The Creator And The Cosmos: How The Greatest Scientific Discoveries Of The Century Reveal God*, (Colorado Springs, Colorado: Navpress, 1994)., p.109.
[303] Ibid, p.108.
[304] Moreland, J.P. and Kai Nielsen, *Does God Exist?: The Debate Between Theists &Athiests*, (Amherst, New York: Prometheus Books, 1993), p.35
[305] Ibid

This is so in order that it starts off expanding at the right rate to fit the eventual number of neutrino types."[306]

Paul Davies, a theoretical physicist at Cambridge summarized the data by saying how hard it was "to resist the impression that the present structure of the universe, apparently so sensitive to minor alterations in the numbers, has been rather carefully thought out…the seemingly miraculous concurrence of these numerical values must remain the most compelling evidence for cosmic design."[307] These are variables necessary for even the simplest, single-cell life such as bacteria to have developed!

No Threat From Evolution

Proponents of Darwinian evolution hold that the complexity we find in the animal kingdom today can be explained by beginning with the simplest, single-cell organisms and positing a chain of successive, gradual mutations. If a mutation proved beneficial, it upped the organism's chance of survival; the organism in turn passed it on to offspring. This is known as "natural selection" – nature favoring the survival of one organism over another. Mutation after mutation occurred with natural selection favoring the resultant, ever-more-complex organisms. Now there are a growing number of scientists who feel that natural selection is an inadequate explanation for the complexity we find not just in higher-level organisms such as human beings, but even at the microscopic level of the cell. Should natural selection prove adequate for explaining all physical life though, it still would not negate belief in a Creator. For those who recognize God, natural selection can be looked upon as one of the great exercises of Divine Providence. Organic life could reach the end He had in mind just as easily through natural selection as if He brought it about with "a snap of His Fingers."

---

[306] Glynn, Patrick, *God: The Evidence : The Reconciliation of Faith and Reason in a Postsecular World*, (Rocklin, CA: Prima Publishing, 1997), p.31.

The Origin of Morality

Possibly the most common objection to God's existence is the presence of evil in the world. If God existed then He would not allow such gross injustice. This was British author C. S. Lewis' argument during the first part of his life. He said it collapsed when he realized that if our world, and he himself, were simply a product of blind evolution, or chance, then we should never have been able to discriminate good and evil. If the universe had always existed in this way and things always operated in this "unjust" manner then we shouldn't know that there is anything wrong; there should be no standard of "good" that we see the world falling dreadfully short of, no evil. As Lewis said, "If the whole universe had no meaning, we should never have found out it has no meaning: just as, *if there is no light in the universe and therefore no creatures with eyes, we should never know it was dark.* Dark would be without meaning."[308] But we do have this "light," this conviction of how things should be; and we have "eyes," to recognize atrocities when they occur and to label them as "evil." Where did this standard come from? It is at odds with the whole world around us. Realizing this, mustn't we conclude that the standard came from *outside* our world?

The alternative is to say that there is no such thing as a right and wrong. And yet, the whole of human history is a witness for the opposing side. When one compares the moral teachings of the ancient civilizations – the Chinese, Egyptians, Babylonians, Hindus, Greeks, and Romans – one finds how remarkably similar they all are.[309] When one considers the purported "differences" in morality between these great cultures, one finds that there are actually universal truths operating below the surface. For example, one culture may say that a man may have one wife and another culture that he may have three. But what "they have always agreed [on is] that you must simply not have any woman you liked."[310] There has never been a civilization with a completely foreign morality – one in which a person was "admired for running away in battle, or where a man felt proud of double-crossing all the people who had been kindest to him."[311] There is this idea

---

[308] Lewis, C.S., *Mere Christianity*, (New York: Macmillan Publishing Co.,1943), p 45-46. Italics added.
[309] Ibid, p.19
[310] Ibid, p.19. Italics added.
[311] Ibid

of what is "just," and it has been with us since the beginning of recorded history.

What I personally find so intriguing about our sense of right and wrong is that it often calls us to a less comfortable life. Who would think up something like "Thou shall not lie," or declare fornication "sin"? It would be so much easier to just give into these behaviors. There is a pesky little voice within each of us telling us what we *ought* to do. If you see someone being mugged you encounter conflicting *instincts*: 1) you want to step in and help the victim, 2) but on the other hand you want to run from a dangerous situation. Then a thought comes to the surface of your consciousness; it tells you which instinct you *ought to honor* and which you *ought to suppress*. There is a right thing to do in this situation, a good thing; and yet, it is the one that may bring you pain. Now where did this standard of behavior come from; *Who* is responsible for it?

Conclusion

There is nothing irrational about belief in God. It is certainly more logical than atheism's assertion of a universal negative. True, God's existence can not be proved through scientific method. If it could He would be a god like those of ancient Greece, part of the cosmos, instead of the Judeo-Christian God Who transcends the universe and lends existence to all that is. But we do catch a glimpse of Him through philosophical method as the Uncaused Cause/ Existence/ Intelligence standing behind the universe. And He apparently cares for us, giving us a standard of good and evil with which to judge our behavior. To go beyond this though, we need God to open up a dialogue, to reveal Himself.

Appendix II – The Uniqueness of Jesus, or Why His Claims Deserve a Hearing

"The God of the universe, the Creator, come in human flesh." That is what Jesus claimed of Himself, and for that reason he cannot be accepted as just one great moral or religious teacher among many. It goes far beyond anything claimed by the founders of other world religions. As C.S. Lewis noted:

> There is no parallel in other religions. If you had gone to Buddha and asked him, "Are you the son of Brahmah?" he would have said, "My son, you are still in the vale of illusion." If you had gone to Socrates and asked, "Are you Zeus?" he would have laughed at you. If you had gone to Mohammed and asked, "Are you Allah?" he would first have rent his clothes and then cut your head off. If you had asked Confucius, "Are you Heaven?" I think he would probably have replied, "Remarks which are not in accordance with nature are in bad taste."[312]

> A man who was merely a man and said the sort of thing Jesus said would not be a great moral teacher. He would either be a lunatic – on a level with a man who says he is a poached egg – or else He would be the Devil of Hell. You must make your choice...But let us not come up with any patronizing nonsense about His being a great human teacher. He has not left that open to us. He did not intend to.[313]

But did Jesus truly make this claim? Well, it is what we find in the earliest writings about Him, the epistles of Paul and the four gospels. The claim is implicit throughout: He spoke of Himself as "Lord of the Sabbath" (Matt.12:8; Mk.2:28; Lk.6:5). He claimed to be "greater than the Temple," God's earthly throne (Matt.12:6). By His own authority He added to and definitively interpreted the Law God had given to Moses (Matt.5:17). He even forgave people's sins, and as his opponents asked, "Who can forgive sins but God alone" (Mark 2:7)? Mark's Gospel, written only thirty years after the crucifixion, tells us that it triggered His death sentence:

---

[312] Lewis, C.S., *The Joyful Christian: 127 Readings from C.S. Lewis*, (New York: Macmillan Publishing Co., 1977), p.74.
[313] Lewis, C.S., *Mere Christianity*, (New York: Macmillan Publishing Co.,1943), p.56

> Again the high priest asked him, "Are you the Christ, the Son of the Blessed?" And Jesus said, "I am; and you will see the Son of man sitting at the right hand of Power, and coming with the clouds of heaven." The high priest tore his clothes. Why do we need any more witnesses? You have heard the blasphemy." They all condemned him as worthy of death (Mark 14:61-64).

To claim to be the "Son of the Blessed" was to claim to be God's offspring, divine, and therefore His equal. The early Christians recorded other instances where this claim was explicitly made: "I and the Father are one" (John 10:30); "Truly, truly, I say to you, before Abraham was, I am"[314] (John 8:58-59).

Could Jesus' claim of divinity be tempered? Could He have meant it in an "Eastern sense"? People involved in the "New Age" movement explain that Jesus realized His "God Consciousness," something potentially true *for all of us*: we are all pieces of God; we just don't know it yet (and that constitutes humanity's largest problem). But this really is not a viable explanation in the case of Jesus:

> There is not a single gossamer thread of evidence that the *thoroughly* Jewish, Scripture-soaked Jesus of Nazareth was even *slightly* influenced by [Eastern] philosophy, much less bent on completely revolutionizing Judaism into a religion that identifies God with the world...Indeed, in the length and breadth of His preaching we do not find the slightest hint that He conceives of either God or human beings in Eastern categories. He does not speak of God as identical with Creation; he speaks of Him in a thoroughly Jewish sense as Transcendent Creator, Judge, and Father (Mt 19:4; 6:14-15). He does not conceive of his disciples as parts of God who have only to realize their own Godhead by letting go of their false consciousness of guilt and sin. Rather, he plainly reminds them they are sinners in need of salvation who are, apart from him alone, incapable of accomplishing their salvation or anything else (John 15:5). So far from affirming that we're okay and he's okay, he frequently reminds us that we are sinners, but he is without sin; we are from below, but he is from above (John 8:1-11; 8:23)...None of this

---

[314] "I AM," or *Yahweh*, is the name of God. He revealed Himself as thus to Moses (Exodus 3:14).

squares very easily with the notion that Christ was really just trying to awaken us to our own deity. Quite the contrary, it looks as though he was attempting to alert us exclusively to his.[315]

In all fairness we should admit that Jesus' claim of divinity was meant in the only way intelligible for a first-century Jew: He was The Eternal, The Almighty come among us, His creations. If he was not Who he claimed, the only options we are left are to label him either delusional or a liar; and neither fit.

We will tackle "delusional" first. Read Jesus' Sermon on the Mount (Matthew 5-7); it is admired by Christians and non-Christians alike for its moral brilliance. Gandhi used it as a basis for his tactic of peaceful non-resistance. The Sermon on the Mount is not the product of someone who is mentally ill. A delusional person doesn't out-maneuver the religious/political leaders of his day in public debate either. Remember that line about "Give to Caesar what is Caesar's, but give to God what is God's" (see Luke 20:20-26)? Crowds were in awe of His teaching and retorts that left opponents speechless (Matthew 21:23-27; 21:46; 22:23; 22:45; Luke 20:39).[316]

The option that Jesus was a liar is untenable as well. A person lies because he or she believes there is something to be gained by it. A first-century Jew with the slightest modicum of intelligence knew that a claim of divinity would be met with cries of blasphemy. A person wouldn't do such a thing to get ahead; He would only do it if it were the truth (we have already said He wasn't delusional). In the end Jesus' testimony led to his execution. He wasn't out to be a politician; instead of selling and ingratiating himself to the elite of the day he told them the painful, unwelcome truth that they were in need of repentance. Instead of sucking up to *them*, he preached mercy and welcomed the "undesirables" into the Kingdom of Heaven – the prostitutes, tax collectors, the uneducated, the rank and file. A liar? No, he had nothing to gain.

So He wasn't delusional, or a lunatic, or an Eastern guru. What else can we know of Jesus? The most exhaustive historical study to date is John

---

[315] Shea, Mark P., *By What Authority?: An Evangelical Discovers Catholic Tradition*, (Huntington, Indiana: Our Sunday Visitor, Inc., 1996), p.40.
[316] The fact that crowds followed Jesus is hardly debatable; historically, what else could explain Him being considered a threat in need of crucifixion?

Meier's three volumes, *A Marginal Jew: Rethinking the Historical Jesus*. Using controlled criteria,[317] Meier has sifted the layers of historical data both in and outside the New Testament to arrive at the points an unbiased historical investigator should be able to affirm:[318] Jesus was a first-century, itinerant preacher, popularly regarded as an exorcist,[319] healer,[320] and even one who could raise the dead.[321] He clashed with prominent Jewish leaders and was crucified under the Roman procurator Pontius Pilate. We also know that shortly afterward his apostles began claiming that he was alive, that he had been raised from the dead. Like Jesus before them - *whom they had seen crucified* – they gained nothing from their claims, save the persecution of Jerusalem and Rome! Within a few decades, rather than recant, they too suffered martyrdom.

What makes sense of Jesus and the apostles' behavior? If not delusion, nor deception, then what? Could Jesus be Who he claimed? The infant church claimed that his image was woven in figure and prophecy throughout the Hebrew Scriptures. Doesn't reason necessitate further investigation on our part? If true, what does He ask of us?

---

[317] Meier employed a five-pronged approach in labeling data historical: 1) multiple attestation, 2) discontinuity, 3) embarrassment, 4) coherence, and 5) the criterion of Jesus' rejection and execution. For further discussion see, Meier, John P., *A Marginal Jew: Rethinking the Historical Jesus*, Volume 2. (New York: Doubleday, 1994), p.5

[318] Meier's work is the product of his imagining what would emerge if a Catholic, Protestant, Jew, and an agnostic – all honest historians cognizant of first-century religious movements – were locked in the bowels of Harvard Divinity School library until they could emerge with a consensus document.

[319] Ibid, p.646-661

[320] Ibid, p.678-727

[321] Ibid, p.773-837

Appendix III – A Christian View of the "New Age" Movement

By the New Age Movement I refer to a "feel good" spirituality which borrows elements from world religions as well as occult beliefs and practices and then assembles them into an amalgam promising enlightenment to its adherents. Actress Shirley Maclaine seemed to emerge as the face of the movement in the 1980's, and it has been going strong since with best-sellers such as Neale Donald Walsch's *Conversations With God* trilogy and Eckart Tolle's *A New Earth*, the literary output and QVC appearances of Sylvia Browne, and television mediums James Van Praagh and John Edwards.

The question I want to address in this appendix is how New Age Movement practitioners claiming spiritual encounters through trances, séances, Ouija boards, automatic writing, etc., could come to such strange and contradictory conclusions about the identity of Jesus. I believe that some people are making it up, milking a public with shallow religious knowledge. In other cases I think we may be dealing with individuals suffering from mental illness, people who are not having spiritual encounters but hallucinations.

There's a third possibility as well, and this will undoubtedly sound to some like I have gone off the deep end: these "spiritual experiences" are encounters with the demonic. The seeking of supernatural experiences, or information, from sources other than the One God is a dangerous undertaking.

You may be stunned that I believe in 'the Devil.' Let's make sure we understand what 'the Devil,' or Satan, or the Adversary is though. Christianity doesn't conceive of him as a being equal but opposite to God. Far from it; he is a creature, one of the angelic realm. As such he is much more powerful than human beings, but still only a finite creature in opposition to an infinite and eternal Creator. Pope Paul VI, the pope who oversaw the closing of Vatican Council II, did not dismiss the Devil as outmoded superstition. During a 1972 address he stated very plainly:

> What are the greatest needs of the Church today? Don't let our answer surprise you as being over simple or even superstitious or unreal: one of the greatest needs is defense from that evil which is called the Devil.

Evil is not merely a lack of something, but an effective agent, a living spiritual being, perverted and perverting. A terrible reality...It is contrary to the teaching of the Bible and the Church to refuse to recognize the existence of such a reality...or to explain it as a pseudoreality, a conceptual and fanciful personification of the unknown causes of our misfortunes...(Nov.15, 1972).

Scripture clearly teaches the existence of such a being. In fact, it speaks of many creatures, demons, allied with the Devil. They are presented as the antitheses of angels, fallen angels. But not only is the Bible very frank on these matters, it is also very firm in its condemnation of the occult practices so prevalent in the New Age movement. In the Old Testament we read:

> Do not turn to mediums or wizards; do not seek them out, to be defiled by them: I am the LORD your God (Leviticus 19:31)

> There shall not be found among you any one who...practices divination, a soothsayer, or an augur, or a sorcerer, or a charmer, or a medium, or a wizard, or a necromancer. For whoever does these things is an abomination to the LORD (Deuteronomy 18:10-12).

> And when they say to you, "Consult the mediums and the wizards who chirp and mutter," should not a people consult their God? Should they consult the dead on behalf of the living? To the teaching and to the testimony [instead]!(Isaiah 8:19-20).

When we turn to the New Testament we have a first person account of how the Apostle Paul reacted to the occult. Luke, his traveling companion, wrote:

> As we were going to the place of prayer, we were met by a slave girl who had a spirit of divination and brought her owners much gain by soothsaying. She followed Paul and us, crying, "these men are servants of the Most High God, who proclaim to you the way of salvation." And this she did for many days. But Paul was annoyed, and turned and said to the spirit, "I charge you in the name of Jesus Christ to come out of her." And it came out that very hour (Acts 16:16-19).

Paul would not accept the testimony of a clairvoyant. Why not? Because he knew what God had said on the matter in the Old Testament. Instead of welcoming her, he performed an exorcism! Had he accepted her testimony, once inside of the Christian community she could have introduced falsehoods, distortions to the gospel. The library books I came across when I started asking questions about Jesus' identity were examples of just this type of thing.

I had grown up in a Christian family, attended a Catholic school and no one had ever warned me of the dangers. Astrology, Ouija boards, mediums, fortune-telling, psychic telephone services – all are at odds with Christianity. When these practices are engaged in they can open the heart to a realm best left untouched. Some people claim that it's harmless fun at parties; others report supernatural manifestations. I look at it as a game of spiritual Russian roulette; play it long enough and you will probably get hurt. God said that it wasn't for His children; that should be enough for us.

Appendix IV – The Old Testament "Apocrypha

In a few instances you will see me quote from books excluded from non-Catholic editions of the Bible. Non-Catholic brothers and sisters refer to these writings (*Tobit, Judith, Wisdom, Baruch, 1 & 2 Maccabees,* an additional 107 verses to the *Book of Esther* and two chapters to the *Book of Daniel*) as the Apocrypha; Catholics refer to them as the "Deutero-canonicals." Initially I came to accept their inspiration because of the resonance I found between them, as a group, and the rest of Scripture. Most convincing was a passage I had "happened upon" in *Wisdom* – it was the most explicit prophecy of Christ I had seen. Observe how closely it mirrors our Lord, especially His passion and death:

Wisdom 2: 12 – 22	Jesus' Ministry and Death
[The wicked said:] "Let us lie in wait for the righteous man, because he is inconvenient to us and opposes our actions; he reproaches us for sins against our training. He professes to have knowledge of God, and calls himself a child of the Lord. He became to us a reproof of our thoughts; the very sight of him is a burden to us, because his manner of life is unlike that of others, and his ways are strange. We are considered by him as something base, and he avoids our ways as unclean; he calls the last end of the righteous happy, and boasts that God is his father. Let us see if his words are true, and let us test what will happen at the end of his life; for if the righteous man is God's son, he will heal him, and will deliver him from the hand of his adversaries. Let us test him with insult and torture, that we may find out how gentle his is, and make trial of his forbearance. Let us condemn him to a shameful death, for, according to what he says, he will be protected."	Consider Jesus' many confrontations with the Pharisees and teachers of the Law recorded in the New Testament. Reminiscent of the Beatitudes: "Blest are the poor in spirit, for theirs is the kingdom of heaven…Blessed are the pure in heart, for they shall see God (Matt. 5:5-12). At the crucifixion: "So also the chief priests, with the scribes and elders, mocked him, saying 'He saved others; he cannot save himself. He is the King of Israel; let him come down now from the cross, and we will believe in him. He trusts in God; let God deliver him now, if he desires him; for he said, 'I am the Son of God'"(Matt. 27:41-44).

I couldn't ignore such prophetic precision. I was grateful to the Holy Spirit for letting me find this and began reading more of the "apocrypha." I wanted to understand why Christians disagreed over the Old Testament.

Through reading and talking with others I learned several interesting facts. First, that the Protestant Old Testament matches that of today's Jewish community; the Protestant Reformers considered it to be more authentic. Second, that St. Jerome, probably the greatest biblical scholar of the first three centuries, chose to distinguish these books from the rest of the Old Testament in his Latin translation, labeling them "ecclesiastical" as opposed to "canonical." These things would seem to argue against the deutero-canonicals acceptance, but there's another side to consider.

So far as the Jewish canon of Scripture goes, it was not decided until close to 100 A.D. The debate over which books to include in the canon was carried on in Jamnia, a Palestinian seacoast town. It was there that Rabbi Johanan ben Zakai had established a center for scribal learning.[322] All of this took place after the fall of Jerusalem and the expulsion of Christians from the Synagogue. Prior to the decisions of Jamnia the Old Testament canon was not "set in stone" and was apparently larger than today's; this was the Old Testament used by the Apostles and the early Church. The Anglican scholar, J.N.D. Kelly writes,

> . . .the Old Testament thus admitted as authoritative in the Church was somewhat bulkier and more comprehensive than the. . .books of the Hebrew Bible of Palestinian Judaism. . .It always included, though with varying degrees of recognition, the so-called Apocrypha, or deutero-canonical books. The reason for this is that the Old Testament which passed in the first instance into the hands of Christians was not the original Hebrew version, but the Greek translation known as the Septuagint.[323]

The Greek translation, begun about 300 B.C., and which included the deutero-canonicals, was what the Church used in her worship and study; after all, Christians were predominantly Greek-speaking. When the Apostles quoted from the Old Testament in their epistles the Septuagint was generally what they used, "Of the 350 quotations of the Old Testament found in

---

[322] Hanson, James E., *If I'm a Christian, Why Be a Catholic?*, (New York: Paulist Press, 1984), p.126
[323] Kelley, John Norman Davidson., *Early Christian Doctrines* (HarperSanFrancisco, 1978), p.53

the New Testament, 300 are taken directly from the Greek Septuagint Bible" as opposed to the Hebrew.[324] Thus, the Christian Church had been making use of an Old Testament containing these books for some sixty years before the Jewish rabbis officially excluded them. It must be recalled that at the time the rabbis set their canon they were no longer the world's teachers; that role had been passed to the Apostles and their successors. When Jerome expressed doubts about the canonicity of the deutero-canonicals a few centuries later, he did so as a scholar living in Bethlehem and performing his translation of the Old Testament alongside rabbis; as such he was susceptible to their opinions. Jerome was free to ask these questions; for although the books had come down to the Church from apostolic times, a formal Church statement (from Peter's successor or an Ecumenical Council) had never been made regarding the Old Testament canon. The local councils of Hippo (393 A.D.) and Carthage (419 A.D.), the latter presided over by St. Augustine, declared the deutero-canonicals to be part of the Old Testament. The decrees of the Council of Carthage received a "semi-binding" status in the minds of most Christians when Pope Boniface gave them his approval.[325]

Now one last objection which I have heard from Protestant brothers and sisters to the Apocrypha is that Jesus did not quote from it as He did the rest of the Old Testament. This objection has two large holes in it, however. First, if quotation from Jesus, or the Apostles after him, as recorded in the New Testament, were our criteria for including books in the Old Testament then all Christians would have to slim their Bibles. They would no longer contain *Ecclesiastes, Obadiah, Zephaniah, Judges, 1 & 2 Chronicles, Ezra, Nehemiah, Lamentations,* or *Nahum.*[326] Second, I maintain that Jesus and the Apostles did draw from the deutero-canonicals. Allow me to list some examples:

---

[324] Rumble, Leslie and Charles M. Carty, *Bible Quizzes To A Street Preacher*,(Rockford, Illinois: Tan Books and Publishers Inc., 1976), p.4
[325] Graham, Henry G., *Where We Got the Bible: Our Debt to the Catholic Church* (Rockford, Illinois: Tan Publishers), p.37.
[326] Shea, Mark P., *By What Authority? : An Evangelical Discovers Catholic Tradition*, (Huntington, Indiana: Our Sunday Visitor, Inc., 1996), p.62.

Sirach 28:2 Forgive your neighbor the wrong he has done, and then your sins will be pardoned when you pray.	*Matthew 6:14* For if you forgive men their trespasses, your heavenly Father also will forgive you.
Sirach 27:6 The fruit discloses the cultivation of a tree; so the expression of a thought discloses the cultivation of a man's mind.	*Matthew 7:16,18* You will know them by their fruits....A sound tree cannot bear evil fruit, nor can a bad tree bear good fruit.
Sirach 28:4 Does he have no mercy toward a man like himself, and yet pray for his own sins?	*Matthew 18:32* Then his lord summoned him and said to him, "You wicked servant! I forgave you all that debt because you besought me; and should not you have had mercy on your fellow servant, as I had mercy on you?"
Sirach 29:10-12 Lose your silver for the sake of a brother or a friend, and do not let it rust under a stone and be lost. Lay up your treasure according to the commandments of the Most High, and it will profit you more than gold. Store up almsgiving in your treasury, and it will rescue you from all affliction...	*Luke 16:9* And I tell you, make friends for yourselves by means of unrighteous mammon [or money] so that when it fails they may receive you into the eternal habitations.

Sirach 33:12-13 Some of them he blessed and exalted, and some of them he made holy and brought near to himself; but some of them he cursed and brought low, and he turned them out of their place. As clay in the hand of the potter – for all his ways are as he pleases – so men are in the hand of him who made them, to give them as he decides.	*Romans 9:18-20* So then, he has mercy upon whomever he wills, and he hardens the heart of whomever he wills. You will say to me then, "Why does he find fault? For who can resist his will?" But who are you to answer back to God…Has the potter not the right to make of the same lump one vessel for beauty and another for menial use?
Wisdom 9:16 We can hardly guess at what is on earth, and what is at hand we find with labor; but who has traced out what is in the heavens? Who has learned thy counsel, unless thou hast given wisdom and sent thy holy Spirit from on high?	*John 3:12-13* If I have told you earthly things and you do not believe, how can you believe if I tell you heavenly things? No one has ascended into heaven but he who descended from heaven, the Son of man.
Wisdom 12:24-25 For they went far astray on the paths of error, accepting as gods those animals which even their enemies despised; they were deceived like foolish babes. Therefore, as to thoughtless children, thou didst send thy judgment to mock them.	*Romans 1:22-25* Claiming to be wise, they became fools, and exchanged the glory of the immortal God for images resembling mortal man or birds or animals or reptiles. Therefore, God gave them up in the lusts of their hearts to impurity, to the dishonoring of themselves, because they exchanged the truth about God for a lie and worshiped and served the creature rather than the Creator, who is blessed for ever! Amen.

Wisdom 7:26 For [Wisdom] is a reflection of eternal light, a spotless mirror of the working of God, and an image of his goodness.	*Hebrews 1:3, NIV* The Son is the radiance of God's glory and the exact representation of his being.
Wisdom 3:5-6 Having been disciplined a little, they will receive great good, because God tested them and found them worthy of himself; like gold in the furnace he tried them, and like a sacrificial burnt offering he accepted them.	*1 Peter 1:6-7* In this you rejoice, though now for a little while you may have to suffer various trials, so that the genuineness of your faith, more precious than gold which though perishable is tested by fire, may redound to praise and glory and honor at the revelation of Jesus Christ.

I think these examples show that Jesus and the Apostles were familiar with the deutero-canonicals. The fact that not all of the deutero-canonicals are quoted from or alluded to should cause us no more difficulty than the fact that so many other Old Testament books were not quoted from or alluded to in the New Testament. So what is a Christian's standard for including some books in the Bible and excluding others? It is the witness of the Church – given through the successors of Peter and the Apostles. As with the New Testament, the Church did not make an "ex cathedra" pronouncement on what books she recognized until the Protestant Reformers began questioning what books really belonged in the Bible (see Chapter 12 for a fuller discussion of this process). It just so happens that the deutero-canonicals contain teaching on the heavenly intercession of the saints as well as purgation of sin following death – doctrines the Reformers rejected. As I share elsewhere in the book, I believe that both of these doctrines belong to the Deposit of Faith.

Appendix V – The Validity of Infant Baptism

For me personally it came down to answering the question, "Was Jesus present in my baptism at the age of three weeks?" I knew Christians who wouldn't hesitate in saying "no." A common justification for their position was: For baptism to have meaning a person has to have sufficient maturity to accept Jesus into his/her heart as personal Lord and Savior. The Apostle Paul said, "…if you confess with your lips that Jesus is Lord and believe in your heart that God raised him from the dead, you will be saved" (Romans 10:9). An infant didn't have the mental, nor the articulatory, ability to make such a confession.

The difficulty I have with that kind of reasoning is that it excludes not just infants from receiving the gift of the Spirit, but adults with profound mental retardation. In fact, if we want to take this passage at absolute face-value, someone who was mute couldn't "confess with [his] lips," and therefore couldn't be saved either.

I am sure that no one reading this is worried about the exclusion of these brothers and sisters from God's kingdom because of their respective challenges. Without a second thought we conclude that the Lord takes these special conditions into consideration. In the case of the mute man, for example, surely the Lord will "hear" his confession of faith offered mentally or via sign language or an augmentative communication device. In the case of the mentally retarded we instinctually believe that God, in His great love for these little ones, extends the grace of Christ to them without requiring "faith" in the same manner as He does from another. God is loving and just; He does not demand what someone is unable to give.

Another situation which we should consider is that of the child who dies before reaching the "age of reason." Is such a child condemned to hell because he/she did not have the chance to "accept Jesus" the way an adult would? I think that even the most legalistic readers of the Bible make a compassionate leap of faith, believing that God has mercy upon the souls of these children. Knowing the great love of God, we believe that these little ones will not be condemned – seeing as how they do not possess the maturity to commit personal sins, they need only to be healed of the effects of original sin by an application of Christ's grace. Again, God is expected to make a merciful exception on behalf of the child. What I find so interesting is that many Christians who cannot accept God bestowing the second birth upon the soul of a *living* child, *can* accept Him doing so for the soul of a deceased child. Why the latter and not the former?

Is it true that the baptism of infants has no basis in Scripture? In my first reading of the New Testament I had not come across any outright mention of it. Taking a second look, however, and considering different biblical passages in light of one another has left me convinced that infants *can* respond to Christ's grace, and therefore should be considered worthy recipients of baptism.

There *is* a good biblical example of an infant receiving God's grace. When the angel Gabriel announced the birth of John the Baptist he told the child's father, "He will be filled with the Holy Spirit *even from his mother's womb*" (Luke 1:15). The filling of the Holy Spirit is an action which the rest of us experience as a consequence of our baptism - John received it before reaching the age of reason, *before even exiting his mother's womb*! If we look a little farther we find that John not only received grace in the womb, he reacted to it; when his mother Elizabeth was visited by Mary, John "leaped for joy" while still in her womb (Luke 1:44).

There are other texts to consider as well. On the day of Pentecost, Peter was asked by the Jewish crowd what they must do to be saved. He replied:

> Repent, and be baptized every one of you in the name of Jesus Christ for the forgiveness of your sins; and you shall receive the gift of the Holy Spirit. For the promise is to you *and your children* and to all that are far off whom the Lord our God calls to him (Acts 2:38-39).

We cannot forget that up until this point in history God had always included infants in His covenant. To have revoked that privilege would have made the New Covenant inferior to the Old. The New Covenant was meant to open the Family of God wider, not limit it. When *Acts of the Apostles* tells us that whole families were baptized (Acts 16:15; 16:31-33; 18:8) it mentions no exclusion of infants.

Something that should be thought-provoking is the Apostle Paul's equating of circumcision in the Old Testament with baptism in the New:

> In [Jesus] also you were circumcised with a circumcision made without hands, by putting off the body of flesh in *the circumcision of Christ*; and

> *you were buried with him in baptism*, in which you were also raised with him through faith in the working of God, who raised him from the dead (Colossians 2:11-12)

I am not offering a new interpretation of this passage; Martin Luther and John Calvin, as well as modern Protestant lights such as Francis Shaeffer, understood it the same way.[327]

This point is pertinent to the present discussion because circumcision was the Old Testament rite whereby male *infants* were brought into God's covenant with Abraham. The Lord had told Abraham:

> I will establish my covenant between me and you and your descendants after you...This is my covenant, which you shall keep, between me and you and your descendants after you: Every male among you shall be circumcised...He that is *eight days old* among you shall be circumcised; every male throughout your generations...Any uncircumcised male who is not circumcised in the flesh of his foreskin shall be cut off from his people; he has broken my covenant (Genesis 17: 7, 10, 12, 14).

The inclusion of infants in His covenant people was a matter of utmost importance in God's eyes. This is amply illustrated by the example of Moses. When God's spokesman was lax in circumcising his own son, it almost cost Moses his life. The only thing that saved him was his quick-thinking, sure-handed wife and a piece of flint (Exodus 4:24-26). My contention is this: if the New Covenant in Christ was not meant to do away with the Old but to bring it to perfection (Matthew 5:17), and baptism is

---

[327] The following citations were found in Stephen Ray's *Crossing the Tiber*, (San Francisco: Ignatius Press, 1997), p.127.
John Calvin wrote, "Hence it is incontrovertible, that baptism has been substituted for circumcision, and performs the same office." *The Institutes of the Christian Religion*, 2:531
Martin Luther said, "We now have baptism instead of circumcision." (*Luther's Works*, ed. Abdel R. Wentz [Philadelphia: Fortress Press, 1959], 36:95,n.)
Francis Schaeffer wrote, "There is a flow between the circumcision of the Old Testament and the baptism of the New. The New Testament speaks of baptism as the Christian's circumcision...We could say it this way...'You are circumcised by Christian circumcision, being baptized'" (*The Complete Works of Francis Schaeffer* [Westchester, Ill: Crossway Books, 1982], 2:225).

meant to be the perfection of circumcision (which God had *required* for infants), then infant baptism should be accepted as legitimate.

During Jesus' earthly ministry all three synoptic gospels record parents bringing their children to Him to be touched and blessed. I found that if we consult Luke's account we are told specifically, "they were bringing even infants to him that he might touch them" (18:15). The rest of the account is equally enlightening:

> ...when the disciples saw it, they rebuked [the parents]. But *Jesus called them to him*, saying: "Let the little children come to me, and *do not hinder them*; for to such belongs the kingdom of God" (Luke 18:15-17).

I believe the Lord Jesus is saying the same thing to disciples of this day who have not yet recognized that His grace is meant even for our infants.

I wish to bring this short discussion on infant baptism to a close with a citation from Alan Schreck's wonderful book, *Catholic and Christian*:

> The most common question about infant baptism is "How can a parent or guardian's faith substitute for the faith of the child?" It is noteworthy that Jesus didn't pose this question. When Jairus asked Jesus to raise his young daughter from the dead (Mark 5:22-23; 35-43) or another father asked Jesus to expel a demon from his son (Mark 9:17-27), Jesus acted with power because of *their* faith, not the faith of their children. How much more would Jesus desire to free children from an even worse bondage, the bondage of sin and eternal death, in response to the faith of their parents and of the whole Christian community?
>
> Infant baptism underscores the fact that salvation is a free gift of God. When someone baptizes it is Christ Who baptizes. He is the One Who saves...The infant did not choose to be baptized, but neither did he or she choose to be born. They are both God's gift, brought about through human agents: the child's parents...The parents of the baptized child must commit themselves to providing an environment for the child to grow in faith. This will prepare [the child] to make a personal faith commitment to Jesus Christ upon reaching maturity. This personal faith commitment is absolutely necessary for the mature Christian.[328]

---

[328] Schreck, Alan, *Catholic and Christian: An Explanation of Commonly Misunderstood Catholic Beliefs*, (Ann Arbor, Michigan: Servant Books, 1984), p.127.

Appendix VI – Does Everyone Receive the Gift of Tongues?

There are some believers who hold that without evidencing the gift of tongues a person cannot have been "baptized in the Holy Spirit." There are others who do not go that far, but claim that each Christian has a prayer language, if they would only *yield to it*. I am convinced, from looking at Scripture and the face of the Church today, that both positions are in error. I will restrict myself to explaining my disagreement with the latter position since those reasons automatically apply to the former.

First, I do not see the gift of tongues *always* accompanying the "release" of the Spirit in *Acts of the Apostles*. We are told in Acts 10:45-47 and 19:6 that tongues accompanied the outpouring of the Holy Spirit on new Christians; in the second example this occurred when the Apostle Paul laid hands on the newly baptized. In Acts 8:14-17, however, we are told that the Holy Spirit came upon the newly-baptized Samaritans through the laying on of Peter and John's hands – but without a mention of tongues. An oversight on the author Luke's part? Well, consider also that there is no mention of the three thousand who were baptized on the day of Pentecost receiving tongues either. In fact, if you went through all the other conversion stories in *Acts* you wouldn't find another mention of the charism.

St. Paul is clear that tongues is not an integral part of everyone's Christian experience. In *The First Epistle to the Corinthians* he wrote:

> Now you are the body of Christ and individually members of it. And God has appointed in the church first apostles, second prophets, third teachers, then workers of miracles, then healers, helpers, administrators, speakers in various kinds of tongues. Are all apostles? Are all prophets? Are all teachers? Do all work miracles? Do all possess the gift of healing? Do all speak with tongues? Do all interpret? But earnestly desire the higher gifts. And I will show you a still more excellent way. If I speak in the tongues of men and of angels, but have not love, I am a noisy gong or a clanging symbol" (1 Corinthians 12:27-13:1).

At this point some "charismatic" believers will object to my citation of the above passage. They interpret Paul as saying that not all Christians should expect to *speak a prophetic message in tongues*, one in need of interpretation; but every Christian *should* expect to *pray in tongues*. I acknowledge that the gift of tongues has two different manifestation – but I see no justification for dividing it up into two different gifts. In the list of gifts given in *First Corinthians 12* Paul listed tongues – just tongues; he did not speak of a gift of praying in tongues and a separate gift of speaking in tongues. He then went on in *Chapter 14* of the same letter to discuss different manifestations of this one gift – primarily a gift of prayer, but sometimes a gift of prophecy when combined with the gift of interpretation. Notice how Paul goes back and forth between the terms "speaking" and "praying" in the following passage:

> Therefore, he who speaks in a tongue should pray for the power to interpret. For if I pray in a tongue, my spirit prays but my mind is unfruitful. What am I to do? I will pray with the spirit and I will pray with the mind also. I will sing with the spirit and I will sing with the mind also. Otherwise, if you bless with the spirit, how can any one in the position of an outsider say the "Amen" to your thanksgiving when he does not know what you are saying? For you may give thanks well enough, but the other man is not edified. I thank God that I speak in tongues more than you all; nevertheless, in church I would rather speak five words with my mind, in order to instruct others, than ten thousand words in a tongue (14:13-18). When you come together…if any speak in a tongue, let there be only two or at most three, and each in turn; and let one interpret. But if there is no one to interpret, let each of them keep silence in church and speak to himself and to God (14:26-28).

Do you see what I mean about the terms *praying in tongues* and *speaking in tongues* referring to one and the same gift? In time I experienced both forms. When I was finally moved to speak a message in tongues at a prayer group I wasn't receiving a new gift; I was only moved to direct toward others what up until that time had been directed only toward God. (An interpretation in English followed and the group heard the message the Lord had for them.)

    I think that the overemphasis some Christians have placed on tongues flows from the blessing it has been in their own lives – because it has been a great blessing for them they conclude that it should be a blessing received by all. It is a pretty common human reaction. The reality, however, is that the Holy Spirit decides which gifts each member of the Body needs to best fulfill their assigned task:

> Now there are varieties of gifts, but the same Spirit...To *each* is given the manifestation of the Spirit for the common good. *To one* is given through the Spirit the utterance of wisdom, and *to another* the utterance of knowledge according to the same Spirit, to another faith...to another gifts of healing...to another the working of miracles, to another prophecy...*to another various kinds of tongues*, to another the interpretation of tongues. All these are inspired by one and the same Spirit, who apportions *to each one individually as he wills* (1 Cor. 12:4-11).

Appendix VII - Scripture is Without Error

At Vatican II, in its *Dogmatic Constitution on Divine Revelation, Dei Verbum* in Latin, the Catholic Church reiterated its ancient conviction that Scripture, as God's written word, could not be at odds with reality, could not deceive:

> Since, therefore, all that the inspired authors, or sacred writers, affirm should be affirmed by the Holy Spirit, we must acknowledge that the books of Sacred Scripture, firmly, faithfully and without error, teach that truth which God, for the sake of our salvation, wished to see confided to the sacred Scriptures. Thus, "all Scripture is inspired by God, and profitable for teaching, for reproof, for correction and for training in righteousness, so that the man of God may be complete, equipped for every good work (2 Tim.3:16)" (DV,11). [329]

Although not employed by *Dei Verbum*, the term "inerrancy" came into vogue in the nineteenth century to denote Scripture's freedom from error.

In discussions of *Dei Verbum*'s teaching on inerrancy, the portion I have italicized is the common citation. As we can see though, this omits the first clause of a very dense, complex sentence, "Since, *therefore, all* that the inspired authors, or sacred writers, affirm *should be affirmed by the Holy Spirit*, we must acknowledge..." The same thought is continued by *2 Timothy 3:16*, "*all Scripture* is inspired by God." Because all of Scripture was produced under the action of the Holy Spirit, for the sake of our salvation, it must be acknowledged as teaching the truth "firmly, faithfully and without error." The Church is not subscribing to fundamentalism, taking every word at face-value; but it is saying that once we take account of literary genres and figurative language, whatever Scripture does in fact affirm is without error.

Admittedly, there are many gifted Catholic scripture scholars and churchmen who do not present *Dei Verbum* in the manner I have. Rather than a reaffirmation of the Church's historic faith in the inerrancy of Scripture, they see it positing a limitation. Fr. George Montague, a dynamic priest and past president of the Catholic Biblical Association of America, has written that Scripture's inspiration extends to historical material but "only to the

---

[329] Flannery, Austin, *Vatican Council II: The Conciliar and Post Conciliar Documents*, (Northport, New York: Costello Publishing Company, 1992), p.757. Italics added

"only to the degree that it contributes to our salvation."[330] "Historical errors," could be admitted in matters not directly bearing upon the message of salvation.[331] The widely used *New Jerome Biblical Commentary*, in its article "Church Pronouncements," says:

> On inerrancy Vatican II made an important qualification as our italics indicate: "The Books of Scripture must be acknowledged as teaching firmly, faithfully, and without error *that truth which God wanted put into the sacred writings for the sake of our salvation*" (3:11)...Thus, it is proper to take the clause as specifying: Scriptural teaching is truth without error to the extent that it conforms to the salvific purpose of God. Decisions about that purpose involves an a posteriori approach in the church, paying attention to literary forms and historical conditions."[332]

Robert Gnuse, associate professor of Old Testament at Loyola University in New Orleans, in his work *The Authority of the Bible*, devoted less than half a page to the issue, concluding that the Church has clearly rejected a position of "total inerrancy":

> Several revisions during the Second Vatican Council between 1962 and 1964 transformed [*Dei Verbum*] from a narrow statement to a more open definition, which could admit the truth of salvation was without error while the written words need not be...The final statement read, "...we must profess of the books of Scripture that they teach with certainty, with fidelity and without error the truth which God wanted recorded in the sacred writings for the sake of our salvation."
> Thus, the Roman Catholic Church has rejected several views in the last two centuries: subsequent approval by the Church or the Spirit, negative assistance by the Spirit, verbal dictation, inspiration of ideas, inspiration of faith and morals, *and total inerrancy*.[333]

---

[330] Montague, George T. *Understanding the Bible: A Basic Introduction to Biblical Interpretation* (New York: Paulist, 1997) p.195.
[331] Ibid, p.195-196.
[332] Brown, Raymond E. and Collins, Thomas Aquinas, "Church Pronouncements" in *The New Jerome Biblical Commentary*, Ed. R.E. Brown, J.A. Fitzmeyer, and R. E. Murphy, p.1169 (Englewood Cliffs, NJ: Prentice Hall, 1990).
[333] Gnuse, Robert. *The Authority of the Bible: Theories of Inspiration, Revelation and the Canon of Scripture.* (New York: Paulist, 1985), p.12.

Avery Dulles, now Avery Cardinal Dulles, writing in 1980, surveyed the landscape as follows:

> The Council makes the rather ambiguous statement that "the books of Scripture" teach "firmly, faithfully, and without error that truth which God wanted to put into the sacred writings for the sake of our salvation" (DV 11). While some commentators interpret this sentence as excluding all error from the Bible, it may be read as asserting that, while there may be erroneous statements here or there, they are corrected elsewhere or do not affect the meaning of the whole. Further, the Council's statement might seem to allow for errors in matters without importance for our salvation…In Roman Catholicism, many prominent theologians still assert inerrancy, but only in a very qualified manner. Norbert Lohfink, for example, has maintained that the unity of the Bible demands that each individual statement be interpreted in terms of the whole, so that it no longer bears the meaning which it would have if read in isolation. Thus an erroneous statement in one or another of the books of Scripture does not compromise the inerrancy of the Bible. Other Catholic theologians, as we have seen, insist only on the "salvific truth" of Scripture, and are willing to admit scientific and historical errors. Oswald Loretz,[334] on the other hand, holds that the Bible is true in the Hebrew sense of being reliable and faithful, but

---

[334] Loretz's position is ably corrected by the work of our Protestant brother, Robert Nicole. After providing a thorough treatment of the OT's use of "emet" and the Septuagint and the NT's use of "aletheia," he concludes by saying, "The biblical view of truth ('emet-aletheia) is that it is like a rope with several intertwined strands. It will not do to isolate the strands and deal with them separately, although they may be distinguished just as various lines in a telephone cable may be distinguished by color. *The full Bible concept of truth involves factuality, faithfulness, and completeness.* Those who have stressed one of these features in order to downgrade either or both of the others are falling short of the biblical pattern. Notably those who have stressed faithfulness, as if conformity to fact did not matter, are failing grievously to give proper attention to what constitutes probably a majority of the passages in which the word *truth* is used."
Nicole, Roger, "The Biblical Concept of Truth" in Ed. Carson, D.A. and Woodbridge, John D., *Scripture and Truth* (Grand Rapids, Michigan: Baker Book House, 1992), p.296.

not in the Greek scientific sense, which would demand conformity between statements and the facts they refer to.[335]

The "salvific truth" of Scripture, often spoken of as matters of faith and morals, seems to place the same truth restrictions on Scripture that have been recognized in papal infallibility.[336] Fr. Raymond Brown, however, sees an even more extensive limit to inerrancy:

> In the last hundred years we have moved from an understanding wherein inspiration guaranteed that the Bible was totally inerrant to an understanding wherein inerrancy is limited to the Bible's teaching of "that truth which God wanted put into the sacred writings for the sake of our salvation." In this long journey of thought the concept of inerrancy was not rejected but was seriously modified to fit the evidence of biblical criticism which showed that the Bible was not inerrant in questions of science, of history, and *even of time-conditioned religious beliefs*.[337]

Brown's statement serves as an example of the slippery slope we begin down when limiting the inerrancy, and I would say, as a result, the authority of Scripture. As Augustine of Hippo wrote so many centuries ago, "…if we once admit in that supreme monument of authority, [the Scriptures], even one polite lie, no shred of those books will remain. Whenever anyone finds

---

[335] Dulles, Avery, "Scripture: Recent Protestant and Catholic Views" in *Theology Today* 37:1 (1980): 7-26, p.20.

[336] Scott Hahn, professor of Scripture and Theology at the Franciscan University of Steubenville, points out the differences between infallibility and inspiration. First, infallibility is a "negative gift." The Holy Spirit prevents the pope, when acting as the Successor of Peter, from teaching error in matters of faith and morals. The words the pope speaks are his own, arrived at, hopefully, through intense study and reflection. His words may not be as clear as we would like, but they are free of error; at a later point he or another pontiff may add greater precision to the pronouncement. Inspiration, on the other hand, is a positive gift. They are the words of not only the human author but of the Holy Spirit Himself. They are free from error because they have come forth from God, the basis of all reality, Who can neither deceive or be deceived.

Hahn, Scott, *Can You Trust the Bible? The Inerrancy of Scripture in Catholic Teaching*, Audio cassette (West Covina, California: St. Joseph Communications, 1990).

[337] Brown, Raymond E. *The Virginal Conception and Bodily Resurrection of Jesus* (New York: Paulist Press, 1973), pp.8-9, italics added. Quoted in Harrison, Brian W, "The Truth and Salvific Purpose of Sacred Scripture According To *Dei Verbum*, Article 11," *Living Tradition* (59) July, 1995, p.6.

anything therein that is difficult to practice or hard to believe, he will refer to this most pernicious precedent and explain it as the idea or practice of a lying author."[338] We can see the fruit of setting such a limit to Scripture's teaching being borne out today in debates among the faithful of the Catholic and a host of other Christian communities: Is Jesus truly the only way to the Father (John 14:6; Acts 4:12), or is that simply time-conditioned religious language, the profession of a small sect trying to establish its identity against its parent Judaism and pagan mystery rites? Shouldn't we Christians living in a pluralistic society recognize other faiths as equally valid, and equally valuable, paths to God? Many Christians today question whether homosexual acts are truly a violation of God's design for humanity (Romans 1:24-27); or again, is that simply the time-conditioned belief of an earlier, less tolerant age? Before I go too far a field let me stop and ask: Did Vatican II really open this Pandora's box?

Much more accomplished theologians than myself maintain that it did not, that what we are dealing with is a false interpretation of *Dei Verbum*. We will proceed to look at a number of reasons for reaching such a conclusion. The first of which, as we have already seen, is context.

After all, isn't one of the cardinal rules of exegesis to look at a statement within its immediate context? Cutting off the first half of a sentence is an odd way to do that. Notice how different the sense is when it is included, "*Since, therefore, all that the inspired authors, or sacred writers, affirm should be affirmed by the Holy Spirit*, we must acknowledge that the books of Sacred Scripture, firmly, faithfully and without error, teach that truth which God, for the sake of our salvation, wished to see confided to the sacred Scriptures."[339]

Obviously I am working from an English translation of the text. Did the original Latin text convey a different meaning? Augustin Cardinal Bea, co-chair of the commission responsible for *Dei Verbum* did not see one. He wrote:

---

[338] Jurgens, William A. *The Faith of the Early Fathers*, Volume 3.(Collegeville, MN: Liturgical Press, 1970), p.2.
[339] Flannery, Austin, *Vatican Council II: The Conciliar and Post Conciliar Documents*, (Northport, New York: Costello Publishing Company, 1992), p.757. Italics added.

...the phrasing we now have does not admit of any such interpretation [limiting inerrancy], because the idea of salvation is not directly linked with the noun "truth" but with the verbal expression "wanted put into the sacred writings;" in other words, the phrase in which the text speaks of salvation explains God's purpose in causing the Scriptures to be written, and not the nature of the truth enshrined therein.[340]

It is wise to take Cardinal Bea as our teacher here.[341] He was in a singular position to speak on the text of *Dei Verbum*. Not only was he co-chair, but he had also served as Director of the Pontifical Biblical Institute for nineteen years prior to the Council. As such, his reputation concerning Scripture was not that of a hardened conservative. He was widely regarded as the principal architect behind the "magna carta" of Catholic biblical studies, Pope Pius XII's *Divino Afflante Spiritu*.[342]

Bea saw no limit being set to inerrancy in *Dei Verbum's* statement. Recognizing the difficulty that had arisen among some interpreters, he explained the development of the statement in earlier versions:

> An earler schema (the third in succession) said that the sacred books teach "truth without error". The following schema, the fourth, inspired by the words of St. Augustine, added the adjective "saving," so that the text asserted that the Scriptures taught "firmly, faithfully, wholly and without error the saving truth." In the voting which followed one hundred and eighty-four council fathers asked for the word "saving" to be removed, because they feared it might lead to misunderstandings, as if the inerrancy of Scripture referred only to matters of faith and morality, whereas there might be error in the treatment of other matters. The Holy Father [Paul VI], to a certain extent sharing this anxiety, decided to ask the Commission to consider whether it would not be better to omit the adjective, as it might lead to some misunderstanding. After a long and wearisome debate, with much discussion and several

---

[340] Bea, Augustin Cardinal, *The Word of God and Mankind* (Chicago: Franciscan Herald Press, 1967), pp.190-191.

[341] Hahn, Scott, *Can You Trust the Bible? The Inerrancy of Scripture in Catholic Teaching*, Audio cassette (West Covina, California: St. Joseph Communications, 1990).

[342] Schmidt, Stjepan, *Augustin Bea: The Cardinal of Unity*. (New York: New City Press, 1992) pp.106-109.

ballots, the present text was accepted, the adjective "saving" being omitted: "the truth which God wanted put into the sacred writings for the sake of our salvation."

Bea goes on to explain that limiting inerrancy had not been part of the theological commission's agenda:

> ...even at the stage of the discussion, when the Conciliar Theological Commission put forward the term "the saving truth," it explained that by this expression it did not mean to restrict inerrancy to matters of faith and morals. In order to show that this had not been its intention, it explained that the text spoke of "truth" in the singular, not of "truths," as if it had wished to discriminate between those which are necessary for salvation and others which are not. Moreover, in spite of this prudent explanation the word "saving" was finally eliminated from the text and replaced with another expression, in order to prevent any possibility of implying that the inerrancy was restricted.

> ...all those (and in the first place the Pope himself) who had been anxious to prevent the possible misunderstanding that might have arisen from the expression "the saving truth" have instead accepted the present form, which means they consider that this does not present the same danger of misunderstanding.[343]

The Pope and the council fathers were obviously mistaken. Providentially, however, the Conciliar Theological Commisson attached a footnote to the statement on inerrancy, referencing portions of two recent papal encyclicals on Scripture, Leo XIII's *Providentissimus Deus*(1893) and Pius XII's *Divino Afflante Spiritu* (1943).[344] This footnote, which none of the "limited

---

[343] Bea, Augustin Cardinal *The Word of God and Mankind* (Chicago: Franciscan Herald Press, 1967), pp.190-191.

[344] Allow Pope John Paul II to place these works in context for us, "*Providentissimus Deus* [1893] appeared in a period marked by vicious polemics against the Church's faith. Liberal exegesis gave important support to these polemics, for it made us of all the scientific resources, from textual criticism to geology, including philology, literary criticism, history of relgions, archaeology and other disciplines besides...[*Providentissimus Deus*] invites Catholic exegetes to acquire genuine scientific expertise so that they may surpass their adversaries in their own field...On the other hand, *Divino Afflante Spiritu* [1943] was published shortly after an entirely different polemic arose, particularly in Italy, against the scientific study of

inerrancy "theologians and exegetes I have read make mention of, should end all debate on the matter. *Dei Verbum* is to be understood as consistent with previous magisterial teaching:

Providentissimus Deus (Enchirdion Biblicum, 121)
There can never, indeed, be any real discrepancy between the theologian and the physicist...If dissension should arise between them, here is the rule...laid down by St. Augustine, for the theologian, "Whatever they can really demonstrate to be true of physical nature, we must show to be capable of reconciliation with our Scriptures, and whatever they assert in their treatises that is contrary to these Scriptures of ours, that is to the Catholic Faith, we must either prove it as well as we can to be entirely false, or at all events we must, without the smallest hesitation, believe it to be so...the [sacred writers] did not seek to penetrate the secrets of nature but rather described and dealt with things in more or less figurative language, or in terms that were commonly used at the time and that in many instances are in daily use at this day, even by the most eminent men of science...God, speaking to men, signified in the way men could understand and were accustomed to.[345]

Providentissimus Deus (Enchiridion Biblicum, 124)
...But it is absolutely wrong and forbidden either to narrow inspiration to certain parts only of Holy Scripture or to admit that the sacred writer has erred. For the system of those who, in order to rid themselves of these difficulties, do not hesitate to concede that divine inspiration regards the things of faith and morals and nothing beyond, be-

---

the Bible. An anonymous pamphlet was widely circulated to warn against what it described as 'a very serious danger for the Church and souls: the critic-scientific system in the study and interpretation of Sacred Scripture, its disastrous deviations and aberrations'...despite the great differences in the difficulties they had to face, the two Encyclicals are in complete agreement at the deepest level. Both of them reject a split between the human and the divine, between scientific research and respect for the faith, between the literal sense and the spiritual sense. They, thus appear to be in perfect harmony with the mystery of the incarnation." Taken from "The relevance of Providentissimus Deus and Divino Afflante Spiritu," in *The Church and the Bible*, Ed. Murphy, Dennis J. (Theological Publications in India, 2001), pp.676-678.
[345] Bechard, Dean P (Ed.), *The Scripture Documents: An Anthology of Official Catholic Teachings* (Collegeville, Minnesota: The Liturgical Press, 2002). pp.53-54.

cause (as they wrongly think) in a question of the truth or falsehood of a passage, we should consider not so much what God has said as the reason and purpose that he had in mind in saying it – this system cannot be tolerated.[346]

Providentissimus Deus (Enchiridion Biblicum, 126-127)
Hence, because the Holy Spirit employed men as his instruments, we cannot therefore say that it was these inspired instruments who, perchance, have fallen into error, and not the primary author...It follows that those who maintain that an error is possible in any genuine passage of the sacred writings either pervert the Catholic notion of inspiration or make God the author of such error...[347]

Divino Afflante Spiritus (Enchiridion Biblicum, 539)
The first and greatest care of Leo XIII was to set forth the teaching on the truth of the sacred Books and to defend it from attack. Hence with grave words did he proclaim that there is no error whatsoever if the sacred writer, speaking of things of the physical order, "went by what sensibly appeared," as [St. Thomas Aquinas] says, speaking either in "figurative language or terms that were commonly used at the time and in many instances are in daily use at this day, even among the most eminent men of science."

...divine inspiration "not only is essentially incompatible with error but excludes and rejects it as absolutely and as necessarily as it is impossible that God himself, the supreme Truth, can utter that which is not true. This is the ancient and constant faith of the Church."[348]

Yes, the "official," and ancient, faith of the Catholic Church is that Scripture is, in the words of *Dei Verbum*, "without error."

---

[346] Ibid, p.55.
[347] Ibid, P.56.
[348] Ibid, pp.116-117.

Bibliography

Albright, W.F. and C.S. Mann, *The Anchor Bible: Matthew*, (Garden City, NY: Doubleday, 1971).

Bea, Augustin Cardinal, *The Word of God and Mankind* (Chicago: Franciscan Herald Press, 1967).

Bechard, Dean P (Ed.), *The Scripture Documents: An Anthology of Official Catholic Teachings* (Collegeville, Minnesota: The Liturgical Press, 2002).

Bennet, Dennis, *How to Pray for the Release of the Holy Spirit*, (South Plainfield, NJ: Bridge Publishing Inc., 1985).

Bonaci, Mary Beth, *Real Love*. (San Francisco: Ignatius Press, 1996).

Brown, Raymond E. *The Virginal Conception and Bodily Resurrection of Jesus* (New York: Paulist Press, 1973).

Brown, Raymond E. and Collins, Thomas Aquinas, "Church Pronouncements" in *The New Jerome Biblical Commentary*, Ed. R.E. Brown, J.A. Fitzmeyer, and R. E. Murphy, p.1169 (Englewood Cliffs, NJ: Prentice Hall, 1990).

Bouyer, Louis, *Introduction to Spirituality*, (New York: Desclee Company, 1961).

Butler, Scott; Norman Dalgren, & David Hess (Eds.), *Jesus, Peter & the Keys: A Scriptural Handbook on the Papacy*, (Santa Barbara, California: Queenship Publishing Company, 1997).

Cantalamessa, Raniero, *The Holy Spirit in the Life of Jesus* (Collegeville, Minnesota: The Liturgical Press, 1994).

Catechism of the Catholic Church, (San Francisco: Ignatius Press, 1994).

Catholic Study Bible, The: New American Bible Including the Revised New Testament. Donald Senior, Mary Ann Getty, Carroll Stuhlmueller, John J. Collins (Eds.), (New York: Oxford University Press, 1990).

Chapin, John (Ed.), *The Book of Catholic Quotations*, (New York: Farrar, Straus, and Cudahy, 1956).

Clark, Stephen, *Redeemer*, (Ann Arbor, Michigan: Servant Books, 1992).

Collins, Raymond F, "Inspiration," in *The New Jerome Biblical Commentary*, Ed. R.E. Brown, J.A. Fitzmeyer, and R. E. Murphy, p.1028 (Englewood Cliffs, NJ:Prentice Hall, 1990).

Currie, David B., *Born Fundamentalist, Born Again Catholic*, (San Francisco: Ignatius Press, 1996).

Currie, David,. *The Rapture* (Manchester New Hampshire: Sophia Institute Press, 2003).

Depuis, Jacques, *Toward a Christian Theology of Religious Pluralism* (Maryknoll, New York: Orbis Books, 1997).

Driscoll, Jeremy, "The Word of God in the Liturgy of the New Covenant," *Letter & Spirit* 1 (2005).

Dulles, Avery, "Scripture: Recent Protestant and Catholic Views" in *Theology Today* 37:1 (1980): 7-26.

Evert, Jason, *If You Really Love Me: 100 Questions on Dating, Relationships, and Sexual Purity.* (Ann Arbor, Michigan: Servant Publications, 2003).

Farmer, William R. and Denis M. Farkasfalvy, *The Formation of the New Testament Canon: An Ecumenical Approach*, (New York: Paulist Press, 1983).

Farrell, Walter, *Companion to the Summa*, Volume 1 (New York: Sheed & Ward, 1938) © Dominicans, Province of St. Albert the Great. Work available at: http://www.domcentral.org/farrell/companion/comp102.htm

Flannery, Austin, *Vatican Council II: The Conciliar and Post Conciliar Documents*, (Northport, New York: Costello Publishing Company, 1992).

Garrigou-Lagrange, Reginald, *The Mother of the Saviour and Our Interior Life*, (Rockford, Illinois: Tan Books and Publishers Inc., 1993).

Girzone, Joseph, *Joshua: A Parable for Today*, (Macmillan Publishing Company, 1987).

Glynn, Patrick, *God: The Evidence : The Reconciliation of Faith and Reason in a Postsecular World*, (Rocklin, CA: Prima Publishing, 1997),

Gnuse, Robert. *The Authority of the Bible: Theories of Inspiration, Revelation and the Canon of Scripture*. (New York: Paulist, 1985).

Graham, Billy, *How To Be Born Again*, (Dallas: Word Publishing, 1977).

Graham, Henry G., *Where We Got The Bible: Our Debt to the Catholic Church*, (Rockford, Illinois: Tan Books and Publishers Inc., 1911).

Hahn, Scott, *The Catholic Gospel* (Audiocassette Series by St. Joseph Communications).

Hahn, Scott, *Can You Trust the Bible? The Inerrancy of Scripture in Catholic Teaching*, Audio cassette (West Covina, California: St. Joseph Communications, 1990).

Hahn, Scott, *Hail Holy Queen: The Mother of God in the Word of God* (San Francisco: Doubleday, 2001).

Hahn, Scott, *Letter and Spirit: From Written Text to Living Word in the Liturgy* (New York: Doubleday, 2005).

Hahn, Scott and Kimberly Hahn, *Rome Sweet Home: Our Journey to Catholicism*, (San Francisco: Ignatius Press, 1993).

Hahn, Scott and Curtis Mitch, *Ignatius Catholic Study Bible: The Gospel of Luke* (San Francisco, 2001).

Hanson, James E., *If I'm a Christian, Why Be a Catholic?*, (New York: Paulist Press, 1984).

Harrison, Brian W, "The Truth and Salvific Purpose of Sacred Scripture According To *Dei Verbum*, Article 11," *Living Tradition* (59) July, 1995.

Holy Bible, The Revised Standard Version, (New York: Collins, 1973).

Jaki, Stanley L., *The Keys of the Kingdom: A Tools Witness to Truth*, (Chicago: The Franciscan Herald Press, 1986).

Jaki, Stanley L., *And On This Rock: The Witness of One Land and Two Covenants*, (Manassas, Virginia: Trinity Communications, 1987).

John Paul II, *That They May Be One: On Commitment to Ecumenism*, <http://www.vatican.va/holy_father/john_paul_ii/encyclicals/documents/hf_jp-ii_enc_25051995_ut-unum-sint_en.html>

Johnson, Kevin Orlin, *Why Do Catholics Do That?: A Guide to the Teachings and Practices of the Catholic Church*, (New York: Ballantine Books, 1994).

Jurgens, William A., *The Faith of the Early Fathers*, Volumes 1-3, (Collegeville, Minnesota: The Liturgical Press, 1970).

Kelly, J.N.D., *Early Christian Doctrines*, (San Francisco: Harper, 1960).

Keating, Karl, *Catholicism & Fundamentalism: The Attack on Catholicism by Bible Christians*, (San Francisco, Ignatius Press, 1986).

Kreeft, Peter, *Summa of the Summa*, (San Francisco: Ignatius Press, 1990).

Kreeft, Peter and Ronald K. Tacelli, *Handbook of Christian Apologetics*, (Downers Grove, Illinois: InterVarsity Press, 1994).

O'Collins, Gerald, *The Tripersonal God* (New York: Paulist Press, 1984).

La Potterie, Ignace de, *Mary in the Mystery of the Covenant* (New York: Alba House, 1992).

Lewis, C.S., *The Joyful Christian: 127 Readings from C.S. Lewis*, (New York: Macmillan Publishing Co.,1977).

Lewis, C.S., *Mere Christianity*, (New York: Macmillan Publishing Co.,1943).

Luther, Martin, *Luther's Works*, Volume 35 (St. Louis: Concordia, 1963).

Madrid, Patrick (Ed.), *Surprised by Truth*, (San Diego, Basilica Press, 1994).

Martin, Ralph, *The Catholic Church at the End of an Age: What is the Spirit Saying?*, (San Francisco, Ignatius Press, 1994).

McKenzie, John L. *The Two-Edged Sword: An Interpretation of the Old Testament* (Garden City, New York: Image Books, 1956).

Meier, John P., *A Marginal Jew: Rethinking the Historical Jesus*, Volume 2. (New York:Doubleday, 1994).

Meier, John P., *A Marginal Jew: Rethinking the Historical Jesus*, Volume 3. (New York:Doubleday, 2001).

Montague, George T. *Understanding the Bible: A Basic Introduction to Biblical Interpretation* (New York: Paulist, 1997).

Moreland, J.P. and Kai Nielsen, *Does God Exist?: The Debate Between Theists & Athiests*, (Amherst, New York: Prometheus Books, 1993).

Most, William G. *Free From All Error.* (Libertyville, Illinois: Prow Books/ Franciscan Marytown Press, 1985).

Murphy, Dennis J. (Ed.), "The relevance of Providentissimus Deus and Divino Afflante Spiritu," in *The Church and the Bible*, (Theological Publications in India, 2001).

The New Jerome Biblical Commentary (Englewood Cliffs, New Jersey: Prentice Hall, 1990), p.1268-1269.

Nicole, Roger, "The Biblical Concept of Truth" in Ed. Carson, D.A. and Woodbridge, John D., *Scripture and Truth* (Grand Rapids, Michigan: Baker Book House, 1992).

O'Collins, Gerald, *Fundamental Theology* (Mahwah, New Jersey: Paulist Press, 1981).

O'Collins, Gerald, *The Tripersonal God* (New York: Paulist Press, 984).

O'Hare, Patrick F., *The Facts About Luther*, (Rockford, IL: TAN Books and Publishers Inc., 1987).

Organ, Barbara E., *Is the Bible Fact or Fiction?: An Introduction to Biblical Historiography*, (New York: Paulist Press, 2004).

Ott, Ludwig, *Fundamentals of Catholic Dogma* (Rockford, Illinois: Tan Books and Publishers Inc., 1960).

Perkins, Pheme, *Collegeville Bible Commentary: The Book of Revelation* (Collegeville, Minnesota: The Liturgical Press, 1983).

Pimentel, Stephen, *Witnesses of the Messiah: On Acts of the Apostles 1-15*, (Steubenville, Ohio: Emmaus Road Publishing, 2002).

Pope Paul VI, *Humanae Vitae (Of Human Life)*, (July 25, 1968), n.17., http://www.vatican.va/holy_father/paul_vi/encyclicals/documents/ hf_p-vi_enc_25071968_humanae-vitae_en.html

Ratzinger, Joseph Cardinal, *Called To Communion: Understanding The Church Today*, (San Francisco: Ignatius Press, 1991).

Ratzinger, Joseph, *Truth and Tolerance: Christian Belief and World Religions*. (San Francisco: Ignatius Press, 2003).

Ray, Stephen K., *Crossing The Tiber: Evangelical Protestants Discover the Historic Church*, (San Francisco: Ignatius Press, 1997).

Ross, Hugh, *The Creator And The Cosmos: How The Greatest Scientific Discoveries Of The Century Reveal God*, (Colorado Springs, Colorado: Navpress, 1994).

Rumble, Leslie and Charles M. Carty, *Bible Quizzes To A Street Preacher*, (Rockford, Illinois: TAN Books and Publishers Inc., 1976).

Rumble, Leslie and Charles M. Carty, *Eucharistic Quizzes To A Street Preacher*, (Rockford, Illinois: TAN Books and Publishers Inc., 1976).

Schmidt, Stjepan, *Augustin Bea: The Cardinal of Unity*. (New York: New City Press, 1992).

Schreck, Alan, *Catholic and Christian: An Explanation of Commonly Misunderstood Catholic Beliefs*, (Ann Arbor, Michigan: Servant Books, 1984).

Shamon, Albert J.M., *Our Lady Says: Let Holy Mass Be Your Life*, (Milford, Ohio: The Riehle Foundation, 1989).

Shea, Mark P., *By What Authority?: An Evangelical Discovers Catholic Tradition*, (Huntington, Indiana: Our Sunday Visitor, Inc., 1996).

Sheed, Frank J., *Theology and Sanity* (San Francisco: Ignatius Press, 1986).

Sheed, Frank, *To Know Christ Jesus* (San Francisco: Ignatius Press, 1980).

Sproul, R.C., *Now That's A Good Question!* (Wheaton, Illinois: Tyndale Publishers, Inc., 1996).

Stravinskas, Peter, *The Bible and the Mass: Understanding the Scriptural Basis of the Liturgy* (Ann Arbor, Michigan: Servant Publications, 1989).

Sri, Edward, *Mystery of the Kingdom* (Steubenville, Ohio: Emmaus Road Publishing, 1999).

Student Bible, The: New International Version. Study Notes by Philip Yancey And Tim Stafford, (Grand Rapids, Michigan: Zondervan Bible Publishers, 1986).

Sullivan, Francis A., *Salvation Outside the Church? The History of the Catholic Response* (Maqwah, New Jersey: Paulist Press, 1992)

Sungenis, Robert A., *How Can I Get to Heaven? The Bible's Teaching on Salvation Made Easy to Understand,* (Santa Barbara, California: Queenship Publishing Company, 1998).

Thigpen, Paul, *The Rapture Trap* (West Chester, Pennsylvania: Ascension Press, 2001).

Tickle, John, *The Book of Revelation: A Catholic Interpretation of the Apocalypse.* (Ligouri, Missouri: Ligouri Publications, 1983).

Treece, Patricia, *Apparitions of Modern Saints* (Ann Arbor, MI: Servant Publications, 2001).

West, Christopher, *Good News About Sex and Marriage: Answers to Your Honest Questions about Catholic Teaching.* (Ann Arbor, Michigan: Servant Publications, 2000).

Whalen, William J., *Separated Brethren*, (Huntington, Indiana: Our Sunday Visitor Press, 1979).

Wuerl, Donald W., Ronald Lawler, & Thomas C. Lawler, *The Gift of Faith: A Question and Answer Catechism Version of the Teaching of Christ*, (Hungtingon, Indiana: Our Sunday Visitor, 1986).

More from Out of the Box
www.outoftheboxrecords.com

Paul Masek
(youth minister from *The God Who is Love*)
Stirring It Up contains practical advice for teens who want to keep the Holy Spirit stirred up in their lives. ***All Bottled Up*** consists of actual letters Paul has received from teens – and his answers – to questions on many of today's hot issues. ***Stirring It Up More*** is an audio CD on which Paul shares some inspirational thoughts and some silliness!

Adam Bitter
Overwhelm Me
Passionate, contemporary songs of worship

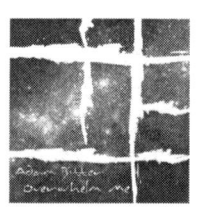

Karl Zimmeman
Love Will Lead Us Home
Rock, reggae, quiet reflection – Karl brings it all on this CD.

Chris Shepherd
The newest addition to the Out of the Box family. Be on the lookout for his forthcoming CD.

Liked the book? Visit the website!
www.explainingchristianity.com

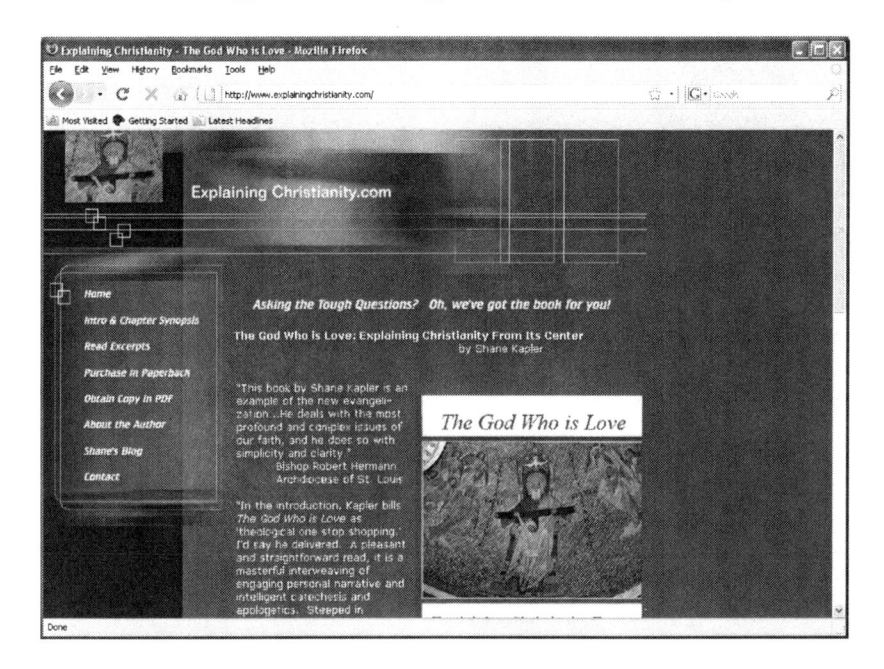

- Share it with friends
- Check out chapter synopsis and excerpts
- Order copies online
- Link to Shane's blog
- Contact information